# LOW-FAT COOKERY

third edition

# LOW-FAT COOKERY

by Evelyn S. Stead and
Gloria K. Warren, R.D.

illustrated by Loring Eutemey

with an introduction by
Eugene A. Stead, Jr., M.D.
and James V. Warren, M.D.

McGraw-Hill Book Company
New York   St. Louis   San Francisco
Düsseldorf   London   Mexico
Sydney   Toronto

First McGraw-Hill Paperback Edition, 1977

3 4 5 6 7 8 9 B P B P 8 7 6 5 4 3 2 1 0

**Library of Congress Cataloging in Publication Data**

Stead, Evelyn S.
  Low-fat cookery.

    1.  Low-fat diet.   I.   Warren, Gloria K., joint author.
II.  Title.
RM237.7.S8 1975        641.5′638        74-14509

    ISBN 0-07-060902-0
    ISBN 0-07-060903-9

# ACKNOWLEDGMENTS

We wish to acknowledge the contribution to this book made by Rosa Saunders, who gave us valuable help in altering and testing recipes.

Technical information on food values of various foods is based on the following sources:

*Cheese Varieties and Descriptions*, U.S. Department of Agriculture, Agriculture Handbook No. 54, Washington, D.C., 1969.

*Composition of Foods, Raw, Processed, Prepared*, U.S. Department of Agriculture, Agriculture Handbook No. 8, Washington, D.C., 1963.

Correspondence with food manufacturers. Copies available in the authors' files.

*Nutritive Value of Foods*, Home and Garden Bulletin No. 72, U.S. Department of Agriculture, Washington, D.C., 1971.

Our approach to individual recipes has varied. In some cases we found existing recipes suitable for inclusion. In other cases we found that existing recipes could be altered to fit low-fat cookery techniques. In still other cases the recipes are original. Several recipes were contributed by interested persons: Helen Clark, Alice Cleland, Jean Estes, Clio Stead Fuller, Marcia Goldner, Leslie Hohman, M.D., Lucy Stead LaVarre, Eleanor Menefee, Margaret Newton, Phyllis Parker, Mary Pfeiffer, Helen Rantz, Simonne Rosse, Ethel Stead, Sally Wallace, and Lucile V. Warren.

In all cases the analyses of the recipes are our own.

E. S. S.
G. K. W.

C
O
N
T
E
N
T
S

# A PHILOSOPHY OF DIET

This book has been compiled on the theory that cooking with less fat can be painless and even pleasant. The publication of a third edition of *Low-fat Cookery* is the "proof of the pudding." After the first edition was published in November, 1956, we continued to follow the principles of low-fat cookery in our homes, to develop new recipes, and to accumulate more information on the fat content of food. More than ninety new recipes were added for the 1959 edition. Now, sixteen years later and still practicing low-fat cookery, we have updated our products lists and our tables of food values and have added still more recipes to broaden the appeal of your table.

We believe that a "diet-by-the-week" scheme, approached with imagination, can turn out to be a treat, not a trial. We even recommend that you forget that word "diet" entirely and enjoy the eating!

For those interested in mastering low-fat cookery techniques, *What to Remember* is a summary in pictures of the important basic points. In cutting down the fat in the diet, one must consider the *invisible* as well as the *visible* fats of both animal and vegetable sources.

The *visible* fats are butter, margarine, lard, vegetable shortenings, vegetable oils, and salad dressings.

*Invisible* sources of fat—the hidden fats—are foods which are not eaten primarily for their fat content but which contain an appreciable amount of fat nonetheless. The cook who wishes to make a success of low-fat cookery must become aware of these hidden fats and of their sources. She must calculate the fat content of these foods with the same care she uses on visible fats. These invisible fats are found in the marbling of meat, the yolk of eggs, most cheeses, whole milk, cream, chocolate, soybeans, olives, nuts except chestnuts and litchi nuts, avocados, and coconuts. Many prepared products contain visible or invisible fats or both.

Labeling of products to describe the ingredients therein has improved. *Read Those Labels!* emphasizes that with the increased information being made available on labels, the consumer can more readily calculate fat content of prepared products. Indeed, if you are following a diet of lowered fat content, it is essential you train yourself to do so. An example is included to show you how to convert to your use the information supplied on the label.

We are interested in outlining foods which will keep the *average* intake of *total* fat at either 25 grams or 50 grams per day. The analyses of the individual recipes and the data on fat content of foods in the Appendix make it a simple matter to calculate one's fat intake. In choosing dishes for your lowered fat menus be sure to "spend" the fat where there is the most nutrition. Principles of good nutrition should be observed regardless of whether one is "on a diet" or not. The meat group will absorb the largest part of the fat allowance. There will be variations in fat content of the diet daily, depending on choice of kind of meat as well as cut. The overall food picture for a period of a week or more would yield a daily diet within the given figures of 25 to 50 grams fat.

The recipes we have devised and compiled will provide a palatable, interesting, and varied menu without adding excessive quantities of fat. In those recipes which use ingredients listed above as containing fat, it will be found that the fat content per serving is compatible with a "diet-by-the-week" scheme.

The real satisfactions of mastering low-fat cookery come when one modifies a family-favorite recipe to fit the lowered-fat pattern. *Do-It-Yourself* points the way, and further information on fat content of foods and the use of herbs appears in the Appendix.

We include a supplementary section at the end of the book which contains suggestions for dovetailing low-fat cookery and special diets (sodium restricted and those using unsaturated vegetable oils).

Evelyn S. Stead
Gloria K. Warren

**A PHILOSOPHY OF DIET**

## The Physician Looks at Low-fat Cookery

Food is one of the paramount interests of man. He spends many hours of his time producing it or obtaining the funds to buy it. His wife spends many hours of her time buying it and preparing it. The eating of it is one of his chief pleasures. Around the daily consumption of food is built much of the family and social life.

Cultural patterns, economic status, habits of cooking and eating, and ideas about health all play a part in determining the individual diet. The lack of adequate food intake, whether in calories, protein, or essential food substances, has been shown to cause illness.

1

Many doctors believe that, on the present American scene, more illness is caused by excessive intake of calories and fat than is caused by diets deficient in essential food substances. All authorities agree that a diet containing too many calories causes obesity and that obesity has an unfavorable effect on the cardiovascular system. Fat in the diet is of particular importance in the problem of obesity because an ounce of fat contains more than twice the calories present in an ounce of carbohydrate or protein. Many doctors believe that the large fat intake in the average American diet plays an important role in hardening of the arteries and that persons of normal weight should derive less of their calories from fat.

We know that obesity is a problem to many people throughout their entire adult life. Atherosclerosis (hardening of the arteries) begins during infancy or childhood and increases as we grow older. If diet is to be a preventive approach to obesity and atherosclerosis, lifelong changes in cooking and eating habits are needed. Such a lifelong restriction of fat intake is impractical with conventional dietary instructions, which center around what you must leave out of your eating. Instead, a philosophy of cooking must be evolved which offers the same variety of tasty dishes to which we are accustomed. The housewife and cook must look at fat in a different light: instead of being a substance used freely in preparing food, it must be relegated to second choice. Fat will not be used when a substitute can be provided. A cherry pie as usually cooked contains 107 grams of fat. By ingenuity, this fat content can be reduced to 10.4 grams.

The caloric values of animal and vegetable fats are approximately the same, and no distinction need be made between them for purposes of weight reduction.

Their chemical structure, however, is different, and

there is evidence that this may be important in the development of atherosclerosis. It has been suggested that a higher percentage of our fat intake should be of the vegetable (unsaturated) type; the average American diet now contains mostly animal (saturated) fats. Your physician may recommend such a change in your diet. If one merely adds vegetable fat to the diet, the caloric content will rise excessively and obesity may result. The use of low-fat cookery will enable you to reduce the basic fat content of your meals so that room is provided for the added calories from the unsaturated fat.

## Effect of Removing Fat from Diet

Our calories come from three food elements: protein, carbohydrate, and fat. Caloric reduction can be accomplished by limiting the intake of all three or by a drastic reduction in one without increasing the intake of the other two. One ounce of fat supplies more than twice as many calories as an equal amount of carbohydrate or protein. Therefore, when one wishes to reduce weight, limitation of fat intake is much more efficient than decreasing the intake of carbohydrates (sugar and starch) or protein.

If one decreases the daily intake of fat from the normal American level of some 100 grams (or often more) to 50 grams of fat or less, weight will be lost unless the total quantity of food eaten is increased. Low-fat cookery is the answer to weight control in those people who enjoy the pleasures of the table. It is rarely prescribed in hospitals and by doctors because such a diet made up in the usual way has always been uninteresting. If this type of cooking is made palatable, however, and is adopted for weight reduction in either healthy or sick persons, the caloric reduction need not be so drastic as on the usual 1200-calorie reduction diet. Such severely restricted diets are often followed for a short time and then discarded. Low-fat cookery can be practiced for years. Therefore there is no need for *rapid* weight loss.

It is worth noting in passing that the figures given on charts showing average weight are too high. They include in their calculation the weights of many patients who are fond of eating and do not know about low-fat cookery. Your doctor's advice should be sought as to your ideal weight. This is of more interest to you, individually, than the average weight of all Americans of your sex, age, and height.

## How to Use This Book

This book is designed primarily for well people who wish to eat less fat, either to control weight or in the belief that they will then be less subject to vascular disease. Sick people should not use this book without the guidance of a physician.

Low-fat cookery will be of particular interest to several groups of persons: (1) persons of normal weight who want to consume less of their calories in fat; (2) those healthy but overweight persons who want to lose weight to improve their appearance or because they believe thin persons live longer than fat ones; (3) patients with heart disease or hypertensive vascular disease who wish to gain in exercise tolerance and longevity by reduction of body weight; (4) patients with coronary artery disease or other forms of atheros-
4    clerosis who are advised by their physician to follow a

diet in the hope of preventing progress of the disease; (5) patients with diabetes.

1. *Healthy people who wish to reduce their intake of fat without reducing weight.* The degree of fat restriction desired will vary greatly. At one extreme will be the housewife who is interested in going to a little but not too much trouble to decrease fat intake; at the other extreme will be the thin doctor interested in vascular disease who is willing to go to a great deal of trouble to reduce his fat intake to an average of 25 grams per day. Many people will be glad to have the cook restrict fat in the cooking but will still like to eat nuts, cheese, and the fat on their ham. This group will reduce their fat intake appreciably by low-fat cookery. They will obtain real satisfaction from the fat eaten but will no longer be eating the hidden fat added in cooking, which they enjoy very little.

Healthy persons using low-fat cookery who do not wish to reduce will have to keep an eye on their weight. For every ounce of fat removed, they will need to add twice as much carbohydrate or protein. This will mean an increase in the total amount of food eaten per day. The weekly menus given for the 25-gram diet and for the 50-gram diet are adequate in minerals and vitamins. If calories are not adequate, they can be added as desired by increasing the intake of foods containing negligible amounts of fat (e.g., skim milk, buttermilk, fruits and vegetables, jelly, jam, certain candies, meringues, and so forth).

2. *Healthy obese people.* Instructions here are very simple. Menus should be planned to give an average daily intake of 25 grams of fat. The usual-size helpings and the usual number of courses may be eaten. Weight will decrease if the usual amount of food is not increased. If the fat left out of the diet is replaced by an equal amount of protein or carbohydrates (sugar and

starch), the caloric intake will be less, even though the amount of food is the same. If more calories are needed to prevent further weight loss, they can be obtained from larger portions, from added courses, or from experimentation with the 50-gram diet.

3. *Patients with heart disease or hypertensive vascular disease.* These are sick people under the care of their doctor. Only he should prescribe their diet, because the salt and protein content of their food may be very important. Weight should be kept below the average for their sex, height, and age. The low-fat schedule will be followed more rigidly by this group than by groups 1 and 2. It is practical by following this book to decrease the fat intake to an average of 15 grams per day or even lower. A specialized diet like Kempner's rice diet reduces the daily fat intake to below 5 grams.

4. *Patients with coronary artery disease or atherosclerosis.* The patient is under the care of his doctor, who will determine the fat and caloric intake. Weight should be kept below the average for the height, age, and sex of the patient, and the selected diet should be followed rigidly.

5. *Patients with diabetes.* It goes without saying that the diabetic person should be under the constant supervision of his doctor, who will find this book helpful if he wishes to use a low-fat schedule. The philosophy of this book as used for normal people— diet by the week instead of the day—must be modified, because in the diabetic person a constant intake of carbohydrate and protein at breakfast, lunch, and dinner is desirable.

The problems differ with the age of the patient. In the young, severely diabetic person, insulin is required to utilize enough calories for growth and development. Gain in weight may be desirable. In the older, less severely diabetic patient, caloric intake is the most important consideration, for weight reduction decreases insulin requirement. Because diabetes is a lifelong illness and vascular disease its chief complication, a diet containing not more than 50 grams of fat is desirable. The patient need not be restricted in sugar or carbohydrate; he should be restricted in calories, and fat restriction is the simplest way to accomplish calorie restriction. Low-fat diets require an increase in carbohydrate and protein but, because of their effect on weight, usually do not increase the insulin requirement. Indeed, they frequently lower it.

To any of the groups of persons interested in low-fat foods, temporary dieting is of no real help. In all, reduction of the fat content in their food must evolve into a way of eating that lasts over many years. This is practical only if the "joy of eating" can be preserved.

Eugene A. Stead, Jr., M.D.
James V. Warren, M.D.

**Iron Will**

**Cooperative Cook**

The problem of decreasing fat in the diet can be moved out of the dining room into the kitchen. When you have mastered the essentials of low-fat cookery, you can forget the word "diet" and enjoy the eating!

In cutting down the fat in the diet, one must consider the *hidden* as well as the obvious fats of both animal and vegetable sources.

9

| **Obvious fats** | **Hidden fats** |
|---|---|
| These you eat because you want to. | These cannot be avoided in conventionally cooked foods. |

## Some Sources of Fat

| | |
|---|---|
| Butter | Marbling of meat |
| Margarine | Egg yolk |
| Lard | Most cheeses |
| Vegetable shortening | Whole milk and cream |
| Vegetable oils | Chocolate |
| Salad dressings | Olives, most nuts, avocados |

## CALORIES DERIVED FROM
## DIFFERENT MIXTURES OF FAT AND
## PROTEIN OR CARBOHYDRATES

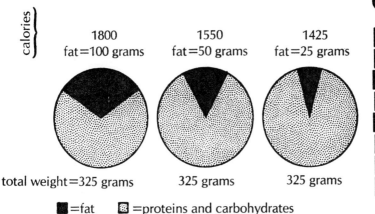

calories }

| 1800 | 1550 | 1425 |
| fat=100 grams | fat=50 grams | fat=25 grams |

total weight=325 grams    325 grams    325 grams

■=fat    ▨ =proteins and carbohydrates

Our calories come from three food elements: protein, carbohydrate, and fat. One ounce of fat supplies more than twice as many calories as an equal amount of carbohydrate or protein. Therefore, reduction of fat intake is the most efficient method of calorie reduction. In servings of equal size, the one containing a lower proportion of fat will contain fewer calories.

11

# READ THOSE LABELS!

Compliance with recent Food and Drug Administration recommendations will require more complete information concerning product content to appear on labels. This new labeling should help you identify new products suitable for lowered fat eating when they appear on the market. Moreover, from time to time some processed foods will require new formulae when basic ingredients or raw materials from which they are made are in short supply or no longer available. The recommendations require that the nutrition information, as well as the ingredient list, reflect such changes. The cook who reads the labels can maintain accurate data on fat content of the food she prepares.

One word of caution: some prepared products may, themselves, be low enough in fat content, but the instructions for cooking may include foods containing

13

fat. For example: "Add one egg" or "Combine with one cup whole milk." Be careful not to increase fat content of the finished dish out of low fat range.

Fat is calculated in grams. Package weights are often given in ounces. This formula will enable you to convert percentage of ounces to grams of fat.

1 ounce = 28.35 grams

ounces × 28.35 = weight in grams

weight in grams × percent of fat = fat content in grams

Example:

An 8-ounce package is labeled as containing 5 percent fat.

8 × 28.35 = 226.8 grams (Round to 227 grams)

227 grams × .05 (5 percent) = 11.35 grams fat

Remember—the more you master the techniques of low-fat planning and cooking, the more satisfying will your table be!

14

Low-fat cookery will succeed in your kitchen—and at your table—when you become familiar enough with the principles involved to modify your own recipes. Two points must always be kept in mind:

1. what substitutions can be made in the ingredients to lower fat content of the recipe?
2. where can the method of cooking be altered to conform to low-fat principles?

On the following pages are two recipes for Baked Lasagne. If you will compare both the ingredients and the method of handling, you will see how the recipe was modified to lower its fat content.

One ingredient, olive oil, was eliminated completely. Onion salt and garlic salt were added to compensate for the fact that the onion and garlic, browned without the oil, would have less flavor.

15

The following substitutions were made:
ground round steak for hamburger
low-fat cottage cheese for ricotta
imitation pasteurized process cheese spread for
   Mozzarella
sapsago for Parmesan

The modifications in seasoning—i.e., more tomato sauce and less tomato paste, and the additional herbs—were a matter of personal taste and were not influenced by low-fat cooking principles.

In the cottage cheese–egg mixture, an additional three-quarters pound of low-fat cottage cheese was used. One egg was found to be enough. This change was made to improve the flavor of the dish, and it also helped decrease the fat content.

The only variation in method necessary was to pan-brown the meat, onion, and garlic in a teflon or treated skillet, without the addition of oil.

**Original Recipe for Baked Lasagne**

   **1 pound lasagne**
   **2 tablespoons olive oil**
   **1 pound chopped meat (assumed to be
      hamburger)**
   **1 medium onion, minced**
   **1 clove garlic, chopped**
   **2 6-ounce cans tomato paste**
   **1 teaspoon parsley**
   **2 eggs**
   **2 cups water**
   **½ teaspoon salt**
   **½ teaspoon pepper**
   **¾ pound Mozzarella cheese**
   **¾ pound ricotta (Italian cottage cheese)**

**Grated Parmesan cheese (estimate 2 ounces used)**

Brown chopped meat in oil with onion, garlic, and parsley. Add tomato paste, 2 cups water, salt and pepper, and simmer for 1½ hours. Add lasagne to 6 quarts boiling water, stirring almost constantly to prevent sticking together, and cook 15 minutes, or until tender. Drain. Mix eggs and ricotta. Arrange lasagne in baking dish in layers, alternating with layers of sauce, Mozzarella, and ricotta, until lasgne is all used. Sprinkle with grated cheese. Bake in moderate over (375°) about 20 minutes, or until Mozzarella is melted.

| Fat content of recipe: | 6–8 servings |
|---|---|
| lasagne: | 4.5–6.8 grams |
| olive oil: | 28.0 grams |
| chopped meat, regular | |
| ground: | 96.2 grams |
| tomato paste: | negligible |
| eggs: | 12.0 grams |
| Mozzarella: | 153.1 grams |
| ricotta: | 13.6–34.0 grams |
| Parmesan: | 18.0 grams |
| Total: | 325.4–348.1 grams |

Fat content per serving, based on 6 servings:
54.2–58.0 grams
Fat content per serving, based on 8 servings:
40.7–43.5 grams

**Modified Recipe for Baked Lasagne**

**1 pound lasagne**
**1 pound round steak, ground**
**1 medium onion, minced**

DO IT YOURSELF

17

1 clove garlic, crushed
½ teaspoon salt
½ teaspoon pepper
1 6-ounce can tomato paste
3 8-ounce cans tomato sauce
2 cups water (more may be used if sauce is too thick)
½ teaspoon sugar
1 teaspoon basil
1 teaspoon oregano
1 teaspoon salt
1 teaspoon pepper
1 teaspoon onion salt
½ teaspoon garlic salt
1½ pounds low-fat cottage cheese (2 12-ounce boxes) (Borden Lite-Line®, Trim n' Light®, Slim n' Light®, Trim®)
1 egg
1 tablespoon chopped parsley (fresh parsley is preferred)
Salt and pepper
¾ pound imitation pasteurized process cheese spread (Chef's Delight® or Count Down®)
Grated sapsago cheese (estimate 2 ounces used)

1. Mix round steak, onion, garlic, salt and pepper. Salt skillet and brown meat mixture. Add tomato paste, tomato sauce, water, herbs, and seasonings. Simmer for 1½ hours; stir occasionally.

2. Mix low-fat cottage cheese, egg, parsley, salt, and pepper.

3. Slice cheese spread in thin slices.

4. Add lasagne to 6 quarts boiling, salted water, stirring almost constantly to prevent sticking together.

Cook 10 to 15 minutes. Lasagne should be almost done but not too tender, to allow for further cooking in the oven. When cooked, pour cold water in pot, drain, and leave noodles standing in cold water until needed. This prevents sticking.

5. Ladle sauce on bottom of baking dish. Arrange layers of lasagne, cottage cheese mixture, sliced process cheese spread, and sauce until lasagne is used. Sprinkle generously with sapsago cheese. Bake in moderate oven (375°) for 20 to 30 minutes or until cheese spread is melted.

6. At table pass remainder of sauce and additional grated sapsago cheese.

| Fat content of recipe: | 6–8 servings |
|---|---|
| lasagne: | 4.5–6.8 grams |
| round steak, separable | |
| lean: | 21.3 grams |
| tomato paste: | negligible |
| tomato sauce: | negligible |
| low-fat cottage cheese: | 6.8–13.6 grams |
| egg: | 6.0 grams |
| imitation pasteurized | |
| process cheese spread: | 3.4–17.0 grams |
| sapsago: | negligible |
| Total: | 42.0–64.7 grams |
| Fat content per serving, based on 6 servings: | 7.0–10.8 grams |
| Fat content per serving, based on 8 servings: | 5.3–8.1 grams |

DO IT YOURSELF

# RECIPES

Though olives, peanuts, and anchovies must be put on the "forbidden" list, there are still many tasty appetizers available. Moreover, they have the advantage of variety!

Pickles: Jerusalem artichoke, cauliflower, cucumber, dill, onions, watermelon rind, cantaloupe, and honeydew

Tiny dill tomatoes

Kosher dill tomatoes (These are considerably larger than the tiny tomatoes above; therefore, they are less suitable for serving as tidbits. However, the flavor is good and they can be sliced and used as topping for other hors d'oeuvres.)

Pickled midget corn (eaten whole—cob and all)

Pickled mushrooms (prepared *without oil*)

Dilly beans (good in salad, too)

Baby pickled okra

23

Pickled garbanzo beans (These are best served as a relish accompanying meat or fish.)

Raw cauliflower buds with Shrimp Dip I (p. 26)

Strips of *small* yellow, summer squash with Clam Dip (p. 28)

Pretzels

Popcorn, unbuttered (There are now several brands of "Butter Flavored Salt" on the market, fat content negligible. Consult the Appendix, p. 337, for fat range.)

Fruit and vegetable juices (Try serving your tomato juice with a cucumber or celery stick as a stirrer. It has eye appeal and provides contrast in texture. Two interesting vegetable juice variations are Mott's Clamato® and Mott's Beefamato®.)

Fresh fruit cup

Crisp, raw vegetables

Grapefruit, plain or broiled with brown sugar or honey and topped with a cherry

Celery, plain or stuffed with one of the cheese dips listed in the chapter on cheeses

Cheese dip with crackers (The fat content of crackers is listed in the Appendix, Table 3, p. 334, and in Appendix, Table 7, p. 371. It is necessary to take this into account in the overall picture. Further reduction of fat content can be achieved by serving these dips with a plate of raw vegetables—carrot strips, cauliflower buds, celery, strips of small yellow squash—instead of with crackers. The cheese dips described in the chapter on cheeses will vary in fat content between 3.4 and 6.8 grams for a 12-ounce recipe. See the Appendix, Table 3, p. 339, for brand names of low-fat cottage cheeses.)

Pickled beets (Use tiny whole beets and prepare according to recipe in chapter on vegetables or check label on canned beets.)

Stuffed beets (Use tiny pickled beets, hollow slightly
and fill with horseradish.)
Melba toast (Remember that there are many varieties
of Melba toast: white, wheat, rye, salty rye, and
even garlic- or onion-flavored rounds. By using
different flavors and different shapes [oblong or
round] you can add both taste and eye appeal to
your cracker tray. There are available, also,
"Melba thin dietslice" breads by Pepperidge
Farm® and Arnold® which make home preparation of Melba toast simple.)
Norwegian Flatbread® or Swedish Crispbread® (a
thin wafer good with dips or with soups)
Water Crackers

### Stuffed Dill Pickles

Cut kosher dill pickles lengthwise. Scoop out inside.
Stuff with mixture of low-fat cottage cheese and pimento blended in electric mixer. Fasten with toothpicks. Chill and slice.

### Swedish Spiced Shrimp

1 pound raw shrimp
1 cup vinegar
1 sliced onion
1 tablespoon pickling spice tied in
cheesecloth
1 cup water

Cook shrimp in salted water for 3 minutes. Drain, cool,
peel, and de-vein.
Combine remaining ingredients. Bring to a boil.
Cool. Pour over shrimp and chill overnight. Drain.
Serve on toothpicks.

*Fat content of recipe:*
*shrimp, raw, in the shell:* 2.5 grams

## Shrimp with Dip

Peel, wash, and drain

### 2 pounds raw shrimp

Drop into boiling water, reduce heat at once and simmer 3 to 4 minutes. Drain at once to prevent curling and overcooking (never overcook shrimp; it toughens them). Serve with one of the following dips.

*Fat content of recipe:*
*shrimp, raw, in the shell:* 5.0 grams

## Shrimp Dip I

**½ cup Special Mayonnaise (see chapter on salads and salad dressings)**
**3½ tablespoons chili sauce[1]**
**1½ teaspoons prepared horseradish[1]**
**¼ teaspoon grated onion (may be omitted)**
**1 teaspoon Worcestershire sauce**
**1 tablespoon lemon juice**
**½ teaspoon salt**
**¼ teaspoon paprika**

To Special Mayonnaise add the other ingredients. Chill.

*Fat content of recipe:*            *Yield: ¾ cup*
*mayonnaise:* 3.2 grams

[1]You may substitute for the chili sauce and prepared horseradish 3½ tablespoons Stokely's Prepared Cocktail Sauce® or Crosse & Blackwell's Seafood Cocktail Sauce®. (See Shrimp Dip III for analysis.)

## Shrimp Dip II

1 cup catsup
2 tablespoons cider or wine vinegar or lemon juice
4 to 6 drops tabasco sauce
1 tablespoon horseradish
1 tablespoon minced chives or grated onion
¼ cup finely chopped celery
1 teaspoon Worcestershire sauce
½ teaspoon salt

Combine all ingredients.

*Fat content of recipe:*          *Yield: about 1¼ cups*
  *catsup:*  1.0 grams

## Shrimp Dip III

**Stokely's Prepared Cocktail Sauce® or Crosse & Blackwell Seafood Cocktail Sauce®**

Prepared with tomatoes, sugar, vinegar, salt, horseradish, spices, flavoring.
  Any other sauce prepared from these ingredients may be used in place of these brands.

*Fat content of product:*
*approximately the content of catsup, per cup:*
                                                    *1.0 gram*

## Shrimp Dip IV

1 cup cooked shrimp or 1 can (6 ounces) frozen cocktail shrimp
1 box (12 ounces) low-fat cottage cheese

27

**3 tablespoons chili sauce**
**¼ teaspoon citric acid**
**½ teaspoon onion powder**
**¼ teaspoon Worcestershire sauce**
**Dash of tabasco sauce**

Chop shrimp fine. Combine all ingredients in electric blender and blend until smooth. Serve with crackers or Melba Toast.

| *Fat content of recipe:* | *Yield: about 1¼ cups* |
|---|---|
| *shrimp:* | 1.8 grams |
| *low-fat cottage cheese:* | 3.4–6.8 grams |
| *Total:* | 5.2–8.6 grams |

## Clam Dip

**6 ounces low-fat cottage cheese**
**1 can minced clams, drained**
**Dash of Worcestershire sauce**

Put ingredients in electric blender and blend until well-mixed but not smooth.

| *Fat content of recipe:* | *Yield: about 1¼ cups* |
|---|---|
| *low-fat cottage cheese:* | 1.7–3.4 grams |
| *clams:* | 2.7 grams |
| *Total:* | 4.4–6.1 grams |

## Tuna Dip

**1 6½-ounce can water-pack white tuna**
**or dietetic-pack tuna[2]**
**½ cup finely chopped cucumbers**

28

[2]For information on other types of tuna see Appendix, Table 3.

2 teaspoons finely chopped chives
1 tablespoon lemon juice
1 8-ounce carton plain yogurt

Mix first four ingredients well and blend into yogurt.

| Fat content of recipe: | Yield: 2 cups |
|---|---|
| *tuna:* | |
| *water-pack, white:* | 1.5 grams |
| *dietetic-pack, Chicken of* | |
| *the Sea® or Star* | |
| *Kist® brand:* | 3.2 grams |
| *yogurt:* | 3.6 grams |
| *Total:* | 5.1 or 6.8 grams |

## Onion Yogurt Dip I

1 8-ounce carton plain yogurt
1 package (1 ounce) Lipton Cup-a-Soup®
Onion Soup mix

Blend dry onion soup mix into yogurt with a wire whisk until smooth. Refrigerate 4 hours or more to allow mixture to thicken. Serve with crackers or bite-sized raw vegetables. If crackers are used, add the fat content of the crackers to the fat content of this recipe.

| Fat content of recipe: | | Yield: 1 cup |
|---|---|---|
| *yogurt:* | 3.6 grams | |
| *soup mix:* | 0.5 grams | |
| *Total:* | 4.1 grams | |

## Onion Yogurt Dip II

1 8-ounce carton plain yogurt
1 tablespoon dehydrated minced onion
½ teaspoon onion salt

Use the dehydrated onions as they come from the jar. They absorb enough liquid from the yogurt to make the addition of water unnecessary.

Blend these ingredients with a wire whisk and refrigerate four hours or more.

This is a well-flavored dip and can be substituted for Onion Yogurt Dip I, if you do not have the Lipton Cup-a-Soup® on hand or if you wish to save the 0.5 grams fat the mix adds.

*Fat content of recipe:*             *Yield: 1 cup*
   *yogurt:*   3.6 grams

## Scallops Broiled in Blankets

**½ pound scallops, fresh or frozen (not breaded)**
**1 3-ounce package smoked sliced beef or dried beef**

If possible, buy small bay scallops. If these are not available, cut the larger ocean scallops into small chunks. Cut the slices of smoked sliced beef or dried beef in half and fold over to strengthen. Roll scallops in beef, and fasten with toothpick. Place on broiler pan and broil 7 inches below the heat. Watch closely. Serve hot.

| *Fat content of recipe:* | *Yield: 24 pieces* |
|---|---|
| *scallops:* | 0.5 grams |
| *smoked or dried beef:* | 5.4 grams |
| *Fat content per piece:* | 0.2 grams |

30

Consommé and bouillon, which are relatively fat free, may be used as desired. These may be canned, made from cubes, or homemade. There are, too, seasoned stock bases both for making bouillon and for seasoning. Among available brands are:

*fat content per teaspoon*

French®
  *Beef Flavor Stock Base:*                   trace
  *Chicken Flavor Stock Base:*       0.2 grams
Maggi®
  *Beef:*                               0.1 grams
  *Chicken:*                        0.1 grams
  *Clam:*                            0.1 grams
  *Onion:*                         0.1 grams
  *Vegetable:*                   0.1 grams
McCormick®
  *Beef Flavor Base:*              0.1 grams
  *Chicken Seasoning Stock Base:*   0.6 grams   31

*Spice Islands®*
*Chicken Seasoning Stock Base:*          0.3 grams

There are several methods of removing fat from homemade soups:

1. Place a lettuce leaf in the hot soup. When it has absorbed the grease, remove it.

2. Float a paper towel on the surface of the soup; when it has absorbed as much grease as it will hold, discard the towel.

3. Put an ice cube in a cloth and agitate it just under the surface of the soup, letting it collect the rising fat.

4. The most effective method: chill the soup, remove solidified grease from cold soup.

Some canned soups that have less than 2 grams of fat per serving when the can contents are either diluted with an equal volume of water or ready to serve (not diluted), as per directions on the label, are listed below. Other canned soups that have more than 2 grams of fat per serving are included in the Appendix, Table 6, p. 368.

Canned Soup                              *Fat grams*

*Campbell®*

*Contents of 1 cup prepared soup when diluted with water according to the directions on can, one can soup plus one can water*

| | |
|---|---|
| *Beef Broth (Bouillon):* | 0.0 |
| *Black Bean:* | 1.6 |
| *Chicken Broth:* | 1.8 |
| *Chicken Gumbo:* | 1.3 |
| *Chicken Noodle:* | 1.7 |
| *Chicken Noodle-O's:* | 1.9 |
| *Chicken with Rice:* | 1.5 |
| *Chicken & Stars:* | 1.5 |

|  | Fat grams |
|---|---|
| *Consommé (Beef), gelatin added:* | 0.0 |
| *Green Pea:* | 1.8 |
| *Onion:* | 1.6 |
| *Tomato:* | 1.8 |
| *Vegetable:* | 1.6 |
| *Vegetarian Vegetable:* | 1.7 |

**S O U P S**

*Crosse & Blackwell®*
*Contents of ½ can (6½ ounces), not diluted*

| *Black Bean:* | 0.6 |
|---|---|
| *Crab:* | 0.9 |
| *French Onion:* | 1.7 |
| *Manhattan Clam Chowder:* | 1.5 |
| *Minestrone:* | 1.5 |

*Swanson®*
*Contents of 1 cup, not diluted*

| *Beef Broth:* | 0.8 |
|---|---|
| *Chicken Broth:* | 1.6 |

*R & R®*
*Contents of 1 cup, not diluted*

| *Chicken Broth—clear:* | 0.8 |
|---|---|
| *Chicken Broth—with rice:* | 1.6 |

The fat content of dry soup mixes is low.

Soup Mix

*Lipton®—Regular Soups*
*Contents of 1 cup prepared soup when diluted with water according to the directions on the package*

| *Beef Flavor Mushroom Mix:* | 0.8 |
|---|---|
| *Beef Flavor Noodle Soup with* | |
| *Vegetables* | 1.3 |
| *Country Vegetable Soup with Noodles* | 1.1 |
| *Green Pea Soup* | 1.7 |
| *Noodle Soup with Real Chicken Broth* | 1.8 |

33

|  | Fat grams |
|---|---|
| Onion Soup | 0.8 |
| Potato Soup | 1.2 |
| Ring-O Noodle Soup with Real Chicken Broth | 1.2 |
| Tomato Vegetable Soup with Noodles | 1.6 |
| Vegetable Beef Soup | 1.5 |

Lipton® Cup-a-Soup (instant soup)

Contents of 1 6-ounce serving when mixed according to directions on package

| Beef Flavored Cup-a-Broth | 0.1 |
|---|---|
| Beef Flavor Noodle | 0.3 |
| Chicken Flavored Cup-a-Broth | 0.7 |
| Chicken Noodle with Chicken Meat | 0.9 |
| Green Pea | 1.4 |
| Noodle Soup—Chicken Flavor | 0.8 |
| Onion | 0.5 |
| Spring Vegetable | 0.8 |
| Tomato | 0.5 |

## Soup Stock

**3 pounds brisket, shinbone, or other soup meat and bone.**

Sprinkle with:

**1 tablespoon salt**

Let stand for 1 hour, then add 3 quarts cold water, and soak ½ hour. Simmer 3½ hours uncovered.
Add:

**2 cups vegetables**
**¾ cup tomatoes**
**½ green pepper**

Simmer, covered, ½ hour. Strain; chill; remove the fat.

Variations may be made by substituting chicken or veal for beef. This is a standard method for making soup stock. The fat content will be negligible if the stock is chilled and the fat removed as directed.

### Jellied Soup

Add 2 tablespoons gelatin, dissolved in small amount of cold water over hot water, to 4 cupfuls of liquid. Chill.

### Ruby Consommé

- **4 cups tomato juice**
- **2 cups chicken broth (fat removed)**
- **1 teaspoon chopped chives or chopped onion**
- **1 stalk celery, chopped**
- **½ teaspoon Worcestershire sauce**
- **¼ clove garlic**
- **1 teaspoon sugar**
- **½ teaspoon salt**
- **2 whole cloves**
- **1 tablespoon lemon juice (fresh, frozen, or canned)**

Simmer tomato juice, chicken broth, chives, celery, Worcestershire sauce, garlic, sugar, and seasonings 45 minutes. Add lemon juice; stir well and strain. Serve hot.

*Fat content of recipe:*     negligible     *6–8 servings*

### Basic Cream Soup

- **2 tablespoons flour**
- **½ cup warm water**

35

2 cups evaporated skimmed milk, undiluted
1 cup water
1½ cups vegetable purée[1] or cooked
minced vegetables
1 teaspoon salt
¼ teaspoon monosodium glutamate
Pepper

Blend flour with ½ cup water until a smooth paste is
made. Add 1 cup of evaporated skimmed milk and
cook about 10 minutes until thick. Add other ingredients. Stir constantly and cook an additional 5
minutes. Other seasonings may be added, such as
chopped onion, chopped celery, depending on the
vegetable used and also on how bland a soup is
desired.

| | |
|---|---|
| *Fat content of recipe:* | *4 servings* |
| *evaporated skimmed milk:* | 1.0 grams |
| *Fat content per serving:* | 0.3 grams |

### Shrimp Bisque

2 tablespoons chopped onion
2 tablespoons chopped celery
3 cups boiling water
1 package Lipton Noodle Soup with Real
Chicken Broth®
1 cup evaporated skimmed milk, undiluted
½ pound cooked shrimp

In saucepan cook onions and celery until soft in small
amount of the boiling water and a teaspoon of the

[1]Jars of puréed baby food may be used (two jars).

soup mix. Stir in water, soup mix, and one-half of
shrimp, finely cut. Cover, simmer for 7 minutes. Stir in
evaporated skimmed milk and remaining shrimp, cut
into bite-size pieces.

*Fat content of recipe:*                                    *4–6 servings*
  *soup mix:*                                    7.2 grams
  *evaporated skimmed milk:*        0.5 grams
  *shrimp:*                                        1.8 grams
  *Total:*                                          9.5 grams
*Fat content per serving, based on 4 servings:* 2.4 grams
*Fat content per serving, based on 6 servings:* 1.6 grams

S
O
U
P
S

### Tomato Orange Blossom Soup

  **1 can (10¾ ounces) condensed tomato
    soup**
  **½ soup can orange juice**
  **½ soup can water**
  **Ground cloves**

Combine soup, juice, water, and cloves. Heat; stir now
and then. To serve cold, place in refrigerator for at
least 4 hours. Serve in chilled mugs or bowls.

*Fat content of recipe:*                                    *2–3 servings*
  *tomato soup:*   4.5 grams
*Fat content per serving, based on 2 servings:* 2.3 grams
*Fat content per serving, based on 3 servings:* 1.5 grams

### Gazpacho

  **1 (1 pound) can tomatoes, chopped**
  **1 No. 2 can tomato juice**
  **Juice of one lemon**
  **1 tablespoon Worcestershire sauce**
  **¼ cup cucumber, finely chopped**

37

¼ cup green pepper, finely chopped
¼ cup green onions, finely chopped
¼ cup celery, finely chopped
2 tablespoons parsley, finely chopped
Salt and freshly ground pepper, to taste
1 clove garlic, crushed

Combine chopped vegetables. Add to liquids and seasonings. (If only slight garlic taste is preferred, add one whole clove garlic, peeled and pierced with a toothpick. Remove after one hour.) Chill at least 5 or 6 hours and serve in small soup plates with a slice of fresh lime.

*Fat content of recipe:*     negligible     *6 servings*

## Chilled Cucumber Soup

2 medium cucumbers
1 cup water
2 slices onion
¼ teaspoon salt
⅛ teaspoon pepper
¼ cup flour
2 cups Swanson® Chicken Broth
¼ bay leaf or 2 cloves
1 8-ounce carton plain yogurt, chilled
1 tablespoon finely chopped dill or chives

Pare, seed, and slice the cucumbers. Combine with water, onion, salt, and pepper and cook, covered, until very soft. Put them through a fine strainer or electric blender. Combine flour with ½ cup chicken broth and stir until smooth. Gradually stir in the remaining chicken broth. Add the cucumber purée, bay leaf, or cloves. Stir the soup over low heat. Simmer 2 minutes. Chill in a covered jar. When ready to serve, stir in yogurt and dill or chives. Serve very cold in chilled bowls.

*Fat content of recipe:*         *4–6 servings*
  *chicken broth:*       3.2 grams
  *yogurt:*            3.6 grams
  *Total:*             6.8 grams
*Fat content per serving, based on 4 servings:* 1.7 grams
*Fat content per serving, based on 6 servings:* 1.1 grams

**Pea Soup, Garnished**

**1 can (11½ ounces) Campbell® green pea soup**
**1 soup can water**
**1 tablespoon yogurt per serving**
**Fresh chives**

Mix soup and water as directed on can. When ready to serve, top with chopped, fresh chives and 1 tablespoon yogurt.

*Fat content of recipe:*         *2–3 servings*
  *green pea soup:*      4.5 grams
  *yogurt, per tablespoon:*   0.2 grams
*Fat content per serving, based on 2 servings:*
  *soup:*        2.3 grams
  *yogurt:*      0.2 grams
  *Total:*       2.5 grams
*Fat content per serving, based on 3 servings:*
  *soup:*        1.5 grams
  *yogurt:*      0.2 grams
  *Total:*       1.7 grams

**Minestrone Soup**

**1 package (7.5 ounces) Reese Italian Home Style Minestrone Soup Mix®**

SOUPS

**2 quarts water**
**1 beef marrow or soup bone**
**1 clove garlic**
**1 large onion, diced**
**1 can (303 size) tomatoes**
**¼ cup uncooked spaghetti**
**1 tablespoon salt or seasoned salt**

The mix consists of pinto beans, black beans, Great Northern beans, green and yellow split peas, lentils, red beans, garbanzo beans, and barley.

Rinse beans, soak contents 3 hours or overnight. Combine with other ingredients. Cook until tender. For quick cooking use pressure cooker. Refrigerate overnight and next day remove congealed fat. Reheat and adjust seasoning.

| *Fat content of recipe:* | *Yield: 8 cups* |
|---|---|
| *beans:* | 3.3 grams |
| *soup bone:* | negligible |
| *spaghetti:* | 0.7 grams |
| *Total:* | 4.0 grams |
| *Fat content per cup:* | 0.5 grams |


### Oriental Beef Broth

**2 (10½-ounce) cans condensed beef broth**
**2 cups water**
**1 cup uncooked thread noodles**
**½ cup dry sherry**
**2 tablespoons thinly sliced green onions**
**2 teaspoons soy sauce**

In a medium saucepan mix beef broth, water and uncooked noodles. Bring to a boil; reduce heat. Cover and simmer 10 minutes. Remove from heat. Add sherry, green onions, and soy sauce.

| Fat content of recipe: | Yield: 6 1-cup servings |
|---|---|
| noodles: | 2.0 grams |
| Fat content per serving: | 0.3 grams |

*Suggested garnishes for soups, to be used according to the type of soup:*

| | |
|---|---|
| Lemon slices | Popcorn (unbuttered) |
| Chopped chives | Paprika |
| Fresh dill | Meringue |
| Parsley, sprigs or chopped | Celery leaves |
| | Watercress |
| Riced, hard-cooked egg white | |

*Suggested accompaniments:*

| | |
|---|---|
| Water crackers | Ry-Krisp® |
| Pretzel sticks | Melba Toast |
| Norwegian Flatbread® | Swedish Crispbread® |

Certain general information on fat content and methods of cooking is helpful in planning the use of meats, fish, and poultry in low-fat menus.

Meats, fish, and poultry vary in fat content both according to kind and cut. In the week's menus a reasonable balance must be maintained between those of higher fat content and those of lower. Beef, lamb, fresh pork, and veal can be included, but they must be cooked according to low-fat methods and must be balanced during the week with main dishes of lower fat content—poultry, fish, or high-protein vegetables such as beans. Cured pork contains more fat than fresh, when compared cut by cut. The light-cure, commercial ham is appreciably lower than the country cure. It is possible to serve a slice or two of breakfast bacon or Canadian bacon occasionally, provided they

43

are carefully drained after cooking. In this case Canadian bacon is to be preferred, since the fat content per pound is considerably lower and the protein content is higher in relation to the amount of fat than in breakfast bacon. In poultry light meat is of lower fat content than dark. Fish, listed per pound, flesh only, raw, range from 0.5 grams fat (haddock) to 90.3 grams fat (Siscowet lake trout).

Study the fat content of meats, fish and poultry listed in Table 3. Choice grade is used because it is the grade most often purchased by the consumer on the retail market. Grades are determined by the amount of marbling (layering of fat between the tissues). "Prime" grade—the top grade in beef and lamb—is also the highest in fat content. It is followed by "choice" and "good." There are other grades, lower on the scale and lower in fat content, but the consumer does not see these on the meat counter.

The fat content is given for raw meat, 1 pound (454 grams) separable lean, where that figure is available. Separable lean is the portion of meat left when it has been trimmed of all visible fat. The figures for veal are for 1 pound (454 grams), medium-fat class, without bone. The figure for separable lean of veal would be somewhat lower. This underscores the point that fat is lowered by trimming and consuming only the lean portion.

Figures on the fat content of fish in Table 3 are, in general, the figure for 1 pound, raw, flesh only. In a few instances where the information might be helpful, the figure is given also for 1 pound, raw, whole, before the fish is dressed.

These figures will give you the basis for making intelligent menu choices. A willingness to eat a varied diet will allow you much more freedom in the use of the cuts containing more fat, because they can be offset by more or less fat-free dishes. In fact, we believe the success of a low-fat bill of fare depends not on narrowing of the diet pattern but on its broadness and versatility.

There are various cooking techniques which will appreciably decrease the fat intake without detracting in any way from the flavor of the food.

Frying is not allowed, but the ready availability of Teflon®-coated cooking utensils has made pan-browning a simple matter. There are several methods of treating non-Teflon®-coated pans to make pan-browning a success. The skillet can be rubbed with a salt bag or sprinkled with salt. Pam®, Lean-Fry®, and Pan Pal® are preparations[1] which, if applied to cooking pans according to the manufacturer's directions, will greatly reduce or eliminate the need for grease. They keep food from sticking, so that many foods can be cooked with no grease and with others much less grease is needed. Similar products are now appearing on the market which contain corn oil. These are not suitable for low-fat cooking. Watch those labels!

Before cooking, the excess fat should always be cut from the meat. In baking or broiling the meat should be placed on racks to allow the fat to drain off during cooking. The fat released by cooking should be drained off before serving.

The most effective method for removing fat released by cooking is to cook the meat partially the day before it is to be used. The meat and broth can then be refrigerated, and the next day it will be possible to lift off the layer of fat which has risen to the top of the broth and congealed. You have left an excellent meat

[1]Pam®, Boyle-Midway, Inc., New York, N.Y. 10017; Lean-Fry®, American Home Products Corp., 685 3rd Ave., New York, N.Y. 10017; Pan Pal®, Blue Cross Laboratories, North Hollywood, Calif., 91605.

MEATS, FISH, AND POULTRY

45

stock which has lost none of its flavor but which is essentially fat-free.

It is possible to absorb some fat by skimming the liquid, while still hot, with a piece of bread to absorb the free fat. This method is not nearly so effective as the refrigeration described in the preceding paragraph, however. The authors find the refrigeration method not only more effective but also easier.

Try seasoning meats, fish and poultry with the herbs and spices suggested in Table 8. You may cook with wine, beer or brandy. These are fat free and leave the food well-flavored.

## For the Outdoor Cook

For anyone with a barbecue pit or grill, cooking on the grill or on a spit over the grill is an excellent low-fat technique. It allows some of the fat to drip away as it cooks. A word of caution: many recipes for barbecue include basting sauces containing oil. Do not use these. The oil is not necessary, because the fat in the meat will prevent drying out. Instead, use one of the Good Seasons® salad dressings made according to the instructions on page 167. The garlic flavor is especially successful in this method of cooking.

There is one basic difference in preparation between oven and outdoor cooking. For the oven, excess fat is trimmed *before cooking*. For the outdoor grill, excess fat is removed *after cooking, but before serving*.

These recipes are suitable for grill or spit:

Beef
    Chuck, shoulder or English cut basted with garlic-
        flavored Good Seasons® salad dressing, page 66
    Shishkebab, page 67

Beef Kabobs, page 68
Lamb
  Leg of lamb butterfly, page 79
  Shashlik en brochette, page 80
Poultry
  Chicken pieces, cooked on the grill and basted with
    barbecue sauce, page 194
  Spit-cooked fryers, page 145
  Spit-cooked Cornish hen, page 151
  Plantation chicken, page 127
  Skewered chicken, page 142
  Rotisserie Chinese duck, page 148
Fish
  Barbecued fish, page 103
  Oysters on the grill, page 120

## Beef

### Hamburgers I

Make thick patties of lean ground beef. Make a deep
thumbprint in the top. Heat an iron skillet, sprinkle
with salt. Place hamburgers in skillet, thumbprint up,
and cook on top of range until bottom of patties
brown. Remove from heat; fill thumbprint with Worcestershire sauce; brown tops under broiler.

*Fat content of recipe:*
  *ground round steak, raw, without bone, separable
    lean, 1 pound:*  21.3 grams

### Hamburgers II

Place hamburgers in broiler and cook till crispy brown.
Prepare following fat-free gravy:

3 tablespoons flour
1 beef bouillon cube
1 cup hot water
¼ teaspoon salt

Brown flour in frying pan. Dissolve bouillon cube in hot water. Slowly add to flour, to make paste. Cook, stirring constantly, until thick. For variation in flavor stir ½ package dehydrated onion soup mix into water before adding to flour. Remove patties to serving dish and pour gravy over them. Serve at once.

*Fat content of recipe:*
  *ground round steak, raw,*
    *without bone, separable*
      *lean, 1 pound:*                21.3 grams
    *flour:*                           negligible
    *Total:*                          21.3 grams
*Fat content of recipe, including onion soup:*
    *onion soup mix:*                1.2 grams
    *Total:*                         22.5 grams


**Beef Stew I**

1½ pounds beef
  Flour, seasoned with salt and pepper
  Boiling water
¼ cup sliced onions
2 bay leaves
  Whole scraped carrots
  Potatoes

Trim all excess fat from beef; cut in 1½-inch cubes; dredge beef with flour. Sear the meat in a hot heavy pot or skillet. Cover meat with boiling water; add onions and bay leaves; cover pot and simmer 1½ hours. Skim fat from top of stew by using a piece of bread or allow to cool and remove the solid sheet of congealed fat (recommended method). Add vegetables. Cook additional 30–40 minutes or until vegetables are done.

*Fat content of recipe:*                    *4–6 servings*
   *chuck beef, raw, without bone, separable lean, 1½*
      *pounds:*     50.4 grams
*This will be decreased by skimming the broth as directed.*

### Beef Stew II (Pressure Cooker Method)

**1½ pounds beef, dredged with seasoned
   flour
1 bay leaf
   Scraped whole carrots
   Onions
   Potatoes, peeled, whole or halves,
   depending on size**

Trim all excess fat from meat; cut in 1½-inch cubes; place on rack in pressure cooker. Add bay leaf and enough water to come up to rack. Bring up pressure and cook 30 minutes. Remove meat from broth and store in covered container in refrigerator. Store broth in separate covered container in refrigerator. Next day lift hardened layer of fat from broth. Place broth in pan or pressure cooker together with vegetables. Cook until vegetables are done. During last 5 minutes of cooking, thicken gravy with flour and return meat for reheating with vegetables and gravy. The stew may simmer a few minutes longer if desired.

*Fat content of recipe:*                    *4–6 servings*
   *chuck beef, raw, without bone, separable lean, 1½*
      *pounds:*     50.4 grams

49

This will be decreased by skimming the broth as directed.

## Monterey Beef Stew

3 pounds stewing beef, cubed
2 large onions, sliced
2 garlic cloves, minced
1 cup chopped celery
¼ cup chopped parsley
2½ cups canned tomatoes
1 bay leaf
½ teaspoon thyme
1 cup peas
12 small carrots
4 potatoes, cut up
½ cup flour
1 tablespoon salt
Freshly ground black pepper

Combine meat, sliced onions, garlic, celery, parsley, tomatoes, bay leaf, thyme, salt, pepper, and 2½ cups of water in large pot. Bring to a boil, reduce heat, cover, and simmer for 2 hours. Add remaining vegetables and simmer for 1 hour. Blend flour with ¾ cup of cold water and stir into stew. Simmer for 5 minutes.

*Fat content of recipe:*          *6 servings*
*chuck beef, raw, without bone, separable lean, 3 pounds:*      100.8 grams
*This will be decreased by skimming the broth as directed. In that case, broth should be refrigerated after the first 2 hours of cooking. Remaining vegetables and flour should be added after broth has been skimmed.*

## Beef Stew with Red Wine

3 pounds lean beef stew meat, cubed
2 tablespoons flour
2 carrots, diced
1 large onion, diced
1 clove garlic, chopped or put through garlic press
Several sprigs parsley, chopped
Pinch of thyme
1 bay leaf, crushed
4 whole allspice
1 10½-ounce can condensed consommé
1½ cups dry red table wine
Salt and pepper to taste
1 1-pound can small whole onions, drained
1 8-ounce can mushrooms, drained
2 tablespoons brandy

Brown cubes of meat on all sides in Teflon® or treated skillet. Sprinkle flour over meat; stir well. Add all remaining ingredients except whole onions, mushrooms, and brandy. Bring to a boil, turn heat very low and simmer, covered, for about two and one-half hours, or until meat is fork tender. Stir frequently, and, if gravy seems too thick, add a little of the liquid drained from the mushrooms. Shortly before serving, add the whole onions, mushrooms, and brandy. Taste and correct seasoning if necessary.

| | |
|---|---|
| *Fat content of recipe:* | *6–8 servings* |
| *chuck beef, raw, without bone,* | |
| *separable lean, 3 pounds:* | 100.8 grams |
| *consommé:* | negligible |
| *Total:* | 100.8 grams |

This will be decreased by skimming the broth as directed. In that case, the broth should be refrigerated and skimmed before adding the onions, mushrooms and brandy.

## Meat Loaf I

> **2 slices dry bread or toast, broken in pieces**
> **½ cup warm liquefied nonfat skim milk**
> **1 beaten egg**
> **¼ cup minced onion**
> **1 pound ground lean beef**
> **1 teaspoon salt**
> **¼ teaspoon pepper**
> **½ cup chili sauce**
> **1 bouillon cube**
> **½ cup hot water**

Soften bread in milk; add egg, onion, meat, seasonings; mix thoroughly. Form into loaf and place in center of square pan. Spread with chili sauce. Dissolve bouillon cube in hot water and pour around loaf. Bake in moderate oven (350°) for 1½ hours.

| Fat content of recipe: | 4–6 servings |
|---|---|
| bread: | 2.0 grams |
| milk: | trace |
| egg: | 6.0 grams |
| beef, round, raw, ground, separable lean: | 21.3 grams |
| chili sauce: | 0.4 grams |
| Total: | 29.7 grams |
| Fat content per serving, based on 4 servings: | 7.4 grams |
| Fat content per serving, based on 6 servings: | 5.0 grams |

## Meat Loaf II

1 egg, beaten
1 pound ground lean beef
4 saltines, broken in pieces
1 teaspoon salt
¼ teaspoon pepper
1 teaspoon rubbed sage or fresh sage, chopped
1 fresh tomato, cut in pieces
¼ cup liquefied nonfat dry milk

To beaten egg add meat, crackers, and seasonings; mix thoroughly. Add chopped tomato, handle carefully, and mix into other ingredients. Form into loaf. Pour milk over top to moisten. Bake in moderate oven (350°) for 1 hour.

| *Fat content of recipe:* | *4–6 servings* |
|---|---|
| *egg:* | 6.0 grams |
| *beef, round, raw, ground, separable lean:* | 21.3 grams |
| *saltines:* | 1.0 grams |
| *Total:* | 28.3 grams |

*Fat content per serving, based on 4 servings:*
7.1 grams
*Fat content per serving, based on 6 servings:*
4.7 grams

## Beef Chunks with Corn and Tomatoes

1¼ pounds top round steak cut in 1½-inch cubes
1 1-pound can tomatoes, drained
1 12-ounce can Niblets® corn
½ teaspoon basil
Pinch nutmeg
Salt and pepper

Pan-brown meat in Teflon® or treated skillet. Place in casserole with tomatoes, corn, and seasonings. Bake in moderate oven for 25 minutes.

*Fat content of recipe:*               *4 servings*
   *beef, round, raw,*
      *separable lean:*        26.6 grams
*Fat content per serving:*      6.7 grams

## Swiss Steak

**2 pounds round steak**
**Garlic clove**
**Flour**
**1 teaspoon salt**
**⅛ teaspoon pepper**
**½ cup chopped onion**
**2 cups boiling tomatoes[2]**

Wipe the steak with a damp cloth and trim the fat off the edges. Rub it with a half clove of garlic. With the edge of a heavy plate pound into both sides as much flour, combined with the salt and pepper, as the steak will hold. Cut the steak into pieces or leave it whole. Pan-brown in a seasoned or salted skillet to prevent it from sticking. Pour off all drippings. Add the chopped onion and tomatoes. Cover the casserole closely and place it in a slow oven (275°) for 2 hours or more. Remove the steak to a hot platter.

*Fat content of recipe:*               *6 servings*
   *beef, round, raw,*
      *separable lean:*        42.6 grams
*Fat content per serving:*      7.1 grams

[2]One cupful boiling water and 2 cupfuls or more chopped carrots, celery, and peppers may be substituted for the tomatoes, or added to them.

### Marinated Swiss Steak

**2-2½ pounds round steak**

Marinade:

> **1½ cups or more claret or burgundy**
> **2 large onions, sliced**
> **1 teaspoon ginger**
> **1 lemon, sliced, including rind**
> **1 tablespoon salt**
> **12 peppercorns**

Marinate from 12 to 24 hours, turning once or twice. Drain, brown in Teflon® or treated pan. Pour off fat. Add marinade and cook slowly, about 1½ hours. When cooked, refrigerate the meat and the marinade separately overnight. The next day, lift off the layer of fat on the chilled marinade. Return meat and marinade to pan and heat thoroughly. Thicken juice with flour to provide gravy.

If you wish to make this recipe ahead of time and store it in the deep freeze, it is best to have somewhat more juice than you ordinarily would. This eliminates the possibility of dryness when defrosted and cooked.

*Fat content of recipe:*          *5 servings*
  *beef, round, raw,*
    *separable lean:*      42.6–53.3 grams
*Fat content per serving:*      8.5–10.7 grams
  *This will be reduced by removing layer of congealed fat from marinade.*

### Beef Burgundy

> **2 pounds lean round beef**
> **2-3 medium onions**
> **1½ tablespoons flour**

**Marjoram**
**Thyme**
**Salt and pepper**
**½ cup beef bouillon**
**½ cup Burgundy**
**½ to ¾ pound sliced fresh mushrooms**
**or 1 large can plain sliced mushrooms**
**(not broiled in butter)**

Peel and slice onions and quick-cook in Teflon®-coated or treated skillet. Remove to separate dish. Remove all fat from beef, cut into strips about 1½ × ½ inches, and quick-cook in same pan. When brown on all sides, sprinkle with flour and add herbs (approximately ¼ teaspoon each). Add beef bouillon and Burgundy. Stir well. Cover and let simmer very gently for 1½ hours. While simmering, it may be necessary to add more bouillon. Add onions and mushrooms. Serve.

This dish freezes well. If frozen, remove from freezer, thaw at room temperature, reheat in covered dish in 350° oven.

| | | |
|---|---|---|
| *Fat content of recipe:* | | *5 servings* |
| *beef, round, raw,* | | |
| *separable lean:* | 42.6 grams | |
| *Fat content per serving:* | 8.5 grams | |

### Beef Fondue

**2 pounds beef, rib-eye fillet**
**2 cups Swanson® chicken broth**
**2 cups dry white wine**
**1 onion thinly sliced**
**3 ribs celery, chopped**
**1 clove garlic, chopped**
**8 juniper berries, crushed[3]**

³Available on speciality spice shelves.

10 peppercorns, crushed
½ teaspoon salt or to taste
1 teaspoon fresh tarragon, chopped, or
    ½ teaspoon dry
2 sprigs parsley
1 bay leaf
2 sprigs fresh thyme or ½ teaspoon dry

Combine all ingredients except beef and bring to a boil; then refrigerate. If possible, make this broth three days ahead to allow flavors to blend.

Trim all fat from meat and cut in bite-size pieces. Put whole quantity of broth in fondue pot and allow to simmer as you cook the meat a serving at a time.

This broth is also excellent for Shrimp Fondue (page 109).

*Fat content of recipe:*                    *4–6 servings*
  *beef, rib, raw,*
    *separable lean:*         105.2 *grams*
  *chicken broth:*              3.2 *grams*
  *Total:*                    108.4 *grams*
*Fat content per serving, based on 4 servings:*
                                  27.1 *grams*
*Fat content per serving, based on 6 servings:*
                                  18.1 *grams*


**Deviled Steak Strips**

1½ pounds round steak
¼ cup all-purpose flour
¼ cup chopped onion
1 clove garlic, minced
1½ cups water
½ cup tomato sauce
1 tablespoon vinegar
1 teaspoon horseradish

1 teaspoon prepared mustard
¾ teaspoon salt
¼ teaspoon pepper

Trim excess fat from meat. Cut into thin strips about 2 inches long; coat with flour. In Teflon®-coated or treated skillet, brown meat, onion, and garlic. Stir in 1 cup water, the tomato sauce, vinegar, horseradish, mustard, salt, and pepper. Cover and simmer for 1 hour or until meat is tender, stirring occasionally. Stir in the remaining ½ cup water, scraping browned bits from bottom of pan; heat through. Serve over noodles or rice.

| Fat content of recipe: | 4 servings |
|---|---|
| beef, round, raw, | |
| separable lean: | 32.0 grams |
| noodles, 2 cups uncooked: | 3.5 grams |
| rice, 1 cup raw: | 1.0 grams |
| Total, over noodles: | 35.5 grams |
| Total, over rice: | 33.0 grams |
| Fat content per serving | |
| over noodles: | 8.9 grams |
| over rice: | 8.3 grams |

## Grilled Flank Steak

Flank steak
Soy sauce
1 teaspoon thyme
Salt and pepper
1¼ cups chopped shallots or green
    onions
1¼ cups red wine
2 tablespoons finely chopped parsley

Brush flank steak with soy sauce and sprinkle well with

salt, freshly ground black pepper and a teaspoon of dried thyme, crumbled. Let stand for an hour or so. Brush again with soy sauce and grill over brisk fire, 3 to 4 minutes on each side for rare steaks. Carve with sharp knife in thin slices on the diagonal. For the sauce: combine shallots or green onions and red wine. Bring just to boiling point. Add salt to taste. Add parsley and spoon over steak slices.

*Fat content of recipe:*
*flank steak, 1 pound, separable lean:* 25.9 grams

### Flank Steak with Spinach Stuffing

1 flank steak (1½ to 2 pounds)
1 cup grated soft breadcrumbs
1 10-ounce package frozen, chopped spinach, cooked and *well* drained
¼ cup grated imitation pasteurized process cheese spread, Chef's Delight® or Count Down®
1 egg, slightly beaten
¼ teaspoon sage
Dash of thyme and marjoram
Salt and pepper to taste
Flour
1 8-ounce can tomato sauce
½ cup dry red table wine
½ cup beef bouillon
1 small onion, chopped
1 clove garlic, chopped or put through garlic press

Have butcher score flank steak. Mix breadcrumbs, spinach, cheese, egg, sage, thyme, marjoram, salt, and pepper. Spread mixture evenly over steak; roll up from one wide side to the other, tucking in the ends as you roll. Tie or skewer securely. Dredge rolled steak with flour. In Teflon® or treated skillet brown steak slowly on all sides. Remove to casserole. Mix tomato sauce, wine, beef bouillon, onion, and garlic; add a dash of thyme and marjoram and salt and pepper to taste; pour over browned steak. Cover tightly and bake at 350° for 1 to 1½ hours or until meat is very tender. Turn steak occasionally during cooking, and add a little water if necessary to keep gravy from becoming too thick. Remove string or skewers; place steak on heated platter and garnish with parsley or watercress; slice, cutting across fibers. Serve gravy separately.

| | |
|---|---|
| *Fat content of recipe:* | *5–6 servings* |
| *flank steak, 1½ to* | |
| *2 pounds, separable* | |
| *lean:* | 38.9–51.8 grams |
| *breadcrumbs:* | 5.0 grams |
| *imitation pasteurized* | |
| *process cheese spread:* | 2.8–0.6 grams |
| *egg:* | 6.0 grams |
| *beef bouillon:* | negligible |
| *Total with Chef's* | |
| *Delight®:* | 52.7–65.6 grams |
| *Total with Count Down®:* | 50.5–63.4 grams |
| *Fat content per serving, based on 5* | |
| *servings:* | 10.1–13.1 grams |
| *Fat content per serving, based on 6* | |
| *servings:* | 8.4–11.0 grams |

## Beef with Green Peppers

**1 pound flank steak, sliced across the grain, ¼ inch thick by 2 inches long**
**4 tablespoons soy sauce**
**1 tablespoon cornstarch**

1 tablespoon dry sherry
1 teaspoon sugar
¼ teaspoon monosodium glutamate
1 slice ginger root
4 tablespoons water
½ chicken bouillon cube
2 green peppers, medium—or 3 small
   ones (large ones have thicker skin)

Mix sliced beef with soy sauce, cornstarch, sherry, sugar, and monosodium glutamate. Set aside. Rinse green pepper, cut in chunks and discard seeds and trim off white soft parts of inside of pepper. (Rinse before cutting so the water will not stay inside the pepper.) Dissolve bouillon cube in water.

Put 2 tablespoons of the chicken bouillon in a hot skillet (Teflon® or treated) over high heat. Add green peppers, stirring constantly until the peppers turn a darker green. Remove peppers and spread out on a plate. In the same skillet add remaining 2 tablespoons of bouillon and ginger root. Stir in beef mixture and turn constantly until the beef is almost cooked. Add green peppers and mix thoroughly. If mixture thickens too rapidly add a small amount of water while cooking. For crispness, do not overcook. Serve immediately over rice.

| *Fat content of recipe:* | *2–3 servings* |
|---|---|
| flank steak, 1 pound, separable lean: | 25.9 grams |
| ½ cup rice, raw: | 0.5 grams |
| Total: | 26.4 grams |
| *Fat content per serving, based on 2 servings:* | |
| | 13.2 grams |
| *Fat content per serving, based on 3 servings:* | |
| | 8.8 grams |

# Steamed Chinese Dumplings

These dumplings are a substantial and tasty dish. By varying the size of the wrappers and the quantity of filling in each you can make tidbits or a dish which, combined with a green salad, makes an interesting supper menu.

For the wrappers:

**2 cups sifted flour**
**1 teaspoon salt**
**2 eggs, slightly beaten**
**Water**

Combine flour and salt, add beaten eggs and enough water to make a stiff dough. Roll out very thin on a slightly floured board. Cut into squares.

| Fat content of recipe: | Yield: 20 4-inch squares |
|---|---|
| flour: | 2.0 grams |
| eggs: | 12.0 grams |
| Total: | 14.0 grams |
| Fat content per 4-inch square: | 0.7 grams |

For the filling:

**1 pound lean ground beef, round**
**2 cups chopped green onion**
**1 cup fresh or canned chopped mush-rooms**
**1 clove garlic put through garlic press**
**1 teaspoon salt**
**1 tablespoon soy sauce**
**1 tablespoon sugar**
**3 tablespoons cornstarch**

Mix filling well. Fill wrappers with 1 to 1½ teaspoons and moisten edges so, when cover is folded to form a triangle containing the filling, the pastry is sealed.

Steam over boiling water 15 minutes. These may be frozen and reheated later.

| Fat content of recipe: | Yield: 60 1- to 1½-teaspoon servings |
|---|---|
| lean ground beef, round: | 21.3 grams |
| soy sauce: | 0.1 grams |
| Total: | 21.4 grams |
| Fat content per teaspoon: | 0.4 grams |

If you wish, you may serve either of the following dipping sauces with these dumplings.

**Sauce with Onion**

1 part soy sauce
1 part white vinegar
    Chopped green onion or garlic

**Sauce with Ginger**

¼ cup soy sauce
¼ cup white vinegar
2 tablespoons minced ginger or 2 teaspoons powdered ginger
1 tablespoon minced garlic
½ teaspoon sugar

## Roasts

Meats should be kept cold and at an even temperature. When a roast is brought home, it should be unwrapped and stored in the refrigerator in an open dish, loosely covered with waxed paper. To prepare, wipe with cloth wrung out in cold water; cut off hard edges and all excess fat. Allow roast to stand until it reaches room temperature. Place on a rack in roasting pan and roast according to the following timetable:

|  | Oven Temperature | Minutes per Pound | Thermometer Reading |
|---|---|---|---|
| Beef, rare | 325°F. | 18–20 | 140°F. |
| Beef, medium | 325°F. | 22–25 | 160°F. |
| Beef, well-done | 325°F. | 27–30 | 170°F. |

An alternate method of roasting is to preheat the oven to 550° and reduce immediately to 350° when the roast is put in the oven.

A meat thermometer is invaluable in either method to make certain the meat is done to your taste. Remove meat shortly before desired thermometer temperature is reached. Meat will continue cooking from internal heat.

Remember that with roasts as well as stew, the fat can be congealed and removed, leaving a low-fat base for gravy. In this case the meat should be partially roasted the day before it is to be used. The pan drippings can then be removed and stored in a covered container in the refrigerator. The following day, the congealed layer of fat will be ready to be lifted off and the broth used as the gravy base. If you do not wish to cook your roast a day ahead, drain the drippings, chill, remove fat, and reserve broth for future use. Substitute the following fat-free gravy with the freshly cooked roast.

### Gravy

3 tablespoons flour
1 beef bouillon cube
1 cup hot water
¼ teaspoon salt

Brown flour in frying pan. Dissolve bouillon cube in hot water. Slowly add to flour, to make paste. Cook, stirring constantly, until thick.

*Fat content of recipe:*
   *rib, raw, 1 pound, separable lean:*   52.6 grams
   *These figures can be appreciably reduced by removing the fat released by cooking by the method described.*

### Sauerbraten

**4–4½ pound chuck beef roast, with bone**
**1½ cups vinegar**
**½ cup red wine**
**1 cup water**
**2 tablespoons sugar**
**½ teaspoon whole black pepper**
**4 bay leaves**
**3 medium onions, sliced**
**12 whole cloves**
**1 teaspoon mustard seed**
**2 teaspoons salt**
**⅓ cup gingersnap crumbs**
**Salt and pepper**
**1 cup liquefied nonfat milk**

Make marinade of liquids and seasonings listed above. Marinate the roast in it in a crock for two to four days, depending upon the degree of sourness you like.

After marinating in a cold place, drain and dry. Add solids from marinade and 1 cup of liquid. Simmer, covered, very slowly about 3½ hours, adding more liquid from marinade if necessary. Sauerbraten may be simmered on top of the stove or in a very slow (300°) oven. Save remaining marinade for use next day. Refrigerate overnight, putting meat and the juices from cooking in separate containers. Next day, lift off layer of fat which has hardened on top of juices. Return roast and defatted juices to pan. Add more marinade. Simmer approximately ½ hour longer. Then add gingersnap crumbs, salt, pepper, and nonfat milk. Allow to simmer until gravy thickens.

*Fat content of recipe:*                                              *8 servings*
   *beef, chuck roast, raw,*
      *separable lean:*                  134.4–151.2 grams
   *gingersnap crumbs:*                            2.8 grams
   *nonfat milk:*                                       negligible
   *Total:*                                      137.2–154.0 grams

*Fat content per serving:*
*The fat content of this recipe is relatively high. However, this is a low-fat method for cooking sauerbraten. On a 50-gram diet, it would be practical to use it.*

### Chuck, Shoulder or English-Cut on the Grill

Purchase chuck (preferably without bone, because it is easier to serve), shoulder, or English-cut roast from 2 to 2½ inches thick. Tenderize thoroughly with Adolph's Unseasoned Meat Tenderizer®. Cook over the outdoor grill basting liberally with garlic-flavored Good Seasons® salad dressing. (See recipe, page 167.) When properly tenderized, this meat can be cooked rare and served as one would a steak.

*Fat content of recipe:*
   *beef, chuck roast, raw,*
      *separable lean, 1 pound:*              33.6 grams
   *beef, shoulder roast, raw,*
      *separable lean, 1 pound:*              33.6 grams

beef, English-cut, raw,
separable lean, 1 pound:     33.6 grams
Good Seasons® salad dressing:     negligible

## Shishkebab

**1 pound beef or veal**
**Cherry tomatoes**
**Small whole onions, parboiled**
**Green pepper chunks**

Place on skewers alternate "layers" of 1½-inch cubes of beef or veal from which all excess fat has been cut, tomatoes, onions and green pepper chunks. Brush with barbecue sauce (recipe below). Wrap tightly in aluminum wrap and lay on grill or in outdoor oven. Cook about 30 minutes. If placed on grill, they must be turned frequently. These may be cooked in the oven if there are no facilities for outdoor cooking available.

## Barbecue Sauce

**12–14 ounces catsup**
**½ cup white distilled vinegar**
**1 teaspoon sugar**
**Red and black pepper**
**⅛ teaspoon salt**

Combine all ingredients in saucepan. Simmer for 15 minutes, stirring frequently.     *Yield: 1½ cups*

Fat content of ingredients:     *4 servings*
beef, round, raw, separable
lean, 1 pound:     21.3 grams     **67**

**MEATS, FISH, AND POULTRY**

veal, loin, raw, medium fat
class, 1 pound:                    50.0 grams
barbecue sauce recipe (12–14
oz. catsup):                     1.4 grams

## Beef Kabobs

**3 pounds beef, round, cut in 2-inch
  cubes
1 cup dry red wine
2 tablespoons vinegar
2 onions, thinly sliced
1 garlic clove, crushed
¼ teaspoon marjoram
¼ teaspoon rosemary
  Cayenne pepper
  Cherry tomatoes
  Whole mushroom caps
2 green peppers, cut up
2 teaspoons salt
  Freshly ground black pepper**

Marinate beef at room temperature for at least 8 hours
in wine, vinegar, onions, garlic, marjoram, rosemary,
cayenne pepper, salt, and black pepper. Drain beef
and save marinade. Put a cherry tomato, two pieces of
beef, a piece of green pepper, and a mushroom cap on
each of the skewers. Repeat until the skewers are full.
Cook over hot charcoal fire for 10 minutes, turning
frequently and basting with marinade. Serve immediately. If necessary, broil instead of using charcoal.

*Fat content of recipe:*                    *6 servings*
  *beef, round, raw, separable
    lean, 3 pounds:*               63.9 grams
**68** *Fat content per serving:*        10.7 grams

### Creamed Dried Beef

**1 jar dried beef**
**1 chicken bouillon cube**
**Hot water**
**2 tablespoons flour**
**Salt and pepper**
**1 cup liquefied nonfat milk**

Prepare white sauce. Dissolve a chicken bouillon cube in ¼ cup of hot water. Blend in flour, salt, and pepper to make a paste. Stir in nonfat milk. Cook, stirring constantly, until of desired thickness.

Add dried beef and serve on toast.

| Fat content of recipe: | 4 servings |
|---|---|
| dried beef (2½ ounces): | 4.5 grams |
| nonfat milk: | 0.2 gram |
| flour: | negligible |
| Total: | 4.7 grams |
| toast, per slice: | trace–1.0 gram |
| Fat content per serving, excluding toast: | 1.2 grams |

### Smoked Sliced Beef, Creamed

For variety try Smoked Sliced Beef in place of dried beef in the recipe above.

### Corned Beef and Bean Casserole

**1 can red kidney beans (1 pound)**
**1 can corned beef (12 ounces), diced**
**1 No. 2 can tomatoes, drained**
**1 medium onion, finely chopped**
**¾ teaspoon salt**
**⅛ teaspoon pepper**

69

1 tablespoon flour
1½ tablespoons sugar
1 teaspoon prepared mustard

Arrange alternate layers of beans, corned beef, tomatoes, and onions in a two-quart casserole. Combine remaining ingredients; pour over bean mixture. Bake at 375° for 1 hour.

| *Fat content of recipe:* | | *4 servings* |
|---|---|---|
| *beans:* | 1.8 grams | |
| *corned beef:* | 40.0 grams | |
| *Total:* | 41.8 grams | |
| *Fat content per serving:* | 10.5 grams | |

### Mock Chop Suey

¾ pound round steak, ground
1 small onion, chopped
½ cup raw rice
1 1-pound can tomatoes
1 1-pound can green peas
½ teaspoon Seasoned Salt
¼ teaspoon Fines Herbes
10 Ritz® crackers

Salt skillet and pan-brown meat and onion, without adding fat. Cook rice; before all the water is cooked out, combine it with the meat, onion, tomatoes (both solids and liquid), peas (both solids and liquid), and seasonings. Place in casserole and top with well-crumbled crackers. Brown in 400° oven for half to three-quarters of an hour. This is a very useful dish. Not only is it easy to prepare, but it can also be prepared the day before and kept in the refrigerator. In this case do not put on the cracker crumbs until you are ready to bake the dish. If you have any leftovers, scrape off the cracker crumbs, as they tend to become soggy if allowed to stand. When you are ready to use the leftovers, moisten with tomato juice and top with fresh cracker crumbs. The leftovers are also excellent for stuffing green peppers. Celery is also a good addition. The flavor of this recipe is not impaired if you vary the quantity of the ingredients. All in all a very adaptable, as well as tasty, dish!

| Fat content of recipe: | 6 servings |
| --- | --- |
| beef, raw, round, separable | |
| lean, ¾ pound: | 16.0 grams |
| rice: | 0.5 gram |
| Ritz® crackers: | 8.0 grams |
| Total: | 24.5 grams |
| Fat content per serving: | 4.1 grams |

## Chopped Beef and Rice, Oriental

1¼ cups Minute Brand® rice
1 pound ground round beef
2 medium onions, sliced
1 can bean sprouts (1 pound), drained
1 box frozen cut green beans
1 can condensed beef bouillon (10½ ounces)
⅓ cup soy sauce
½ cup water
½ teaspoon ground ginger

Combine all ingredients in two-quart casserole. Mix lightly with fork. Cover; bake in hot oven (425°) 40 minutes, or until rice is tender. This casserole can be frozen.

Fat content of recipe:                    4–6 servings
beef, raw, round, separable

MEATS, FISH, AND POULTRY

| | |
|---|---|
| *lean, 1 pound:* | 21.3 grams |
| *vegetables:* | negligible |
| *Total:* | 21.3 grams |

*Fat content per serving, based on 4 servings:*

5.3 grams

*Fat content per serving, based on 6 servings:*

3.6 grams

## Veal

### Veal Roll-ups in Tomato Sauce

4 tablespoons grated onion
1½ cups soft breadcrumbs
2 tablespoons minced parsley
¼ teaspoon salt
   Pepper
1 chicken bouillon cube
3 tablespoons water
6 slices veal, pounded thin, as for scallopini (page 73)
6 thin slices of cooked tongue
1 tablespoon butter
2 8-ounce cans tomato sauce
½ cup water
1 tablespoon chopped parsley
¼ teaspoon thyme
½ teaspoon salt

To make stuffing mix grated onion with breadcrumbs,
minced parsley, ¼ teaspoon salt, and a dash of pepper.
Blend well with 3 tablespoons water in which chicken
bouillon cube has been dissolved. Spread each slice of
veal with some of the stuffing. Cover with a thin slice of
72    cooked tongue, cut the same size as the veal, if

possible. Roll and fasten securely with thread. Sauté in a skillet in 1 tablespoon hot butter until evenly browned. Remove from the pan and roll in paper toweling to absorb the excess fat. Drain the skillet; then into the skillet pour tomato sauce and ½ cup water. Season with chopped parsley, thyme, ½ teaspoon salt, and a dash of pepper. Simmer, covered, for 45 minutes until rolls are tender. Remove thread and serve rolls with rice or noodles.

| Fat content of recipe: | 6 servings |
|---|---|
| breadcrumbs: | 7.5 grams |
| veal, round, medium fat, | |
| separable lean, 2 pounds: | 82.0 grams |
| tongue, canned, 8 ounces: | 46.0 grams |
| tomato sauce: | negligible |
| butter: | 12.0 grams |
| Total: | 147.5 grams |
| Fat content per serving: | 24.6 grams |

**Veal Scallopini**

**8 slices veal ¼ inch thick, 4 inches**
**square, from 2 pounds of veal cutlet**
**1 clove garlic, minced**
**1½ teaspoons salt**
**¼ teaspoon pepper**
**⅛ teaspoon oregano**
**½ cup chopped mushrooms**
**2 tablespoons Marsala or sherry**

Pound veal to ¼-inch thickness. Get the butcher to do this for you with the flat side of his large cleaver. Pan brown in a skillet sprinkled with salt. Add the garlic, salt, pepper, oregano, mushrooms, and wine. Cover and cook over low heat 15 minutes or until veal is tender.

73

*Fat content of recipe:*                    *4 servings*
    *veal cutlet (round), medium*
        *fat, separable lean,*
        *2 pounds:*                    82.0 grams
*Fat content per serving:*            20.5 grams


## Veal Stew

Veal may be used in place of beef in the Beef Stew recipes, pages 48–49.

*Fat content of recipe before congealed fat is removed from broth:*
  *veal, raw, round, medium fat, 1½ pounds:*
                              61.5 grams
*Fat content per serving, based on 4 servings:*
                              15.4 grams
*Fat content per serving, based on 6 servings:*
                              10.3 grams


## Veal with Wine Sauce

1½ pounds veal cutlet, round, cut in 2-inch cubes, trimmed of excess fat and sprinkled with salt
¾ cup thinly sliced onions
½ cup thinly sliced carrots
1 pound thinly sliced mushrooms or 1 can mushrooms (plain)
¼ teaspoon paprika
1 tablespoon flour
¾ cup claret or port
1½ cups water

Placed trimmed, cubed veal in skillet and pan brown. Remove from fire and add vegetables and seasonings.

Stir in wine. Simmer uncovered until meat is tender. As liquid simmers down, gradually add water to maintain gravy. Serve with noodles.

Fat content of recipe:                              5 servings
   veal, raw, round, medium fat, 1½ pounds:
                                       61.5 grams
Fat content per serving, before addition of noodles:
                                       12.3 grams

### Veal with Lemon (Veal Piccata)

**1 pound lean veal round, thin sliced**
**Salt**
**Freshly ground black pepper**
**Flour**
**1 tablespoon corn oil**
**1½ cups beef broth or bouillon**
**8 paper-thin lemon slices**
**1 tablespoon lemon juice**

Remove the transparent filaments or the skin and any fat from the veal. Place it between waxed paper and pound using a smooth surface mallet until it is about ¼ inch thick. Cut into pieces (scallops) easy to handle for browning. Season with salt and pepper; dip in flour and *shake off excess*. Use a seasoned heavy iron skillet. Rub the bottom with 1 tablespoon oil. When the skillet is hot sauté the veal quickly on both sides. Transfer the browned veal to a hot plate and set aside. Add bouillon or beef broth. Boil it briskly for 1 or 2 minutes, stirring constantly and scraping in any browned bits in the skillet. Add the lemon juice. Return the veal to the skillet and arrange the lemon slices on top. Cover and simmer over low heat for 10 minutes. Serve with the sauce and lemon slices.

| Fat content of recipe: | 4 servings |
|---|---|
| veal, raw, round, 1 pound: | 41.0 grams |
| oil: | 14.0 grams |
| Total: | 55.0 grams |
| Fat content per serving: | 13.8 grams |

## Lamb

### Chops and Rice

> 4 thick shoulder lamb chops
> 1 cup uncooked rice
> 4 thick slices Bermuda onion
> 4 thick slices fresh tomato
> 4 thick slices green pepper without
> seeds
> 2½ cups beef bouillon
> ½ teaspoon thyme
> ½ teaspoon marjoram
> Salt and pepper

Trim fat from chops. Pan-brown. Put them in a shallow casserole. Place 1 tablespoon of rice on each chop, with a slice each of onion, tomato, and green pepper. Pour bouillon over all, and sprinkle with herbs, salt, and pepper. Cover and simmer in a slow oven for 50 minutes.

| Fat content of ingredients: | 4 servings |
|---|---|
| lamb, shoulder, raw, separable lean, 1 pound: | 34.9 grams |
| rice, raw, 1 cup: | 1.0 gram |

### Lamb Roast with Rosemary

> Lamb roast, trimmed
> Flour

1 cup consommé or bouillon
1 cup dry white wine
1 clove garlic, minced
2 teaspoons fresh or dried rosemary
1 onion, minced or shredded
  Salt and pepper

Salt and pepper lamb roast. Dredge with flour. Place on roast rack in roasting pan. Put in hot oven to brown and then reduce heat to 325°. Baste every 15 minutes with the liquor made from the consommé, white wine, garlic, rosemary, and onion, which has been mixed, and simmer 5 minutes. Do not use pan drippings, because you wish to eliminate fat. After each basting, sprinkle a little salt over the meat. Cook until tender. If you wish, you may substitute ¼ cup white vinegar and ½ cup water for the wine.

*Fat content of recipe:*
  *lamb, leg, raw, separable lean, 1 pound:*
                                                    22.7 grams

### Roast Leg of Lamb with Vermouth

1 small (5-pound) leg of lamb, trimmed
3 tablespoons lemon juice
2 cloves garlic, minced
1 tablespoon curry powder
2 teaspoons salt
¼ teaspoon pepper
2 onions, sliced
½ cup dry vermouth

Sprinkle the lamb with the lemon juice. Mix the garlic, curry, salt, and pepper with a little lemon juice to make a paste; rub into the lamb. If possible, season the lamb the day before it is to be roasted. Place leg on rack in roasting pan; arrange onions around it. Roast in a 400°

oven for 30 minutes. Drain off fat. Add vermouth; reduce heat to 350°. Roast 1½ hours longer or until lamb is tender, basting frequently. If you prefer rare lamb, use a meat thermometer. Serve hot.

*Fat content of recipe:*
  *lamb, leg, raw, separable lean, 1 pound:*
                                                  22.7 grams

## Barbecued Leg of Lamb

Trim a 6-pound leg of lamb and wipe with a damp cloth. Rub thoroughly with salt, and dredge with flour. Brown quickly in a hot oven (450°). Reduce heat to 350° and roast until nearly done, about 2 to 2½ hours. Remove from oven. Drain off drippings. Refrigerate roast and drippings separately overnight, so that fat may be removed from drippings next day. The following day, return the roast to the pan and place sliced onions in bottom of roasting pan. Combine:

**1 cup water**
**½ cup catsup**
**2 tablespoons A.1. sauce®**
**2 tablespoons Worcestershire sauce**
**½ teaspoon cayenne**

Pour over meat. Continue cooking meat in moderate oven for 45 minutes or an hour, basting frequently with sauce.

*Fat content of recipe:*
  *lamb, leg, raw, separable lean, 1 pound:*
                                                  22.7 grams
  *Appreciably reduced by refrigerating and removing*
  *fat from drippings.*

## Lamb Bundles

4 lamb shanks
2 tablespoons Worcestershire sauce
4 or more small onions
4 carrots sliced
    Salt and freshly ground black pepper
    Minced garlic

Using meaty lamb shanks that are each enough for one serving, trim off excess fat. Tenderize thoroughly with Adolph's Unseasoned Meat Tenderizer®. Place each one on a large square of heavy-duty aluminum foil. Brush with Worcestershire sauce. Add the vegetables, dividing them among the packages, and sprinkle each with salt, pepper, and garlic. Seal foil to make tight packages and place in a shallow pan. Bake at 325° for 1 to 1½ hours. Serve packages on plate, or to reduce further the fat content, serve the meat and vegetables without the broth released by cooking.

*Fat content of recipe:*                    *4 servings*
    *lamb shanks, raw, separable lean, 1 pound:*
                                         34.9 grams

## Leg of Lamb Butterfly

Leg of lamb, 5 to 6 pounds
Seasoned salt
1 package Good Seasons® salad dressing
    mix, French flavor

Have butcher bone lamb and cut open butterfly fashion. Prepare Good Seasons® salad dressing according to instructions on page 167; pour over lamb in shallow pan and let stand about 1 hour. Sprinkle generously with seasoned salt. Place the marinated lamb, fat side up, over medium hot coals and broil 45 minutes to one hour, basting with the marinade and turning to brown both sides. (If you have never tasted rare leg of lamb, we recommend you try this while it is still pink on the inside. The relatively short cooking time is designed to provide a new taste treat.) Slice across the grain.

*Fat content of recipe:*
  *lamb, leg, raw, separable*
    *lean, 1 pound:*                 22.7 grams
  *Good Seasons® salad dressing:*    negligible

### Shashlik en Brochette

**2 pounds lamb, cut from the leg**
**2 cups Burgundy**
**½ cup minced onion**
**2 bay leaves**
**1 tablespoon Worcestershire sauce**
**1 garlic clove, crushed**
**1 teaspoon salt**
**Freshly ground black pepper**

Trim lamb and cut into 1½-inch cubes. Marinate 48 hours in wine, onion, bay leaves, Worcestershire, garlic, salt, and pepper. Cook on skewers.

*Fat content of recipe:*            *4 servings*
  *lamb, leg, raw, separable*
    *lean, 2 pounds:*               45.4 grams
*Fat content per serving:*          11.4 grams

## Pork

### Sweet-Sour Pork

**6 loin pork chops**
**1 cup pineapple chunks, drained (re-serve juice)**

6 small sweet pickles, sliced
1 green pepper, cut into 1-inch squares
3 small carrots, sliced
1 clove garlic, minced
½ cup water

Bone and trim the pork chops and slice meat paper thin. Brown meat in a Teflon® or treated skillet. Add pineapple chunks, sweet pickles, green pepper, carrots, garlic, and ½ cup water. Cover and cook 10 minutes.

Blend together:

2 tablespoons vinegar
1½ tablespoons sugar
1 tablespoon Chinese molasses
1 tablespoon cornstarch
½ cup pineapple juice drained from chunks

Add to meat mixture. Mix thoroughly and cook 5 minutes. Watch closely to prevent sticking.

*Fat content of recipe:*                     *4 servings*
  *pork, loin, medium fat, 1 pound, separable lean:*
                                            51.7 grams

## Variety Meats

### Broiled Liver I

**Slices of beef liver ⅓ inch thick.**

Sprinkle all surfaces of liver evenly with Adolph's Unseasoned Meat Tenderizer®. Place in covered dish in refrigerator and allow to stand until ready to cook.

Dry liver slices on paper towel. Place liver on broiling rack about 3 inches from moderate flame. Leave door of broiling oven open. Broil the liver exactly 1 minute on each side. Season with salt and pepper, if desired.

Slices of calves' liver may be broiled by this same method, but they will not require the use of the meat tenderizer. Beef liver is appreciably less expensive than calf liver and also has a lower fat content; therefore the authors found beef liver more attractive for use in this recipe.

*Fat content of recipe:*
| | |
|---|---|
| *beef liver, raw, 1 pound:* | 17.2 grams |
| *calf liver, raw, 1 pound:* | 21.3 grams |

### Broiled Liver II

Beef or pork liver may be prepared by sprinkling with meat tenderizer as directed in Broiled Liver I. Brown in broiler and simmer in low-fat gravy until tender. Prepare low-fat gravy by following rule:

**3 tablespoons flour**
**1 beef bouillon cube**
**1 cup hot water**
**¼ teaspoon salt**

Brown flour in frying pan. Dissolve bouillon cube in hot water. Add to flour, slowly, to make paste. Cook, stirring constantly, until thick. Place browned liver in gravy and simmer until tender.

*Fat content of recipe:*
| | |
|---|---|
| *beef liver, raw, 1 pound:* | 17.2 grams |
| *pork liver, raw, 1 pound:* | 16.8 grams |

### Tomatoes with Chicken Livers

**6 firm tomatoes**
**1 cup finely chopped, cooked chicken livers**

¼ teaspoon dried basil
¼ teaspoon grated onion
½ cup finely dried breadcrumbs
   Salt, pepper, garlic salt to taste
1 tablespoon parsley

Remove slice from top of tomato and gently scoop out pulp. Drain and salt inside of tomato shell. Mix pulp with remaining ingredients and return to tomato shell. Bake in 325° oven for about 20 minutes or until shells are soft.

*Fat content of recipe:*
   *1½ cups raw chicken livers:*        14.7 grams
   *½ cup breadcrumbs:*                  2.5 grams
   *Total:*                             17.2 grams
*Fat content per cooked tomato:*        2.9 grams

## Miscellaneous

### Spaghetti

6 ounces dry spaghetti
2 quarts boiling water
1 teaspoon salt

Drop spaghetti into boiling water and cook 9 to 12 minutes. Drain. Serve with any of the following sauces.

*Fat content of recipe:*                *4 servings*
   *spaghetti:*   2.0 grams

### Creole Sauce

1 can Campbell® tomato soup (10¾ ounces)

83

## ½ cup chopped green peppers, onion, celery, pickle relish

Simmer above ingredients until blended. Pour over spaghetti which has been placed in casserole. Grate sapsago cheese over all (see Cheeses, page 155). Place in oven until top browns.

*Fat content of recipe:*
| | |
|---|---|
| *tomato soup:* | 4.5 grams |
| *sapsago cheese:* | negligible |

*Fat content per serving (including spaghetti) based on 4 servings:*     1.6 grams


## Lawry's Spaghetti Sauce Mix®

*Fat content of recipe:*
*Lawry's Spaghetti Sauce Mix®:*   3.4 grams
*Fat content per serving (including spaghetti) based on 4 servings:*     1.4 grams

For variety, pan-brown in Teflon® or treated pan ½ pound round steak ground. Pour off fat released by cooking, and add meat to sauce. Adjust fat content of recipe to include meat:

*beef, round, raw, separable lean, ½ pound:*
10.7 grams


## Lasagne Sauce

See Baked Lasagne, page 86. This sauce is suitable for use with spaghetti, also. One making of this sauce will dress eight servings of spaghetti.

| *Fat content of recipe:* | *8 servings* |
|---|---|
| *round steak, raw, ground,* | |
| *separable lean:* | 21.3 grams |
| *Fat content per serving:* | 2.7 grams |

### Curried Spaghetti

1 10¾-ounce can Campbell® cream of chicken soup, undiluted
1 10¾-ounce can Campbell® cream of mushroom soup, undiluted
½ cup liquefied nonfat dry skim milk
¼ cup water
8 ounces thin spaghetti
⅛ cup warm water
2 teaspoons curry powder
4-ounce can whole mushrooms (with liquid)
½ tablespoon scraped onion
¼ teaspoon dried thyme
⅛ teaspoon dried basil
⅛ teaspoon dried oregano
1 can water-pack, white, or dietetic-pack tuna, slightly broken up

In saucepan, combine first four ingredients; stir until blended. Simmer mixture over low heat 10 minutes, stirring. Meanwhile, cook spaghetti (broken in halves) until tender, as directed on package. Combine warm water and curry powder; add to hot soup mixture, along with mushrooms, onion, thyme, basil, oregano. Simmer 10 minutes, stirring. Add tuna; heat. Place drained, cooked spaghetti in a two-quart casserole. Pour soup mixture over spaghetti; toss lightly with fork. Brown in oven.

| Fat content of recipe: | 4–5 servings |
|---|---|
| chicken soup: | 12.5 grams |
| mushroom soup: | 24.8 grams |
| milk: | trace |
| spaghetti: | 2.7 grams |
| tuna: | |
| water-pack, white: | 1.5 grams |

*dietetic pack,*
   *Chicken of the Sea®*
   *or Star Kist®*
   *brands:*                3.2 grams
*Total:*             41.5–43.2 grams
*Fat content per serving, based on 4 servings:*
                     10.4–10.8 grams
*Fat content per serving, based on 5 servings:*
                     8.3–8.6 grams

### Baked Lasagne

1 pound lasagne
1 pound round steak, ground
1 medium onion, minced
1 clove garlic, crushed
½ teaspoon salt
½ teaspoon pepper
1 6-ounce can tomato paste
3 8-ounce cans tomato sauce
2 cups water (more may be used if
   sauce is too thick)
½ teaspoon sugar
1 teaspoon basil
1 teaspoon oregano
1 teaspoon salt
1 teaspoon pepper
1 teaspoon onion salt
½ teaspoon garlic salt
1½ pounds low-fat cottage cheese (2 12-
   ounce boxes) (Borden Lite-Line®,
   Trim n' Light®, Slim n' Light®, Trim®)
1 egg
1 tablespoon chopped parsley (fresh
   parsley is to be preferred)

Salt and pepper
¾ pound imitation pasteurized process
cheese spread (Chef's Delight® or
Count Down®)
Grated sapsago cheese (estimate 2
ounces used)

1. Mix round steak, onion, garlic, salt, and pepper. Salt skillet and brown meat mixture. Add tomato paste, tomato sauce, water, herbs, and seasonings. Simmer for 1½ hours; stir occasionally.

2. Mix low-fat cottage cheese, egg, parsley, salt, and pepper.

3. Slice cheese spread in thin slices.

4. Add lasagne to six quarts boiling, salted water, stirring almost constantly to prevent sticking together. Cook 10 to 15 minutes. Lasagne should be almost done, but not too tender, to allow for further cooking in the oven. When cooked, pour cold water in pot, drain, and leave noodles standing in cold water until needed. This prevents sticking.

5. Ladle sauce on bottom of baking dish. Arrange layers of lasagne, cottage cheese mixture, sliced process cheese spread, and sauce until lasagne is used. Sprinkle generously with sapsago cheese. Bake in moderate oven (375°) for 20–30 minutes or until cheese spread is melted.

6. At table pass remainder of sauce and additional grated sapsago cheese.

| Fat content of recipe: | 6–8 servings |
|---|---|
| lasagne: | 4.5–6.8 grams |
| round steak, separable | |
| lean: | 21.3 grams |
| low-fat cottage cheese: | 6.8–13.6 grams |
| egg: | 6.0 grams |
| imitation pasteurized | |

*process cheese*

|  |  |
|---|---|
| *spread:* | 3.4–17.0 grams |
| *sapsago:* | negligible |
| *Total:* | 42.0–64.7 grams |

*Fat content per serving, based on 6 servings:*

7.0–10.8 grams

*Fat content per serving, based on 8 servings:*

5.3–8.1 grams

## Pasta E Fagioli

2 cans tomatoes (No. 303)
1 can tomato paste (6 ounces)
2 cups water
1 teaspoon salt
¼ teaspoon pepper
1 teaspoon oregano
1 teaspoon basil
1 teaspoon onion salt
½ teaspoon garlic salt
2 1-pound, 4-ounce cans white kidney
  beans
½ pound spaghetti (broken into 2-inch
  pieces)

Put the two cans of tomatoes through a sieve. Combine with them the tomato paste, water, and seasonings. Simmer for 1½ hours. Add the kidney beans. Cook the spaghetti in rapidly boiling salted water until the spaghetti is almost done but not tender. Drain and add to the tomato and bean mixture. Heat together until the spaghetti is tender. Serve hot. It refrigerates well.

| *Fat content of recipe:* | *6 servings* |
|---|---|
| *white kidney beans:* | 5.8 grams |
| *spaghetti:* | 2.7 grams |
| *Total:* | 8.5 grams |
| *Fat content per serving:* | 1.4 grams |

### Beef and Polenta Casserole

1 cup yellow corn meal
2 cups grated Count Down® imitation
   pasteurized process cheese spread
1 large onion, chopped
1 clove garlic, chopped or put through
   garlic press
1 pound ground round steak
1 1 pound, 13 ounces–can tomatoes
¼ cup tomato paste
½ cup dry red table wine
   Pinch each of oregano, rosemary, and
   basil
½ teaspoon sugar
   Salt and pepper to taste

Cook corn meal according to directions on package for corn meal mush, adding salt to taste. To the hot mush add one cup of the grated cheese; pour into a loaf pan that has been rinsed with cold water; chill until firm, preferably overnight.

Prepare sauce as follows: in Teflon® or treated skillet cook onion, garlic and beef, stirring with a fork until meat has lost its red color. Drain off all fat from skillet. Add tomatoes, tomato paste, wine, and seasonings; bring to a boil, then cover and cook gently, stirring frequently, for one hour. Refrigerate overnight and remove congealed layer of fat the next day.

To assemble dish: unmold chilled mush and cut crosswise in thin slices. Arrange half of these slices in the bottom of a lightly greased shallow casserole (8 × 12 × 2 inches is a good size); cover slices with half of the meat sauce. Repeat layers; sprinkle remaining one cup grated cheese over the top. Bake in 350° oven for one hour.

*Fat content of recipe:*                    *6 servings*    **89**

**MEATS, FISH, AND POULTRY**

| | |
|---|---|
| *corn meal:* | 2.0–5.0 grams |
| *Count Down®:* | 4.8 grams |
| *beef, raw, round,* | |
| *separable lean:* | 21.3 grams |
| *Total:* | 28.1–31.1 grams |
| *Fat content per serving:* | 4.7–5.2 grams |

## Italian Supper Casserole

½ pound shell or bow-tie macaroni
1 pound beef, round, ground
1 onion, chopped
1 clove garlic, chopped or put through
  garlic press
1 8-ounce can tomato sauce
1 6-ounce can tomato paste
½ cup dry red table wine
1 4-ounce can mushroom stems and
  pieces, drained (not broiled in butter)
  Pinch each of thyme, rosemary and
  oregano
  Salt and pepper to taste
1 10-ounce package frozen chopped
  spinach, cooked and *thoroughly*
  drained
¼ cup chopped parsley
½ cup fine, dry breadcrumbs
2 eggs, well beaten
½ teaspoon powdered sage

Quick-cook beef, onion, and garlic in Teflon® or treated skillet until meat is no longer red, stirring with a fork so that meat is broken into small pieces. Add tomato sauce, tomato paste, wine, mushrooms, thyme, rosemary, oregano, salt, and pepper. Bring to a boil, then cover and simmer 20 minutes. Refrigerate overnight to allow fat to rise and congeal.

90    The following day cook macaroni in boiling salted

water *just* until tender; drain. Remove sauce from refrigerator and lift off congealed layer of fat. Mix spinach, parsley, breadcrumbs, eggs, sage, salt, and pepper. In two-quart casserole spread half of the macaroni; cover with half of the spinach mixture; cover spinach with half of the meat sauce. Repeat layers with remaining ingredients. Bake in a 350° oven for 45 minutes.

| Fat content of recipe: | 5–6 servings |
|---|---|
| macaroni: | 2.7 grams |
| beef, round, separable lean: | 21.3 grams |
| breadcrumbs: | 2.5 grams |
| eggs: | 12.0 grams |
| Total: | 38.5 grams |

*Fat content per serving, based on 5 servings:*
7.7 grams

*Fat content per serving, based on 6 servings:*
6.4 grams

## Baked Beans and Brown Bread

Canned baked beans, vegetarian style in tomato sauce, are not high in fat content. Check carefully ingredients listed on can label. Combined with brown bread, they make a substantial dish for either breakfast or lunch.

*Fat content:*
canned baked beans, vegetarian
  style, 1 pound:                          2.3 grams
canned brown bread with
  raisins: 1 slice, 3 by ¾
  inches:                                  1.0 gram

## Baked Eggs in Creole Sauce
**1 10¾-ounce can Campbell® tomato soup, undiluted**
**2 tablespoons finely chopped celery**

2 tablespoons finely chopped green pepper
2 tablespoons finely chopped onion
2 tablespoons sweet-pickle relish
4 eggs
Cracker crumbs
Salt and pepper

Pour condensed tomato soup into a saucepan. Add celery, green pepper, onion, and sweet-pickle relish. Heat until well blended. Grease four ramekins. Place in each 3 tablespoons sauce. Sprinkle with cracker crumbs. Break 1 egg into each dish. Sprinkle with salt and pepper. Cover each egg with 2 tablespoons sauce and another sprinkle of cracker crumbs. Bake in a moderate oven (350°) for about 15 minutes or until eggs are medium firm.

| *Fat content of recipe:* | *4 servings* |
|---|---|
| *soup:* | 4.5 grams |
| *eggs:* | 24.0 grams |
| *Total:* | 28.5 grams |
| *Fat content per serving:* | 7.1 grams |

## Chili

2 medium or large onions
1 10¾-ounce can Campbell® tomato soup
1 8-ounce can tomato sauce
½ pound ground round steak
1 can kidney beans (1 pound)
1 beef bouillon cube
¼ cup water
Salt, pepper, chili powder

92    Brown onions and meat together. Stir with fork and it

will not be necessary to grease pan. When meat and onions are browned, add bouillon cube dissolved in water. Add tomato soup, sauce, and drained kidney beans. Add salt and pepper. Add chili powder while tasting until chili is seasoned enough. This dish freezes well.

| *Fat content of recipe:* | *4 servings* |
|---|---|
| *beef, raw, round, separable* | |
| *lean, ½ pound:* | 10.7 grams |
| *tomato soup:* | 4.5 grams |
| *beans:* | 1.8 grams |
| *Total:* | 17.0 grams |
| *Fat content per serving:* | 4.3 grams |

### Fried Rice

> 3 cups cooked rice
> 3 eggs, slightly beaten
> 2 strips of bacon, cut fine (2 teaspoons Durkee Imitation Bacon Bits®, French's Imitation Bacon Crumbles®, or McCormick Baconbits® may be substituted)
> 1½ cups cooked meat (chicken, shrimp, crab, tuna, etc.)
> 2 tablespoons green onions, cut fine
> ½ pound fresh bean sprouts or 1 small can bean sprouts
> ½ cup sliced button mushrooms, canned (plain, not broiled in butter)
> 2 tablespoons soy sauce
> Salt and pepper to taste

Fry bacon until crisp. Remove bacon from skillet, drain off all fat possible. Fry beaten eggs until hard-cooked. There will be enough grease on the pan to prevent sticking. Add cooked rice and fry for 5 minutes, stirring constantly. Add all other ingredients, cooked bacon, and seasoning. Mix thoroughly and cook for 10 minutes.

| Fat content of recipe: | 5 servings |
|---|---|
| rice: | 0.7 gram |
| bacon: | 8.0 grams |
| Bacon Bits®, Bacon Crumbles®, or Baconbits®: | 0.6–0.8 gram |
| eggs: | 18.0 grams |
| water-pack white or dietetic tuna: | 1.5–3.2 grams |
| 5-ounce can chicken: | 16.6 grams |
| 5½-ounce can crabmeat: | 3.9 grams |
| shrimp, cooked, drained, 1 pound: | 5.0 grams |

Adjust fat content according to ingredients used. Note that the fat content can be markedly reduced by using water-pack white tuna and imitation bacon bits.

## Fish

Certain fish can be recommended particularly, because their fat content is so low. The following fish contain less than 1 gram of fat per pound as purchased:

Burbot, raw, whole
Clams, hard or round, raw, in shell
Cod, raw, whole
Crayfish, fresh water; spiny lobster, raw, in shell
Cusk, raw, drawn and flesh only
Drums, red (redfish), raw, whole

Frog legs, raw
Haddock, raw, whole and flesh only
Hake, including Pacific hake, squirrel hake, and
    silver hake or whiting, raw, whole
Oysters, Eastern, raw in shell
Scallops, bay and sea, raw, muscle only
Tomcod, Atlantic, raw, whole

The next group contains less than 5 grams of fat per
pound as purchased:

Abalone, steaks, raw
Bass, Black Sea, raw, whole
    Smallmouth and largemouth, raw, whole
    White, raw, whole
Burbot, fillets, raw
Clams:
    Soft. raw, in shell
    Hard, raw, meat only
Cod, fillets, raw
    Dried, salted
Crab whole in shell
Crappie white, raw, flesh only
Crayfish fresh water; spiny lobster, raw, flesh only
Croaker, Atlantic, raw, whole
    White, raw, flesh only
    Yellowfin, raw flesh only
Drum, red (redfish), raw, flesh only
Finnan haddie (smoked haddock), raw, flesh only
Flatfishes (flounder, soles, and sanddabs), raw,
    whole and flesh only
Grouper, including red, black, and speckled hind,
    raw, whole and flesh only
Haddock, smoked
Hake, including Pacific hake, squirrel hake, and
    silver hake or whiting, raw, flesh only
Halibut, Atlantic and Pacific, raw, whole

Lobster, raw, whole
Mussels, Atlantic and Pacific, raw, in shell
Octopus, raw
Perch, ocean, Atlantic and Pacific, raw, whole
Perch, yellow, raw, whole and flesh only
Pickerel, chain, raw, whole and flesh only
Pike, blue, raw, whole and flesh only
    Northern, raw, whole
    Walleye, raw, whole
Pollock, raw, drawn and fillets
Red and gray snapper, raw, whole and flesh only
Redhorse, silver, raw, drawn
Sauger, raw, whole and flesh only
Seabass, white, raw, flesh only
Sheepshead, Atlantic, raw, whole
Shrimp, raw, in shell and flesh only
Skate (raja fish), raw, flesh only
Squid, raw, flesh only
Suckers, including white and mullet suckers raw,
    whole
Tautog (blackfish), raw, whole
Tilefish, raw, whole and flesh only
Tomcod, Atlantic, raw, flesh only
Trout, brook, raw, whole
Turtle, green, raw, muscle only

Although oysters, meat only, contain more than 5 grams of fat per pound, they are highly useful. The fat content (4.0 grams per cup) must be evaluated in the light of the fact that there is no waste to be considered and that most recipes serving four or five persons require only 1 pint (8 grams of fat). In such recipes, therefore, the fat content per serving would be 1.6–2.0 grams.

Most canned fish can be used quite freely. Even tuna fish may be included, if you use tuna packed in water or dietetic-pack tuna (Chicken of the Sea Brand®). If you use oil-pack tuna, drain and wash it under hot water to remove the oil. This brief checklist of canned fish will let you see where you stand.

| | Fat grams |
|---|---|
| Clams, minced, solid and liquid (8-ounce can) | 1.6 |
| Cod, canned, 1 pound | 1.4 |
| Crab, canned or cooked, meat only (5½-ounce can) | 3.9 |
| Lobster, meat only (6½-ounce can) | 2.8 |
| Oysters, canned, solids and liquid, 1 pound | 2.2 |
| Shrimp, dry pack or drained solids (5-ounce can) | 1.6 |
| Tuna fish: | |
| solids and liquids (7-ounce can) | 40.7 |
| drained solids (7-ounce can) | 13.8 |
| in water, solids and liquid (7-ounce can) | 1.6 |
| dietetic pack (6½-ounce can) | 3.2 |

Table 3 in the Appendix gives more detailed information on these and other fish. Do beware—some types of fish are distinctly high in their fat content.

**Baked Fish Fillets I**

**1½ pounds fish fillets, frozen or fresh**
**Salt, pepper, paprika**
**1 chicken bouillon cube**
**¼ cup hot water**

M
E
A
T
S,
F
I
S
H,
A
N
D
P
O
U
L
T
R
Y

97

3 tablespoons flour
1½ cups liquefied nonfat dry milk
1 teaspoon Worcestershire sauce
1½ tablespoons sherry
½ teaspoon rosemary
½ cup canned mushrooms (use plain type; not those described on label as "broiled in butter")

Place fish fillets in shallow casserole; season well with salt, pepper, and paprika. Make white sauce by dissolving bouillon cube in water and blending in flour. Add the hot milk slowly, stirring constantly. When it is well blended, stir in Worcestershire sauce, sherry, and rosemary. Add mushrooms. Pour over fish fillets. Bake about 25 minutes in 350° oven.

*Fat content of recipe:*             *6 servings*
*(This calculation is based on the use of haddock fillets. You may use perch or flounder fillets, but recalculate the fat content accordingly.)*

| | |
|---|---|
| *haddock fillets:* | 0.8 gram |
| *bouillon cube:* | negligible |
| *flour:* | negligible |
| *nonfat milk:* | 0.3 gram |
| *Total:* | 1.1 grams |
| *Fat content per serving:* | 0.2 gram |

**Baked Fish Fillets II**

1½ pounds fish fillets, frozen or fresh
1 chicken bouillon cube
¼ cup hot water
3 tablespoons flour
1½ cups liquefied nonfat dry milk
Salt, pepper
1 teaspoon Worcestershire sauce or 2

tablespoons sherry
½ teaspoon dry mustard
1 cup boiled shrimp
Chopped chives

Place fish fillets in shallow casserole. Prepare cream sauce by dissolving bouillon cube in water and blending in flour which has been seasoned with salt, pepper, and dry mustard. Slowly stir in milk and, when blended, add Worcestershire sauce or sherry. Pour this sauce over the fish and place in moderate oven (350°) until fish is tender—about 20 or 25 minutes. Remove the sauce and fish to an ovenproof platter and sprinkle over it the cooked shrimp. Run the dish under broiler until shrimp is heated through. Remove, sprinkle with chopped chives, and serve.

*Fat content of recipe:*          *6 servings*
   *(This calculation is based on the use of haddock fillets.)*

| | |
|---|---|
| *haddock fillets:* | 0.8 gram |
| *bouillon cube:* | negligible |
| *flour:* | negligible |
| *nonfat milk:* | 0.3 gram |
| *boiled shrimp:* | 1.8 grams |
| Total: | 2.9 grams |
| *Fat content per serving:* | 0.5 gram |

## Marinated Fish Fillets

1½ pounds fish fillets, frozen or fresh
1 package Good Seasons® salad dressing mix (any flavor)
2 tablespoons pectin (Sure-Jell®)
3 tablespoons lemon juice
¾ cup water
1 cup breadcrumbs

Make up Good Seasons® salad dressing mix as follows: place contents of package in jar; add pectin, lemon juice, and water, and shake well.

Place fish fillets in shallow Pyrex® baking pan and marinate in salad dressing for about 2 hours. Remove fish from marinade; sprinkle with breadcrumbs; place in broiler and broil about 10 minutes until breadcrumbs are well browned. When fish is partially cooked, it may be basted with the remaining marinade while in the broiler.

*Fat content of recipe:*                      *6 servings*
*(This calculation is based on the use of haddock fillets.)*

| | |
|---|---|
| *haddock fillets:* | 0.8 gram |
| *breadcrumbs:* | 5.0 grams |
| *Total:* | 5.8 grams |
| *Fat content per serving:* | 1.0 gram |

## Fillets Florentine

**2 packages of chopped frozen spinach
Salt and pepper
4 fish fillets
¼ cup white wine
¼ cup water
¾ cup liquefied nonfat dry milk
Grated sapsago cheese**

Cook spinach according to directions on package; drain; add salt and pepper and pack in an ovenproof serving dish. Keep warm. In a baking dish, place the defrosted fillets. Cover with white wine and water, and poach in a preheated 375° oven for 10 to 15 minutes, or until fish is opaque. Pour off liquid into a saucepan and reduce to ⅓ cup. Use this liquid and ¾ cup liquefied nonfat dry milk to make Basic White Sauce, page 198.

Drain fillets well, and place on spinach bed. Pour cream sauce over, sprinkle generously with grated sapsago cheese, and brown lightly under the broiler. This is a bland but good dish.

*Fat content of recipe:*                      *4 servings*
   *flounder fillets, 1 pound:*        3.6 grams
   *nonfat milk:*                              trace
   *Total:*                                    3.6 grams
*Fat content per serving:*            0.9 gram

### Baked Fish in Wine

**2 pounds fish fillets, frozen or fresh**
**3 medium-sized fresh tomatoes finely**
**  cut *or* 1 cup canned tomatoes**
**1 onion, chopped**
**1 green pepper, chopped**
**½ cup dry sherry**
**Salt and pepper**

Place fish in a baking dish. Cover with tomatoes, onion, green pepper, salt and pepper, and sherry wine. Bake uncovered in a moderate oven (350°) about 20 minutes or until fish is tender.

*Fat content of recipe:*                      *6 servings*
   *(This calculation is based on the use of flounder fillets. If you use another variety of fish, recalculate the fat content accordingly.)*
   flounder fillets:              5.4 grams
*Fat content per serving:*            0.9 gram

### Baked Bluefish

**1 3-to-4 pound bluefish, cleaned with**
**  head removed**

101

**Salt and freshly ground black pepper
to taste
1 large onion, thinly sliced
2 tomatoes, skinned and thinly sliced
½ teaspoon oregano
2 tablespoons parsley
½ cup dry white wine
½ cup plain yogurt**

Preheat oven to 375°. Season the fish inside and out
with salt and pepper. In a shallow baking dish large
enough to accommodate the fish, arrange a layer of
onion and a layer of tomato. Season with salt, pepper,
oregano, and parsley. Set the fish on top and pour over
the wine. Cover tightly with aluminum foil. Bake the
fish 40 minutes or until the flesh is opaque all the way
down to the bone at the thickest part. Remove the fish
to a warm platter. Stir the yogurt into the onion and
tomato mixture. Reheat but do not boil and spoon
around the fish.

| Fat content of recipe: | 4 servings |
|---|---|
| bluefish  raw  as purchased | |
| before removal of head: | |
| 3 pounds: | 22.8 grams |
| 4 pounds: | 30.4 grams |
| yogurt, ¹₂ 8-ounce carton: | 1.8 grams |
| Total: | |
| with 3-pound fish: | 24.6 grams |
| with 4-pound fish: | 32.2 grams |
| Fat content per serving: | |
| with 3-pound fish: | 6.2 grams |
| with 4-pound fish: | 8.1 grams |

## Red Snapper Creole

**2 10-ounce packages, red snapper fillets
2 chicken bouillon cubes dissolved in ½
cup hot water**

2 medium onions, minced
1 green pepper, chopped fine
1 cup finely chopped celery stalks and
   leaves
1 teaspoon salt
¼ teaspoon paprika
1 10-ounce can tomatoes

Thaw snapper. Pour bouillon into shallow baking dish. Spread onion, pepper, and celery over bottom of dish. Place fillets on top of vegetables. Sprinkle with salt and paprika. Top with tomatoes and juice. Cover. Bake in 325° oven for 1 hour.

| | | |
|---|---|---|
| *Fat content of recipe:* | | *6 servings* |
| *red snapper:* | 5.1 grams | |
| *Fat content per serving:* | 0.9 gram | |

**Barbecued Fish**

2 pounds haddock or flounder fillets
½ cup soy sauce
¾ cup sherry
¼ cup lemon juice
2 cloves garlic, minced or mashed
1 teaspoon powdered ginger
Lemon wedges

Cut fish into finger-size pieces 1 inch wide, 2 inches long, and 1 inch thick. Combine soy sauce, sherry, lemon juice, garlic, and ginger. Marinate fish in this mixture for 2 hours. Skewer carefully or slip inside a wire toaster and place on the barbecue grill over low coals. Cook until fish flakes with a fork, about 10 or 15 minutes. Baste occasionally with the remaining marinade. Instead of barbecuing, fish may be baked in a very hot oven (450°) for 12 minutes. Slip the fish under the broiler a minute if you want it browner. Serve with lemon wedges.

103

| Fat content of recipe: | | 5 servings |
|---|---|---|
| soy sauce: | 0.8 gram | |
| haddock: | 1.0 gram | |
| flounder: | 7.2 grams | |
| Total: with haddock: | 1.8 grams | |
| with flounder: | 8.0 grams | |
| Fat content per serving: | | |
| with haddock: | 0.4 gram | |
| with flounder: | 1.6 grams | |

## Salt Broiled Fish

This is a Japanese cooking technique which produces a delicately flavored, moist fish and is as simple as a recipe can be.

Use small fish, one per person. Have the fish market remove the head and tail, and remove the bones as in fillet, *but* leave the fish whole, so it can be folded back together. *Important:* you *must* have the skin on the fish. This keeps it from burning without the protection of butter or sauce.

About 20 to 30 minutes before cooking, salt the fish on both sides. Use about the amount you would if you were salting after cooking. Let stand until time to cook. Broil on lightly oiled aluminum foil on both sides. Watch carefully to avoid burning and turn with spatula when half done. This takes only a few minutes per side.

| Fat content of recipe: | |
|---|---|
| bluefish, whole, per pound as purchased: | 7.6 grams |
| brook trout, whole, per pound as purchased: | 9.5 grams |
| weakfish (gray trout), whole, per pound as purchased: | 12.2 grams |

### Salmon Steaks

>   5 salmon steaks
>   ¼ cup flour
>   ½ teaspoon salt
>   ¼ teaspoon paprika
>   1½ cups boiling, liquefied nonfat dry
>     milk
>   2 medium-sized onions
>   1 teaspoon rosemary leaves, crumbled

Pour milk in bottom of pan. Dip salmon steaks in flour which has been seasoned with salt and paprika. Place in pan. Place sliced onions over steaks and sprinkle with rosemary. Bake in 375° oven about 30 to 35 minutes, or until onions are tender.

| *Fat content of recipe:* | *5 servings* |
|---|---|
| salmon, Atlantic, raw, flesh only, 1 pound: | 60.8 grams |
| salmon, Chinook (king), raw, flesh only, 1 pound: | 70.8 grams |

### Herb-Broiled Fish Steaks

>   2 pounds fish steaks (halibut, haddock,
>     salmon, cod, swordfish)
>   ⅜ cup boiling water
>   2 level teaspoons chicken stock base or
>     2 chicken bouillon cubes
>   1 tablespoon grated onion
>   Juice of 1 lemon
>   1 teaspoon salt
>   ¼ teaspoon pepper
>   ½ teaspoon marjoram
>   1 tablespoon minced chives or green
>     onion
>   2 tablespoons chopped parsley

105

Put fish on a greased broiler rack. Dissolve chicken stock base or bouillon cubes in hot water. Mix with remaining ingredients and pour half of sauce over fish. Broil about 6 minutes. Turn and pour remaining sauce over fish. Broil 6 to 8 minutes, or until fish flakes easily with a fork.

| *Fat content of ingredients:* | *4 servings* |
|---|---|
| *halibut, Atlantic and Pacific,* | |
| *raw, flesh only, 1 pound:* | 5.4 grams |
| *California, raw, flesh* | |
| *only, 1 pound:* | 6.4 grams |
| *Greenland, raw, flesh* | |
| *only, 1 pound:* | 38.1 grams |
| *haddock, raw, flesh only,* | |
| *1 pound:* | 0.5 gram |
| *salmon, Atlantic, raw, flesh* | |
| *only, 1 pound:* | 60.8 grams |
| *Chinook (king), raw, flesh* | |
| *only, 1 pound:* | 70.8 grams |
| *cod, raw, flesh only, 1 pound:* | 1.4 grams |
| *swordfish, raw, flesh only,* | |
| *1 pound:* | 18.1 grams |
| *chicken stock base, 2 level teaspoons:* | |
| *French®:* | 0.4 gram |
| *Maggi®:* | 0.2 gram |
| *McCormick®:* | 1.2 grams |
| *Spice Islands®:* | 0.6 gram |

## Baked Stuffed Flounder

**2 whole fresh flounder, heads removed, cleaned (2 pounds; use two 1-pound fillets if you wish)**
**½ package Pepperidge Farm® Herb Seasoned Stuffing (4 ounces)**

**½ cup cut-up boiled shrimp**
**1 chicken bouillon cube**
**½ cup water**
**Salt, pepper, and monosodium gluta-mate**
**Lemon juice**

Make dressing by combining Pepperidge Farm® mix with shrimp and adding enough chicken bouillon to moisten. Stuff the flounder. Rub the fish with lemon juice and sprinkle with seasonings. Wrap in aluminum foil, using double fold to seal in moisture. Bake in moderate oven (350°) for 30 minutes.

| *Fat content of recipe:* | | *6 servings* |
|---|---|---|
| *flounder:* | 7.2 grams | |
| *stuffing mix:* | 1.5 grams | |
| *bouillon cubes:* | negligible | |
| *shrimp:* | 0.9 gram | |
| *Total:* | 9.6 grams | |
| *Fat content per serving:* | 1.6 grams | |

### Stuffed Swordfish Steak

Use preceding rule for Baked Stuffed Flounder. Package in individual servings in aluminum foil. Freeze. When ready to use, place frozen in 350° oven for 1½ hours. If you wish to use it immediately without freezing, you can reduce the cooking time.

*Fat content of recipe:*
  *swordfish, raw, 1 pound, flesh only:* 18.1 grams
  *Other ingredients as in preceding recipe.*

### Baked Stuffed Bass

From the recipe above for Baked Stuffed Flounder omit the shrimp and proceed as directed. Sprinkle the bass

**MEATS, FISH, AND POULTRY**

107

liberally with marjoram before wrapping in aluminum foil.

*Fat content of recipe:*
   *bass, 1 pound, raw, whole as purchased:*

| | |
|---|---|
| *Black Sea:* | 2.1 grams |
| *smallmouth and largemouth:* | 3.7 grams |
| *striped:* | 5.3 grams |
| *white:* | 4.1 grams |
| *stuffing mix:* | 3.0 grams |

When preparing baked stuffed fish of a delicate flavor, try this Green Dressing for a pleasant change in taste, texture, and color.

### Green Dressing

**2 tablespoons chopped shallots**
**1 egg**
**½ cup tender celery with leaves**
**½ cup parsley tops**
**¼ cup water cress tops**
**½ cup crumbled, crustless bread**
**½ teaspoon salt**
**⅛ teaspoon dried basil**
**½ cup bread which has been pulled apart in irregular pieces and lightly toasted in the oven**
**¼ cup sliced water chestnuts**

Quick-cook the shallots until transparent in a Teflon®-coated saucepan or one treated with Pam®, Lean-Fry®, or Pan Pal®. Cool slightly. Place in a blender and blend to a paste with all ingredients *except* pulled bread and water chestnuts. Blend in with a fork these last two ingredients.

108

*Fat content of recipe:*

| | |
|---|---|
| *egg:* | 6.0 grams |
| *breadcrumbs:* | 2.5 grams |
| *pulled bread:* | 2.0 grams |
| *Total:* | 10.5 grams |

### Shrimp and Celery Bake

**2 pounds shrimp**
**1 cup chopped celery**
**¾ cup Basic White Sauce (page 198)**
**Salt**
**⅛ teaspoon paprika**
**½ teaspoon Worcestershire sauce (optional)**
**Breadcrumbs**

Cook, shell, and devein shrimp. Cook celery in small amount of lightly salted boiled water until tender, allowing it to absorb the water if possible. Drain if necessary. Prepare white sauce and bring to a boil; add celery, shrimp, and seasoning. Place in greased casserole and sprinkle the top with breadcrumbs. Brown under broiler.

*Fat content of recipe:*                          *5 servings*

| | |
|---|---|
| *shrimp:* | 7.2 grams |
| *white sauce:* | negligible |
| *Total:* | 7.2 grams |
| *Fat content per serving:* | 1.4 grams |

### Shrimp Fondue

**3 pounds raw shrimp in the shell**
**Fondue broth: see Beef Fondue, page 56** 109

Shell and devein raw shrimp.

Prepare fondue broth as described in recipe for Beef Fondue, page 56. Put whole quantity of broth in fondue pot and allow to simmer as you cook the shrimp a serving at a time.

| *Fat content of recipe:* | *6 servings* |
|---|---|
| *shrimp, in shell:* | 7.5 grams |
| *chicken broth:* | 3.2 grams |
| *Total:* | 10.7 grams |
| *Fat content per serving:* | 1.8 grams |

### Shrimp—or Lobster—with Lobster Sauce

This delicious Chinese dish is served on boiled rice. The lobster sauce may be used to dress either cooked shrimp or cooked lobster.

**1 to 1½ pounds cooked shrimp or lobster**
**½ pound ground pork**
**1 chicken bouillon cube dissolved in ¼ cup water**
**1 clove garlic, chopped fine or mashed**
**1 teaspoon Chinese black beans, washed and drained thoroughly (available in Chinese grocery stores)**
**1 tablespoon chopped green onion**
**2 eggs**
**4 tablespoons cornstarch**
**2 tablespoons soy sauce**
**1 cup water**
**1 pinch gourmet powder (or monosodium glutamate)**

Brown pork in 12-inch skillet slowly for 15 minutes. Pour off all fat. Add bouillon cube (dissolved in water), garlic, and black beans which have been mashed together, and onion. Mix thoroughly and cook for 5 minutes. While this is cooking, place cornstarch in a small saucepan, and add a small amount of water to make a smooth paste. Gradually add remainder of water and soy sauce. Add gourmet powder and cook until sauce thickens. Set aside. Beat eggs slightly and pour over meat mixture in skillet, stirring and turning constantly for a few minutes. Now add sauce from saucepan and mix well. Add cooked shrimp or lobster and simmer a few minutes until all is well heated. Serve on cooked rice.

| Fat content of recipe: | 5 servings |
|---|---|
| 1–1½ pounds, shrimp, | |
| raw, in shell: | 2.5–3.8 grams |
| ½ pound ground pork, | |
| loin, separable lean: | 25.9 grams |
| bouillon cube: | negligible |
| eggs: | 12.0 grams |
| soy sauce: | 0.2 gram |
| Total: | 38.8–42.6 grams |
| Fat content per serving: | 7.8–8.5 grams |

This is appreciably reduced by pouring off the fat from the cooked pork. Recalculate if lobster is used in place of shrimp.

**Crab Meat and Eggs**

2 eggs
1 chicken bouillon cube
¼ cup hot water
2 tablespoons flour
1 cup liquefied nonfat dry milk
Salt, pepper, paprika
1 can crab meat (5½ ounces)

111

½ cup chopped celery
¼ cup chopped green pepper
1 teaspoon Worcestershire sauce or 1 tablespoon sherry
¼ cup breadcrumbs
1 tablespoon margarine

Hard cook eggs, cool, shell, and slice thin. Make white sauce by dissolving bouillon cube in water and blending in flour seasoned with salt, pepper, and paprika; add hot milk, stirring constantly until smooth and blended. When the sauce is boiling, add crab meat, celery, and green pepper. Remove the crab from the fire and add Worcestershire sauce or sherry and sliced eggs. Place these ingredients in baking dish, top with breadcrumbs, and dot with margarine. Brown the crumbs under a broiler or bake the crab meat in a pan of hot water in a moderate oven (375°) until crumbs brown.

| *Fat content of recipe:* | *4 servings* |
|---|---|
| *eggs:* | 12.0 grams |
| *bouillon cube:* | negligible |
| *flour:* | negligible |
| *milk:* | trace |
| *crab meat:* | 3.9 grams |
| *breadcrumbs:* | 1.3 grams |
| *margarine:* | 12.0 grams |
| *Total:* | 29.2 grams |
| *Fat content per serving:* | 7.3 grams |

## Crab Meat Florentine

2 10-ounce packages frozen chopped spinach
1 10¾-ounce can Campbell® cream of mushroom soup

2 cups grated Count Down® imitation
   pasteurized process skim milk cheese
   spread
¼ cup evaporated skimmed milk
¼ cup dry or medium sherry
1 teaspoon Worcestershire sauce
   Dash of pepper
1 pound fresh crab meat
½ cup fine, dry breadcrumbs
   Paprika

Cook spinach without salt; drain *thoroughly.* In a
saucepan combine the mushroom soup, one cup of
the cheese, evaporated skimmed milk, sherry,
Worcestershire sauce, and pepper; stir over low heat
until cheese melts and ingredients are nicely blended.
Mix one-half of this sauce with the spinach; spread in
bottom of a 10 × 6 × 2-inch baking dish. Arrange crab
meat evenly over spinach; cover with remaining sauce
and sprinkle with crumbs. Top with remaining cheese
and dust with paprika. Bake in 350° oven for 25 to 30
minutes.

| Fat content of recipe: | 6 servings |
| --- | --- |
| mushroom soup: | 24.8 grams |
| cheese (Count Down®): | 4.8 grams |
| evaporated skimmed milk: | 0.1 gram |
| crab meat: | 8.6 grams |
| breadcrumbs: | 2.5 grams |
| Total: | 40.8 grams |
| Fat content per serving: | 6.8 grams |

**Toasted Rolls with Crab Salad**

3 cups boned cooked crab meat, fresh
   or canned
1 cup diced celery

MEATS, FISH, AND POULTRY

113

**Juice of ½ lemon**
**1 small onion, grated**
**¼ cup finely minced parsley**
**½ cup Special Mayonnaise (page 164)**
**Salt**
**Pepper**
**Dash of hot red-pepper sauce**

Mix all ingredients. Fill toasted soft rolls with the salad and a piece or two of crisp lettuce.

| Fat content of recipe: | To fill 8 rolls |
|---|---|
| crab meat, fresh or canned (cooked): | 12.9–17.0 grams |
| Special Mayonnaise: | 3.2 grams |
| Total: | 16.1–20.2 grams |
| Fat content per serving: | |
| crab salad: | 2.0–2.5 grams |
| roll: | 2.0 grams |
| Total: | 4.0–4.5 grams |

### Mock Newburg

**1 can lobster (6½ ounces)**
**1 chicken bouillon cube**
**¼ cup hot water**
**3 tablespoons flour**
**1½ cups liquefied nonfat dry milk**
**Salt, pepper**
**1 teaspoon Worcestershire sauce**
**2 tablespoons tomato catsup**
**1 can mushrooms, solids and liquid (4 ounces)**

Make sauce by dissolving bouillon cube in water, blending in flour and seasoning; stir in the hot milk

and mushroom liquid until blended and smooth. Add

Worcestershire sauce, catsup, and mushrooms. Heat well, stirring constantly. Add lobster, and simmer until lobster is heated through. It may be more convenient to make this in a double boiler so that it will not be necessary to watch it so closely.

| Fat content of recipe: | 4 servings |
|---|---|
| lobster: | 3.3 grams |
| bouillon cube: | negligible |
| flour: | negligible |
| milk: | trace |
| catsup: | trace |
| Total: | 3.3 grams |
| Fat content per serving: | 0.8 gram |

### Tuna Fish and Potato Casserole

1 No. 303 can potatoes
1 can water-pack white tuna or dietetic-
  pack tuna (6½ ounces)
1 tablespoon diced onion
1 can condensed Campbell® celery soup
  (10¾ ounces)
6 tablespoons water
Salt, pepper

Place in casserole alternate layers of sliced potatoes, diced onions, and tuna fish which is water packed or dietetic pack or which has been washed under hot water to remove oil. Mix together soup and water and pour over contents of casserole. Add seasoning. Bake in hot oven 25 minutes.

| Fat content of recipe: | 4 servings |
|---|---|
| tuna: | |
| water-pack, white: | 1.5 grams |
| dietetic-pack, Chicken of | |

the Sea® or Star Kist®

| | |
|---|---:|
| brands: | 3.2 grams |
| celery soup: | 11.0 grams |
| Total: | 15.7 grams |
| Fat content per serving: | 3.9 grams |

## Chicken and Crab Casserole

- 1 10¾-ounce can Campbell® cream of mushroom soup
- 1 10¾-ounce can Campbell® cream of chicken soup
- ½ cup liquefied nonfat dry milk
- 1 tablespoon grated onion
- 1–1½ teaspoons turmeric
- ½ teaspoon paprika
- 1 5-ounce can boned chicken, cut in chunks
- 1 5½-ounce can crab meat, drained and flaked
- 1 4-ounce can mushrooms, drained
- 1 cup uncooked rice

Boil rice and place in casserole. Mix together all other ingredients and pour over rice in casserole. Place in moderate oven until heated through thoroughly.

| Fat content of recipe: | 6 servings |
|---|---:|
| mushroom soup: | 24.8 grams |
| chicken soup: | 12.5 grams |
| milk: | trace |
| chicken: | 16.7 grams |
| crab meat: | 3.9 grams |
| rice: | 1.0 gram |
| Total: | 58.9 grams |
| Fat content per serving: | 9.8 grams |

### Skewered Scallops

**2 pounds fresh or frozen scallops (not breaded)**
**2 slices bacon, raw**

If possible, buy small bay scallops. If these are not available, cut the larger ocean scallops into small chunks. Cut bacon strips into half-inch squares.

Thread several scallops onto a thin skewer followed by one square of bacon. Repeat until ingredients are used.

Broil a few minutes until bacon begins to crisp and scallops brown lightly at the edges. Watch closely.

*Fat content of recipe:*
| | |
|---|---|
| *scallops:* | 1.8 grams |
| *bacon:* | 8.0 grams |

### Scallops Broiled in Blankets

See Appetizers, page 30.

### Sweet-Sour Tuna

**1 9-ounce can pineapple tidbits, drained**
**⅓ cup pineapple syrup**
**1 cup green pepper, cut in ½-inch pieces**
**1 5-ounce can water chestnuts, sliced**
**2 tablespoons sugar**
**1 tablespoon cornstarch**
**1 teaspoon soy sauce**
**1 tablespoon vinegar**
**½ cup chicken bouillon**
**¼ teaspoon salt**

MEATS, FISH, AND POULTRY

117

Dash pepper
1 6½-ounce can water-pack white or dietetic-pack tuna

Cook pineapple in a Teflon® or treated skillet for 5 minutes. (The use of Pam®, Lean-Fry®, or Pan Pal® will prevent the pineapple from sticking.) Add pineapple syrup, green pepper, and water chestnuts; cover and simmer for 10 minutes. Combine sugar, cornstarch, soy sauce, vinegar, chicken broth, and seasonings; add to pineapple. Cook, stirring constantly until thickened. Add tuna. Heat through thoroughly. Serve over boiled rice.

| *Fat content of recipe:* | *4 servings* |
|---|---|
| *soy sauce:* | negligible |
| *chicken bouillon:* | negligible |
| *tuna:* | |
| *water-pack, white:* | 1.5 grams |
| *dietetic-pack, Chicken of the Sea® or Star Kist® brands:* | 3.2 grams |
| *Total:* | 1.5–3.2 grams |
| *Fat content per serving:* | 0.4–0.8 gram |
| *If served over rice, cook 1 cup raw rice. This will add the following fat content:* | |
| *to the total for the recipe:* | 1.0 gram |
| *to the serving:* | 0.3 gram |

## Tuna Fish Creole

1 6½-ounce can water-pack white or dietetic-pack tuna
1 chicken bouillon cube
2 tablespoons flour
1 cup liquefied nonfat milk

**2 tablespoons chopped green pepper**
**1 small tomato cut in eighths**
**¼ cup hot water**
**Salt and pepper**

Dissolve bouillon cube in hot water. Simmer green pepper and tomato in this broth for a few minutes. Blend in flour, salt, and pepper. Slowly blend in the milk until the mixture is smooth. Cook to desired thickness. Add tuna which has been separated into chunks. Heat thoroughly. Serve on rice or toast.

| *Fat content of recipe:* | *4 servings* |
|---|---|
| *bouillon cube:* | negligible |
| *flour:* | negligible |
| *nonfat milk:* | trace |
| *tuna:* | |
| *water-pack, white:* | 1.5 grams |
| *dietetic-pack, Chicken* | |
| *of the Sea® or Star* | |
| *Kist® brands:* | 3.2 grams |
| *Total:* | 1.5–3.2 grams |
| *Fat content per serving:* | 0.4–0.8 gram |

### Steamed Clams

For those who live too far from the seacoast to obtain fresh steamed clams, a canned product is available. Whole clams in the shell packed in brine and broth and ready to heat and serve can be obtained from:

HCA Food Corp., Baltimore, Maryland, 21237: Doxee Bucket of Steamed Clams, 24 fl. oz. (1 pt. 8 fl. oz.), about 12 clams

A. M. Look Canning Co., Inc., East Machias, Maine, 04630: Atlantic Steamed Clams in the Shell, 44 oz., 30–40 clams

Reese Finer Foods Division, Pet., Inc., 1750 West Wrightwood Ave., Chicago, Illinois 60614: Steamed Clams in Shell, 24 oz. (1 pt. 8 oz.)

## Clams Cockaigne

**48 freshly opened clams on the half shell**
**¼ cup finely chopped shallots or green onions**
**2 tablespoons dry white wine**
**1 tablespoon finely chopped parsley**
**4 cloves garlic, finely chopped**
**Salt to taste**
**½ teaspoon freshly ground black pepper**
**2 tablespoons breadcrumbs**
**48 1-inch squares Natural Swiss Cheese ( ⅛ pound)**

Preheat oven to 400°. Arrange the clams on the half shell in a large baking dish. Heat the shallots with wine in a small saucepan and cook until most of the liquid evaporates. Let cool. Combine shallots, parsley, garlic, salt, pepper, breadcrumbs. Spread on clams. Top with squares of cheese. Bake until cheese just melts.

*Fat content of recipe:*

| | |
|---|---|
| *clams:* | 6.6 grams |
| *breadcrumbs:* | negligible |
| *Natural Swiss cheese:* | 25.4 grams |
| *Total:* | 32.0 grams |
| *Fat content per clam as served:* | 0.7 gram |

## Oysters on the Grill

Leave oysters in shell and place on charcoal grill when fire reaches white ash stage. Cover with a *wet* burlap bag and when oysters pop open, serve immediately. Delicious as an hors d'oeuvre when you are having a barbecue.

*Fat content of recipe:*
  *oysters:*
      *1 pound, raw, Eastern,*
        *in shell:*                     0.8 gram
      *1 pound, raw, Eastern,*
        *meat only:*                    8.2 grams
      *1 pound, raw, Pacific*
        *and Western (Olympia),*
        *meat only:*                    10.0 grams

**Oysters and Macaroni au Gratin**

**1 pint oysters**
**3 tablespoons flour**
**¾ cup nonfat dry milk powder**
**1 teaspoon salt**
**⅛ teaspoon pepper**
**1⅓ cups water**
**1 cup cooked macaroni**
**1 cup grated imitation pasteurized process cheese spread: Chef's Delight® or Count Down®**

Drain oysters. Combine dry ingredients and gradually stir in water, cooking over low heat and stirring constantly until smooth and thick. Place a layer of cooked macaroni in a lightly oiled casserole, cover with a layer of oysters, then sprinkle with grated cheese. Repeat layers; pour sauce over and cover with grated cheese. Bake at 350° for about 30 minutes or until brown.

*Fat content of recipe:*                   *4 servings*
  *oysters:*                              6.0 grams

MEATS, FISH, AND POULTRY

121

| flour: | negligible |
|---|---|
| nonfat dry milk: | 0.8 gram |
| macaroni: | 0.7 gram |
| cheese: | 2.4–12.0 grams |
| Total: | 9.9–19.5 grams |
| Fat content per serving: | 2.5–4.9 grams |

## Sardines in Tomato Sauce or Mustard Sauce

Most sardines are packed in one kind of oil or another, and this oil is difficult to remove. However, several manufacturers pack sardines in tomato sauce or mustard sauce. These are not suitable for appetizers because their fat content is too high to include them on a "free" snack list. However, they fit well in a luncheon menu, where they can be eaten on crackers as an accompaniment to soup.

*Fat content of recipe:*

| *Underwood Sardines in Tomato Sauce®, 4-ounce can:* | 10.4 grams |
|---|---|
| *Underwood Sardines in Mustard Sauce®, 4-ounce can:* | 15.2 grams |

## Poultry

Two points of general information are helpful in dealing with poultry in low-fat menus. First, dark meat contains more fat than light meat. You can, therefore, control your individual intake somewhat by the selection of your pieces. Second, in poultry there is a high concentration of fat in the skin and directly beneath it. Fat content can be lowered by not eating the skin.

## Time Table for Roasting Poultry

| Bird | Oven Temperature, F° | Time per pound, minutes |
|---|---|---|
| Chicken, roasting | 350 | 20 |
| Duck | 350 | 20 |
| Turkey (unstuffed): | | |
| 8–10 pounds | 350 | 20–25 |
| 10–16 pounds | 350 | 20 |
| 18–25 pounds | 300 | 13–15 |

Add 5 minutes per pound for stuffed bird. Preheat oven to 450°. Put bird in oven and reduce heat immediately according to chart.

### Roast Chicken

Place chicken on rack in roasting pan. Rack allows fat to drain off. Moisten the dressing not with fat but with chicken bouillon cubes dissolved in hot water. Make your gravy by using chicken bouillon as the base instead of the chicken fat.

*Fat content of recipe:*
*roaster, raw, ready-to-cook,*
  *per pound:*     59.3 grams
*light meat, roasted, 3½*
  *ounces, without skin:*     4.9 grams
*dark meat, roasted, 3½*
  *ounces, without skin:*     6.5 grams
*The fat content of the raw roaster will be appreciably reduced by removal of the fat released by cooking.*

### Stuffing Balls

**¼ cup chicken bouillon made from cube**
**½ cup chopped onion**

MEATS, FISH, AND POULTRY

123

½ cup chopped celery
1 12-ounce can whole kernel corn,
   drained
1 8-ounce package Pepperidge Farm®
   Herb Seasoned Stuffing
½ teaspoon salt
¼ teaspoon pepper
½ teaspoon marjoram, crushed
2 eggs
1 cup liquefied nonfat milk

Quick-cook onion and celery in the chicken bouillon in a Teflon® or treated pan. Add corn, stuffing mix, seasonings, eggs, and milk; mix well and shape into 1¼- to 1½-inch balls.

Place in shallow 9 × 13–inch or 10-inch round pan. Bake, uncovered, in a preheated 375° oven for 15 minutes. Serve with leftover turkey or chicken gravy.

| Fat content of recipe: | | Yield: 25 to 28 balls |
|---|---|---|
| chicken bouillon: | negligible | |
| stuffing mix: | 3.0 grams | |
| eggs: | 12.0 grams | |
| milk: | trace | |
| Total: | 15.0 grams | |
| Fat content per ball, based on 24 balls: | | 0.6 gram |
| Fat content per ball, based on 28 balls: | | 0.5 gram |

## Stewed Chicken

You can proceed with stewed chicken with the same low-fat method recommended for beef, lamb, or veal stews: cook the day before, refrigerate the broth, and next day lift off the layer of fat which will have formed on the top. Here again, it is possible to skim the fat immediately after cooking with a piece of bread, but it is much more effective to refrigerate it. Stewing chickens should simmer—never boil—in a closely covered pot 2 hours or more until tender. A 5-pound stewing chicken serves 5 or 6 people.

*Fat content of recipe:*
*hens and stewing chicken, raw,*
    *ready-to-cook, per pound:*      82.1 grams
*light meat, stewed, 3½*
    *ounces, without skin:*      4.7 grams
*dark meat, stewed, 3½*
    *ounces, without skin:*      9.5 grams
*The fat content of the raw hen or stewing chicken will be appreciably reduced by removal of the fat released by cooking.*

### Baked Chicken

**1 2-pound fryer, cut up**
**Sliced onion**
**Parsley, fresh or dried**
**Rosemary**
**Salt and pepper**

Place cut-up fryer in pan. Season with salt, pepper, sliced onion, parsley, and rosemary. Cover pan tightly with aluminum foil and bake in 375° oven about 45 minutes. Make gravy by using chicken bouillon, flour, salt, and pepper in place of the pan drippings. Serve with rice.

*Fat content of recipe:*      *4 servings*
*breast, raw, per pound:*      8.6 grams
*drumstick, raw, per pound:*      10.6 grams
*thigh, raw, per pound:*      19.1 grams
*wing, raw, per pound:*      16.5 grams

125

## Barbecued Chicken

1 2-pound fryer, cut up
¼ cup vinegar
½ cup catsup
Dash tabasco
1 cup water

Place cut-up fryer in baking pan. Mix together vinegar, catsup, tabasco, and water. Pour over chicken in baking dish. Bake at 350° about 1 hour.

| Fat content of recipe: | 4 servings |
|---|---|
| breast, raw, per pound: | 8.6 grams |
| drumstick, raw, per pound: | 10.6 grams |
| thigh, raw, per pound: | 19.1 grams |
| wing, raw, per pound: | 16.5 grams |

## Chicken in a Garden

Cut-up fryers (allow 2 to 3 pieces of
   chicken per person)
Medium potatoes, 1 per person
Medium tomatoes, 1 per person
Medium onions, 1 per person
Mushrooms, fresh or canned (plain varie-
   ty, not "broiled in butter")
Green peppers, 2 slices per person
Packaged precooked rice (Minute®)
Worcestershire sauce
Salt, pepper, paprika
40-inch length of aluminum foil per per-
son

For each person: fold aluminum foil in half to give double thickness. Just off center of foil place 2 or 3 pieces of chicken, 1 pared potato, 1 tomato, 1 peeled onion, 2 mushroom caps if fresh (several if canned), and 2 green pepper rings. Sprinkle with 2 tablespoons rice, 1 teaspoon Worcestershire sauce, ¾ teaspoon salt, and dash of pepper and paprika. Fold foil in "drugstore" wrap.[4] Place on shallow pan and bake in very hot oven (450°) about 1¼ hours, or until all is tender, turning packages every 20 to 30 minutes.

*Fat content of recipe:*
| | |
|---|---|
| *breast, raw, per pound:* | 8.6 grams |
| *drumstick, raw, per pound:* | 10.6 grams |
| *thigh, raw, per pound:* | 19.1 grams |
| *wing, raw, per pound:* | 16.5 grams |

**Plantation Chicken**

**1 2-pound fryer, cut up**
**Chopped onion**
**Parsley, fresh or dried**
**Rosemary**
**Salt and pepper**

Cut five pieces of aluminum foil. Place on foil pieces of chicken sprinkled with onion, parsley, rosemary, salt, and pepper. Wrap with drugstore wrap described under "Chicken in a Garden." Cook on outdoor grill about 30 minutes, turning once. Serve and eat from foil packet. (This may be cooked in stove oven, if it is not convenient to cook outdoors.)

*Fat content of recipe:*
| | |
|---|---|
| *breast, raw, per pound:* | 8.6 grams |
| *drumstick, raw, per pound:* | 10.6 grams |

[4]Drugstore wrap: fold foil over food at center; fold over opposite edge three times for tight seal. Fold ends same way. This allows you to cut pack open at center and remove food or eat from pack.

**MEATS, FISH, AND POULTRY**

127

| thigh, raw, per pound: | 19.1 grams |
| wing, raw, per pound: | 16.5 grams |

## Chicken Chop Suey

**1 2-pound frying chicken**
**½ cup chopped green pepper**
**½ cup chopped onion**
**1 cup chopped celery with leaves**
**1 cup canned bean sprouts**
**2 tablespoons flour**
**2 tablespoons soy sauce**
**½ cup mushrooms**

Cook chicken in pressure cooker or simmer in pot on top of stove until meat will fall away from bones. Separate meat and broth and chill broth so that layer of congealed fat may be removed from top. Place ½ cup of remaining chicken broth or jelly in skillet and add pepper, onion, celery. Cook these ingredients slowly until they are soft and tender. Add shredded chicken and bean sprouts. Make a paste of the remaining chicken broth and the flour. Add this to the other ingredients, and stir and cook until they boil. Stir in soy sauce and mushrooms. Serve on rice.

| *Fat content of recipe:* | *4 servings* |
| *fryer, raw, ready-to-cook,* | |
| *1 pound:* | 15.1 grams |
| *soy sauce:* | 0.2 gram |

*Calculate the fat content by the weight of your ready-to-cook fryer. This will be further reduced by removal of the chicken fat from the broth.*

## Broiled Chicken with Lemon Sauce

**1 1½- to 2-pound frying chicken, cut in**
**serving pieces**
**1 small clove garlic**

½ teaspoon salt
½ cup lemon juice
2 tablespoons chopped onion
½ teaspoon black pepper
½ teaspoon dried thyme
¼ cup water
2 tablespoons pure pectin[5]

Mash clove garlic with salt in a bowl. Stir in remaining ingredients. (If sauce is allowed to stand overnight, the flavors will blend especially well, but this is not necessary.) Marinate the chicken in this sauce for 1 hour or longer. Remove the broiling rack and place chicken in broiling pan well down from flame. Broil slowly for 1 hour, basting with remaining marinade.

*Fat content of recipe:*

| | |
|---|---|
| *breast, raw, per pound:* | 8.6 grams |
| *drumstick, raw, per pound:* | 10.6 grams |
| *thigh, raw, per pound:* | 19.1 grams |
| *wing, raw, per pound:* | 16.5 grams |

### Chicken Creole

1 1½- to 2-pound frying chicken, cut in serving pieces
2 tablespoons chopped onion
2 tablespoons chopped green peppers
½ cup tomato purée or strained tomatoes
1 cup chicken broth (chicken bouillon cube dissolved in hot water)
¼ teaspoon salt
¼ teaspoon paprika
3 tablespoons flour
1 teaspoon lemon juice
½ teaspoon horseradish

[5]Powdered pectin is sold under the trade name Sure-Jell®.

½ cup mushrooms, sliced (or canned, without butter)
½ cup pimento

Bake chicken in covered pan in 375° oven for about 45 minutes. Place in skillet, stir and cook until tender: onion, peppers, tomato purée, chicken broth, salt, paprika. When peppers and onion are tender, thicken with flour. Add remaining ingredients, including chicken, and simmer a few minutes. Add salt as needed. Serve on rice or noodles.

| Fat content of recipe: | 6 servings |
|---|---|
| breast, raw, per pound: | 8.6 grams |
| drumstick, raw, per pound: | 10.6 grams |
| thigh, raw, per pound: | 19.1 grams |
| wing, raw, per pound: | 16.5 grams |
| rice, raw, 1 cup: | 1.0 gram |
| noodles, uncooked, 1 pound: | 20.9 grams |

### Chicken Tetrazzini

2 to 3 cupfuls of canned chicken
½ package of spaghetti, boiled (4 ounces)
¾ cup mushrooms (plain, not "broiled in butter")
1 chicken bouillon cube
¼ cup water
2 tablespoons flour
2 cups chicken broth or chicken bouillon
2 tablespoons sherry
Seasoning
Grated sapsago cheese (see under Cheeses, page 155)

130 Make sauce by dissolving bouillon cube in water and

blending in flour and seasoning. Then gradually add broth from which fat has been skimmed, stirring until the sauce is smooth. Remove from fire and add sherry. Add mushrooms to meat. Add half of sauce to the meat and the other half to the spaghetti. Place spaghetti in a greased casserole. Make a hole in the center. Place chicken in it. Sprinkle the top with grated sapsago cheese. Bake in moderate oven (375°) until lightly browned.

| *Fat content of recipe:* | *6 servings* |
|---|---|
| *1 pound canned chicken, meat only, boned:* | 53.1 grams |
| *spaghetti:* | 1.6 grams |
| *Total:* | 54.7 grams |
| *Fat content per serving:* | 9.1 grams |

### Chicken Divan (Modified Fat Content)

1 3-pound fryer
1 large bunch fresh broccoli or 2 pack-
    ages frozen broccoli
2 chicken bouillon cubes, dissolved in 2
    cups hot water
4 tablespoons flour
½ cup evaporated skimmed milk, un-
    diluted
3 tablespoons sherry
    Salt, pepper
    Grated sapsago cheese (see under
    Cheeses, page 155)

Wrap chicken in aluminum foil and bake in 325° oven about 2 hours. Cook broccoli in boiling salted water until tender; drain and set aside.

Make a sauce by using about ¼ cup of the chicken bouillon with the flour. Blend these in a saucepan over

131

a low flame. When flour and bouillon are smoothly blended, gradually add the remaining 1¾ cups chicken bouillon, stirring constantly until thick and smooth. Cook over a low flame for about 10 minutes, stirring frequently. Remove from fire and fold in evaporated skimmed milk, which has been whipped. (To whip evaporated skimmed milk, chill well the milk, bowl, and beater.) Add sherry. Season to taste with salt and pepper.

Place the cooked broccoli on a hot ovenproof platter and pour over it half the sauce. To the remaining sauce, add ¼ cup grated sapsago cheese. Over the broccoli arrange chicken meat which has been removed from the bones. Cover the chicken meat with the remaining sauce and sprinkle with grated sapsago cheese. Set the dish under the broiler until the sauce bubbles and is lightly browned.

| Fat content of recipe: | 6 servings |
|---|---|
| fryer, raw, ready-to-cook, | |
| 1 pound: | 15.1 grams |
| bouillon cubes: | negligible |
| flour: | negligible |
| evaporated skimmed milk, | |
| undiluted: | 0.3 gram |
| sapsago cheese: | negligible |

*Calculate the fat content by the weight of your ready-to-cook fryer. This will be further reduced by reserving the broth released by cooking for future use when it has been defatted and by removing the skin from the chicken meat.*

### Chicken Curry

**1 cup chopped onions**
**¾ cup catsup**

1½ cups buttermilk
2 teaspoons ground turmeric
1 teaspoon ground ginger
½ teaspoon ground clove
½ teaspoon ground cinnamon
⅛ teaspoon pepper
6 cardamon seeds (remove from pod), crushed
2 garlic cloves, minced
2½ pounds fryer breasts and legs

Combine all ingredients in large skillet. Add chicken. Cover; simmer 1 hour or until chicken is tender. Remove cover; cook 15 minutes or until sauce is of desired consistency. Serve over hot, cooked rice.

| Fat content of recipe: | 6 servings |
|---|---|
| breast, raw, per pound: | 8.6 grams |
| drumstick, raw, per pound: | 10.6 grams |
| thigh, raw, per pound: | 19.1 grams |
| rice, raw, 1 cup: | 1.0 gram |
| sauce: | |
| catsup: | 0.8 gram |
| buttermilk: | trace |

### Chicken in White Wine

2 2-pound chickens, cut up
2 teaspoons salt
¼ teaspoon pepper
2 tablespoons chopped (or dried) parsley
¼ teaspoon rosemary
¼ teaspoon tarragon
½ cup white wine

Put chicken in shallow baking dish. Sprinkle with the salt, pepper, parsley, rosemary, tarragon, and wine.

133

Cover. Bake in a 350° oven 45 minutes, or until tender.

| Fat content of recipe: | 4 servings |
|---|---|
| breast, raw, per pound: | 8.6 grams |
| drumstick, raw, per pound: | 10.6 grams |
| thigh, raw, per pound: | 19.1 grams |
| wing, raw, per pound: | 16.5 grams |

### Chicken and Mushrooms

**1 2- to 2½-pound fryer, cut up
1 pint mushroom sauce (page 196)
  Grated sapsago cheese (see under
  Cheeses, page 155)**

Place fryer in casserole, cover with mushroom sauce, and sprinkle generously with sapsago cheese. Bake in moderate oven (350°) about 1 hour or until tender.

| Fat content of recipe: | 4 servings |
|---|---|
| fryer, raw, ready-to-cook, | |
| 1 pound: | 15.1 grams |
| mushroom sauce: | negligible |
| sapsago cheese: | negligible |

### Oven Fried Chicken

**1 2-pound fryer
  Kellogg's Corn Flake Crumbs® (coating mix)
  Evaporated skimmed milk
  Salt and pepper**

Cut up fryer. Season crumbs with salt and pepper. Dip pieces of chicken in milk and then in crumbs. Place on Teflon® or treated cooky sheet. Bake in 375° oven for 45 minutes.

Fat content of recipe:
  breast, raw, per pound:          8.6 grams
  drumstick, raw, per pound:    10.6 grams
  thigh, raw, per pound:       19.1 grams
  wing, raw, per pound:        16.5 grams
  evaporated skimmed milk,
     undiluted, 1 cup:         0.5 gram
  cornflake crumbs, 1 cup:     0.8 gram

### Pennsylvania Dutch Chicken Pot Pie

**Stewing hen or roasting chicken to yield
  2 cups cooked chicken
2 quarts chicken broth
1 tablespoon minced onion
½ cup celery, sliced
1 medium potato, diced
1 carrot, sliced
½ contents package Pennsylvania Dutch®
  broad noodles
  Parsley**

Cook stewing hen. Remove meat from bones. Store broth overnight and remove chilled layer of fat. If hen does not yield two quarts of broth, supplement with chicken bouillon cubes dissolved in hot water. Heat broth to boiling and add noodles slowly. Add vegetables and cook uncovered at a rolling boil for 30 minutes. Before serving add cooked chicken and garnish with parsley.

Fat content of recipe:         *6 servings*
  roaster, raw, ready-to-cook,
     per pound:          59.3 grams
  hens and stewing chicken, raw,
     ready-to-cook, per pound:  82.1 grams
  noodles, dry, 1 pound:     20.9 grams

*The fat content will be reduced by following the low-fat method indicated of chilling the broth and removing the congealed fat.*

### Chicken Chowder

**1 envelope Lipton® dry tomato–vegetable soup mix**
**1 quart water**
**1 1-pound can (2 cups) kidney beans, drained**
**1 1-pound can (2 cups) mixed vegetables, drained**
**1 8-ounce can (1 cup) tomatoes, cut up**
**2 5-ounce cans boned chicken**

In large saucepan combine dry soup mix, water, beans, mixed vegetables and tomatoes. Add chicken, heat to boiling; reduce heat and simmer, uncovered, for 10 minutes.

| | |
|---|---|
| *Fat content of recipe:* | *8 servings* |
| *dry tomato–vegetable soup mix:* | 6.4 grams |
| *kidney beans:* | 2.0 grams |
| *chicken:* | 33.2 grams |
| *Total:* | 41.6 grams |
| *Fat content per serving:* | 5.2 grams |

### Pineapple Chicken Curry

**1 4–5 pound stewing hen or roasting chicken**
**1 large onion, chopped**
**⅔ cup chicken bouillon**
**1 tablespoon curry powder**
**⅔ cup flour**

**4 cups** strained chicken broth from cooking chicken (add chicken bouillon if needed to make that amount)
**1 cup** evaporated skimmed milk
**1 9-ounce can** crushed pineapple, well drained
**½ cup** seedless raisins
**2 tablespoons** dry or medium sherry
Salt to taste

Cook, cool and cut up stewing chicken. Strain broth and refrigerate so fat can be removed.

Cook onion gently in chicken bouillon. Blend in curry powder and flour. Gradually add broth and cook, stirring constantly, until mixture is thickened and smooth; simmer 5 minutes, stirring frequently. Stir in evaporated skimmed milk; add pineapple, raisins, chicken, sherry, and salt. Heat gently, but thoroughly. Serve with rice and condiments.

| *Fat content of recipe:* | *8 servings* |
|---|---|
| roaster, raw, | |
| ready-to-cook: | 237.2–296.5 grams |
| stewing hen, raw, | |
| ready-to-cook: | 328.4–410.5 grams |
| chicken bouillon: | negligible |
| flour: | 0.7 gram |
| evaporated skimmed | |
| milk: | 0.5 gram |
| Total: | |
| with roaster: | 238.4–297.7 grams |
| with stewing hen: | 329.6–411.7 grams |
| Fat content per serving: | |
| from 4-pound roaster: | 29.8 grams |
| from 5-pound roaster: | 37.2 grams |
| from 4-pound stewing | |
| hen: | 41.2 grams |

from 5-pound stewing
hen:                          51.5 grams
*The fat content will be appreciably reduced by chilling the broth and removing the fat as directed.*

Suggested condiments of low-fat content: minced scallions; chutney; minced green peppers; white of hard-cooked egg, chopped.

### Sherried Chicken with Herbs

4 deboned chicken breasts
1 teaspoon monosodium glutamate
½ teaspoon salt
½ teaspoon paprika
1 can sliced mushrooms (plain, *not* broiled in butter)
½ cup sherry
  Pinch of savory
  Pinch of thyme
  Pinch of rosemary
  Pinch of marjoram
1 tablespoon parsley, minced
1 bay leaf
  Pepper to taste

To bone chicken breasts, place breast on a flat surface. Using a paring knife, make a small incision between the meat and the breast bones, at a point away from the main wing portion. Using the fingers and the knife, carefully pull and scrape the meat away from the bones, taking care not to tear the meat.

Sprinkle chicken on both sides with monosodium glutamate, salt, pepper, and paprika. Brown chicken in Teflon® or treated skillet. Drain mushrooms, adding liquid and sherry to chicken. Sprinkle with herbs and parsley, add bay leaf, cover and simmer until tender. Add mushrooms last 10 minutes of cooking time.

*Fat content of recipe:*                 *4 servings*
   *chicken breast, raw, ready-to-cook, per pound:*
                               8.6 grams

### Chicken Cerise

- 4 fryers, quartered
- 2 teaspoons salt
- ¼ teaspoon pepper
- 1 cup water
- ½ cup raisins
- ½ cup brown sugar
- 1 teaspoon garlic (optional)
- 2 medium onions, sliced
- 1 12-ounce bottle chili sauce
- 1 16-ounce can Bing cherries
- 1 cup sherry

Place chicken in shallow roasting pan, skin side down. Season with salt and pepper. Broil under medium heat until golden brown. Combine remaining ingredients except cherries and wine, mix thoroughly. Pour sauce over chicken and cover entire pan with aluminum foil, bake about 1½ hours in 325° oven. Fifteen minutes before serving remove foil, add cherries and wine.

*Fat content of recipe:*            *16 servings*
   *fryer, raw, ready-to-cook,*
      *per pound:*            15.1 grams
   *chili sauce:*            2.0 grams

### Chicken Scallops Ratatouille

- 3 whole chicken breasts
- ½ cup all-purpose flour
- 1½ teaspoons salt
- ¼ teaspoon pepper
- 1 chicken bouillon cube dissolved in ⅓ cup water

**MEATS, FISH, AND POULTRY**

139

2 large onions, sliced
2 zucchini, sliced
2 large tomatoes, sliced
2 green peppers, cut in strips
1 small eggplant (not peeled), diced
2 cloves garlic crushed
2 tablespoons salt
1 teaspoon crumbled thyme
¼ teaspoon pepper

Remove skin from chicken breasts. Bone. Slice length-wise into 2 large cutlets and then into 4 smaller cutlets. To slice the second time run the fingers and then the knife along the white tendon which diagonally crosses the underside of each larger cutlet. Pound cutlets thin between two sheets of waxed paper or foil. In a bowl mix flour, the 1½ teaspoons salt and ¼ teaspoon pepper, and dip cutlets in mixture. Press firmly to coat. Shake off excess. Chill.

In a large Teflon® or treated skillet pan-brown cutlets, 3 or 4 at a time, 2 to 3 minutes per side. Remove from skillet and keep warm until all are cooked and vegetables prepared.

To the pan add bouillon, onions, zucchini, tomatoes, peppers, and eggplant. Sprinkle with crushed garlic, thyme and the remaining 2 tablespoons of salt and ¼ teaspoon pepper. Cook covered until vegetables are just tender (about 20 minutes) stirring occasionally. Top with cutlets; cook, uncovered, 10 minutes more. Arrange vegetables as a bed, cutlets on top.

*Fat content of recipe:*       *6 servings*
*chicken breast, raw, ready-to-cook, 1 pound:*
8.6 grams

## Chicken in Martini

1 roasting chicken
3 slices bacon

⅓ cup gin
⅓ cup dry vermouth
10 juniper berries[6]
 2 onions
   Seasoning
 1 10 × 16-inch brown-in-bag

Season fowl inside and out. Peel onions and place in bird's cavity. Lay 3 strips of bacon on high points of breast and legs to prevent burning and add flavor. Slide bird into bag. Place gin, vermouth, and juniper berries inside bag; tie bag and puncture according to maker's instructions. Bake at 400°.

This recipe may be used, also, for baking in a pan. Place bird on rack to allow fat to drip off. Baste frequently with the mixture of gin, vermouth, and juniper berries.

Fowl will be done when thermometer inserted in thickest part of thigh registers 185° (between 20 and 30 minutes to the pound.)

With either method: to maintain low-fat principles, drain off liquid when bird is done. The greatest part of the drippings from the bacon become part of this liquid, and the bacon can be calculated as "broiled and drained."

*Fat content of recipe:*
   *roaster, raw, ready-to-cook,*
        *1 pound:*                    59.3 grams
   *3 strips bacon, broiled and*
        *drained:*                    13.2 grams


### Sherried Artichoke Chicken

**1 2 to 2½-pound frying chicken, cut in
   serving pieces**

[6]Available on specialty spice shelves.

Salt and pepper
Paprika
1 can (1 pound) artichoke hearts,
 drained
¼ pound fresh mushrooms, sliced
3 tablespoons chopped scallions
2 tablespoons flour
⅔ cup Swanson® chicken broth
¼ cup sherry
½ teaspoon crumbled dried rosemary

Sprinkle chicken generously with salt, pepper and paprika. In Teflon® or treated skillet, brown chicken pieces on all sides. Transfer to 2-quart, shallow casserole. Arrange artichoke hearts between chicken pieces. In same skillet quick cook mushrooms and scallions until just tender. Sprinkle flour over mushrooms and stir in chicken broth, sherry and rosemary. Cook, stirring, a few minutes; pour over chicken. Cover and bake in moderate oven (375°) 40 minutes or until chicken is tender.

| | |
|---|---|
| *Fat content of recipe:* | *4 servings* |
| *fryer, ready-to-cook, raw,* | |
| *per pound:* | 15.1 grams |
| *chicken broth:* | 2.1 grams |

## Skewered Chicken

2 chicken breasts or 6 thighs, boned,
 skinned, and cut into 1-inch pieces
8 green onions cut in pieces, or slices of
 quartered large onions
1 green pepper cut in squares
1 cup soy sauce
1 cup dry sherry

¼ cup beef broth
1 teaspoon sugar
1 clove garlic crushed
1 tablespoon minced, preserved ginger
   or 1 teaspoon powdered ginger

Combine soy sauce, sherry, beef broth, sugar, garlic, and ginger. Marinate chicken, onions, and green pepper in this sauce for one hour. Put chicken, onions, and green peppers on skewers. Grill 3 inches above white-hot charcoal fire for 10 to 15 minutes. Brush with marinade as you turn the skewers over the charcoal.

If it is not possible to cook this over a charcoal grill, it can be broiled in the broiler pan in the oven.

| Fat content of recipe: | 4 servings |
| --- | --- |
| breast, raw, per pound: | 8.6 grams |
| thigh, raw, per pound: | 19.1 grams |
| soy sauce: | 1.6 grams |

**Turmeric Chicken**

   1 2 to 2½-pound frying chicken, cut in
      serving pieces
   1 cup uncooked long grain rice
   2 cups boiling water
   3 teaspoons salt
1½ teaspoons ground turmeric
   ¼ teaspoon freshly ground black pepper
   1 bay leaf
   ½ cup minced onion
   1 tablespoon lemon juice

Preheat oven to 325°. Combine all ingredients and turn into 2-quart casserole. Cover and bake until rice and chicken are tender, about 1¼ hours. During cooking, add water if necessary to keep rice moist.

143

*Fat content of recipe:*
*fryer, raw, ready-to-cook,*
*per pound:*      15.1 grams
*rice, 1 cup:*      1.0 gram

## Chicken Bulgarian

**1 2 to 2½-pound frying chicken, cut in serving pieces**
**1 cup yogurt**
**1½ teaspoons salt**
**1 clove garlic minced**
**½ teaspoon ground cardamon**
**1 teaspoon chili powder**
**¼ teaspoon cinnamon**
**2 tablespoons flour**

Combine yogurt, salt, garlic, cardamon, chili powder, and cinnamon. (Fold, do not stir, other ingredients into yogurt to maintain its thick consistency.) Marinate chicken in yogurt mixture for at least 4 hours or overnight. Place chicken in baking pan, skin side up. Combine flour with marinade and spoon over chicken. Bake at 350° for about 1½ hours or until chicken is tender. Baste occasionally with marinade.

*Fat content of recipe:*      *4 servings*
*fryer, raw, ready-to-cook,*
*per pound:*      15.1 grams
*yogurt:*      3.6 grams

## Chicken Wings with Oyster Sauce

**2 pounds chicken wings—about 10 pieces**
**1 slice ginger root**
**1 teaspoon dry sherry**

2½ tablespoons soy sauce
3 tablespoons oyster sauce[7]
1 teaspoon sugar

Cut the joints of the wing into three sections, and discard the wing tip section.

Put the ginger root and half the wings in a Teflon® or treated skillet and gently brown both sides. Remove the browned wings and brown the rest of the wings in the same manner. After the wings are browned, put wings, sherry, soy sauce, oyster sauce, and sugar into same skillet. Pour in 1 cup of water. Bring to a boil. Simmer with cover on for 10 minutes and baste the wings for another 10 minutes without cover, turning occasionally, or until a half cup of liquid remains. Serve hot or cold. It is not necessary to reheat leftovers.

*Fat content of recipe:*
  *chicken wings, raw,*
    *ready-to-cook, per pound:*     16.5 grams
  *soy sauce:*                      0.3 gram
  *oyster sauce:*                   negligible

### Spit-Cooked Fryers

Spit-cooked chicken is an easily prepared and mouth-watering dish. Medium-sized fryers (from 2 to 2½ pounds) should be rinsed in cold water and the cavity sprinkled generously with salt and oregano. Truss securely with string so legs and wings cannot break away during cooking. Place on spit and cook over an open fire. Sprinkle liberally from time to time with Accent® or Seasoned Salt or both. These fryers should cook slowly for a considerable period of time. The length of time will vary both with the heat of the fire

[7]Available in Oriental food stores and specialty food shops.

and the out-of-doors temperature. Experiment once or twice until you find the time best suited to your set-up.

*Fat content of recipe:*
  *fryer, raw, ready-to-cook, per pound:*   15.1 grams

### Roast Turkey

Roast turkey in roaster and follow low-fat technique by:

  Using no additional fat
  Placing on rack so that fat will drain off
  Moistening dressing with bouillon, not turkey fat
  Making gravy with bouillon, not turkey fat

*Fat content of recipe:*
  *turkey, raw, ready-to-cook,*
      *per pound:*                48.7 grams
    *light meat, roasted,*
      *3½ ounces (100 grams):*      3.9 grams
    *dark meat, roasted,*
      *3½ ounces (100 grams):*      8.3 grams
*This will be reduced by draining off fat released by cooking and by not eating the skin.*

## Duck

The next two recipes are included despite the fact that the fat content of duck is considerably above that of chicken, and therefore it is probably wise to recommend chicken! But if you *are* going to cook duck, *do* cook it by one of these methods which remove the maximum amount of fat and taste delicious at the same time.

146

### Duck à l'Orange

5-pound duckling
2 carrots
2 onions, sliced
Thyme
1 bay leaf
½ cup white wine
½ cup consommé
2 tablespoons sugar
1 teaspoon vinegar
Juice of 2 oranges and ½ lemon
2 tablespoons flour
Cold water
Peeled sections of 2 oranges
¼ cup orange curaçao (optional)

Wash a 5-pound duckling and place in the cavity carrots, sliced onions, a little thyme, and a bay leaf. Roast in an uncovered pan in a 350° oven about 1½ hours, until done. Remove duck from roasting pan and keep hot. Discard excess fat from pan. Add wine and consommé and cook 5 minutes. Melt sugar in heavy saucepan. As it caramelizes, add vinegar and orange and lemon juice. Strain sauce from pan into juice, bring to boil, and thicken with the flour which has been mixed with a little cold water. Season and simmer 10 minutes. Carve duck and garnish slices with peeled sections of 2 oranges. Add curaçao to sauce and pour over duck.

*Fat content of recipe:*          *4 servings*
*The only fat of any consequence is in the duckling itself.*
*domestic duck, raw,*
    *ready-to-cook, per pound:*     106.4 grams
    *flesh only, 3½ ounces:*      8.2 grams

*wild duck, raw,*

| | |
|---|---:|
| *ready-to-cook, per pound:* | 41.6 grams |
| *flesh only, 3½ ounces:* | 5.2 grams |

*These figures for per pound, ready-to-cook, and 3½ ounces, flesh only, show an extreme range. They are the figures available in our sources. From practical experience in cooking duck, the authors feel the actual figure lies somewhere in between.*

## Rotisserie Chinese Duck

**1 duckling, about 5 pounds, dressed**
**Salt**
**Few sprigs of parsley**
**½ lemon**
**¼ cup dark molasses (preferably Chinese bead molasses)**
**½ cup soy sauce**
**½ cup sherry**
**1 small clove garlic, minced**

Wash the duck and dry with paper towels, inside and out. Sprinkle inside cavity with salt and insert parsley and lemon. Truss bird securely. Fold wings under and tie close to body. Tie ends of legs together, then bring cord under tail, over breast and tie securely. Make certain thighs are close to body so they will not break away during cooking.

In a sauce pan, combine molasses, soy sauce, sherry and garlic. Cook over low heat five minutes.

Insert spit rod through center of duck cavity, balancing carefully. Be sure one set of skewers is inserted firmly into the legs before tightening screws.

Spit-cook over open fire two hours or until tender, basting every 15 minutes with sauce. The duck skin will darken considerably while cooking. Because of the considerable amount of fat in a duck which is released by cooking, the fire may flare up as the fat drips down on the coals. Be prepared to extinguish these flare-ups with a cup of water to prevent burning the duck. When done, drumstick meat is soft when pressed with fingers and thigh joint moves easily.

*Fat content of recipe:*
*domestic duck, raw,*
*ready-to-cook, per pound:*          106.4 grams
*flesh only, 3½ ounces:*               8.2 grams
*Fat content will be reduced by not eating the skin.*
*Note comment on fat content under preceding recipe.*

## Cornish Hens

### Cornish Hen Roasted

> **4 Cornish hens with giblets (about 1 pound each)**
> **2 chicken bouillon cubes**
> **1¾ cup boiling water**
> **¼ cup lemon juice**

Thaw Cornish hens as directed on package, remove wrapped giblets from hens, rinse hens in cold water, dry, and place on rack in uncovered roasting pan, breast side up. Roast at 350° for an hour; raise oven temperature to 400° and continue cooking 10 minutes. Baste frequently with bouillon cubes which have been dissolved in water with lemon juice added. Serve garnished with slices of orange, topped with a little currant jelly.

If you wish to serve the hens with rice and gravy,

simmer giblets until tender in boiling water; cut giblets up; pour off drippings from pan and add flour, salt, pepper, and water in which giblets have been cooked to the remaining brown crust. Additional fat will be eliminated if the skin is not eaten as most of the fat appears directly under the skin.

*Fat content of recipe:*
*roasting chicken, raw,*
    *ready-to-cook, per pound:*     59.3 grams
*without skin, roasted,*
    *3½ ounces (100 grams):*
        *light meat:*     4.9 grams
        *dark meat:*     6.5 grams
*giblets, raw, 1 pound:*     21.8 grams

## Orange Sauce for Baked or Roasted Cornish Hen

2 beef bouillon cubes
10 ounces water
1 cup orange juice
¼ cup Cointreau or Grand Marnier
2 tablespoons cornstarch
1 tablespoon honey
1 teaspoon lemon juice
1 tablespoon orange rind cut in thin
   strips

Dissolve bouillon cubes in water. Moisten cornstarch in ¼ cup of the orange juice. Combine all ingredients except orange rind in sauce pan and cook over medium heat, stirring constantly, until thickened. Add orange rind just before serving.

*Fat content of recipe:*   negligible     *Yield: dresses*
*4 to 6 hens*

150

## Spit-Cooked Cornish Hen

Rinse Cornish hens in cold water and dry inside and out with paper towels. Place on spit and truss securely so legs or wing tips will not break away during cooking. Roast over open fire. Sprinkle liberally from time to time with Aćcent® and Seasoned Salt. Cooking time will vary with the heat of the fire and the outdoor temperature. Allow 1½ hours.

*Fat content of recipe:*
*roasting chicken, raw,*
    *ready-to-cook, per pound:*     59.3 grams
*without skin, roasted,*
    *3½ ounces (100 grams):*
        *light meat:*     4.9 grams
        *dark meat:*     6.5 grams
  *giblets, raw, 1 pound:*     21.8 grams
*This will be reduced by the fat which drips away during spit cooking.*

LOW-FAT COTTAGE CHEESE

Most cheeses commonly available in this country contain appreciable amounts of butterfat and must therefore be used with care in low-fat menus. See pages 338–340 for the fat content of various cheeses. Federal standards specify the minimum amount of butterfat that each kind of cheese must contain to be legal. In special lowered-calorie cheese spreads, some statement must be made on the label that the product is below government standards for special reasons, i.e., the lowered caloric content. The fat content of cheese spreads in general, while lower than the fat content of processed cheese and natural cheese, is still high enough to require careful use. These good-tasting, cheddar flavor "imitation pasteurized process cheese spreads" are now on the market:

153

| Fat content of imitation pasteurized process cheese spreads | 2-pound block | 1-inch slice from 2-pound block |
|---|---|---|
| Chef's Delight®[1] (5% fat) | 45.4 grams | 5.6 grams |
| Count Down®[1] (1% fat) | 9.1 grams | 1.1 grams |

also available in 8-ounce cups in Cheddar and Blue Cheese flavors (1% fat) *fat content per 8-ounce cup:* 2.3 grams

Some imported cheeses are produced from skim milk and have a very low fat content. Two dessert cheeses low in fat are:

(1) *Gammelost*, a national delicacy of Norway, which has a strong taste and odor and the consistency of a meat spread. Its fat content is only 0.7 percent.[2] It is found chiefly in large cities where there is a concentration of Norwegian population or in specialty stores catering to Scandinavian trade.[3]

| Fat content: | |
|---|---|
| *per 6-ounce jar:* | 1.2 grams |
| *per serving:* | negligible |

(2) Harzer Hand Cheese (*Harzkäse*). This German cheese has a very sharp, pungent flavor and aroma. Its texture is smooth and semisoft. Its fat content ranges between 1 and 2 percent.[4,5]

[1]Manufactured by The Fisher Cheese Co., Wapakoneta, Ohio 45895.

[2]Estimate from Office of Agricultural Attaché, Norwegian Embassy, Washington, D.C.

[3]Importer: S. A. Haram & Co., Inc., 34 Beach Street, New York, New York 10013.

[4]*Cheese Varieties and Descriptions*, U.S. Department of Agriculture, Agriculture Handbook No. 54, Washington, D.C., 1953. Slightly revised 1969.

[5]Importer: Otto Roth & Co., Inc., 14 Empire Boulevard, Moonachie, New Jersey 07074.

*Fat content:*
    *per 6½-ounce roll:*       1.8–3.6 grams
    *per serving:*            negligible

Both these cheeses require constant refrigeration, and each has so distinctive a taste that it will not be palatable to everyone.

A third imported cheese of lowered fat content is now available. Made in Switzerland, St. Otho® cheese is a firm, yellow cheese of good flavor. It is tasty on crackers and will bubble up if placed under broiler heat. The fat content is five percent (1.4 grams per ounce of cheese) and must be counted in the daily fat intake. This is a satisfactory "eating" cheese, not as strongly flavored as *Gammelost* or Harzer Hand Cheese. Distributed by Otto Roth & Company, Inc.,[5] it is available in cheese specialty shops.

Sapsago, Geska® brand,[6] a Swiss green cheese, is approximately one percent fat. It is a grating type of cheese which we have used as flavoring for some of our recipes.

The most readily available lowered fat cheeses are dry cottage cheese, low-fat cottage cheese, and the imitation pasteurized process cheese spreads described earlier in this chapter. Nonetheless we have found it possible to include some cheese dishes in this book.

First, with dry cottage cheese there need be no limitation whatever. The fat content of a 12-ounce box is 1.0 gram. This can be purchased from any local dairy and is labeled "Dry" or "Uncreamed" in contrast to "Creamed Cottage Cheese," which does contain some fat. If you cannot obtain dry cottage cheese, wash

[6]Food specialty stores in various parts of the country stock sapsago cheese. If you are unable to obtain it in your locality, write the distributer, Otto Roth & Co., Inc., 14 Empire Boulevard, Moonachie, New Jersey 07074.

155

creamed cottage cheese by placing it in a strainer and running cold water over it. Also on the national market are a number of low-fat cottage cheeses with fat content per 12- to 16-ounce carton ranging from 3.4 to 6.8 grams. These are listed by brand names in Table 3, page 339, in the Appendix. These low-fat cottage cheeses have more of the characteristics of a creamed cottage cheese, but the fat content remains low. Any of the following spreads or dips may be made with dry cottage cheese or with one of the low-fat cottage cheeses.

## Cheese Spreads and Dips

### Chive Cheese

Place dry or low-fat cottage cheese in electric mixer and blend at heavy-batter speed until smooth. An electric blender may also be used. Add chopped, fresh chives and celery salt to taste. Serve as a spread for crackers.

*Fat content of recipe:*
  *depending upon type of cottage cheese used:*
                                          1.0–6.8 grams

### Garlic Cheese

Place dry or low-fat cottage cheese in electric mixer or blender as in preceding recipe. Season with garlic salt to taste. This is good either as a cracker spread or for stuffing celery.

*Fat content of recipe:*
  *depending on type of cottage cheese used:*
156                                       1.0–6.8 grams

## Onion Cheese

Place 12 ounces of dry or low-fat cottage cheese in electric mixer or blender. Blend in one-half package Lipton® dry Onion Soup. Serve as a spread for crackers.

*Fat content of recipe:*
*cottage cheese, depending*
    *on type used:*           1.0–6.8 grams
*onion soup mix:*            1.2 grams

## Brown-Bread Sandwiches

Blend dry or low-fat cottage cheese in electric mixer at heavy-batter speed without further seasoning. Spread between slices of Boston brown bread with raisins.

*Fat content of recipe:*
*cottage cheese, depending*
    *on type used:*           1.0–6.8 grams
*Boston brown bread,*
    *1 slice, 3 by ¾ inches:*     1.0 gram

## Pimento Cheese Spread

**12 ounces Count Down® imitation pasteurized process cheese spread; approximately 3 inches cut from a 2-pound block**
**1 4-ounce can pimento**
**3 tablespoons Special Mayonnaise (page 164)**

Grate cheese spread, add pimento and mayonnaise, and blend well in electric mixer.

157

| Fat content of recipe: | Yield: 2½ cups |
|---|---|
| Count Down®: | 3.3 grams |
| mayonnaise: | 1.2 grams |
| Total: | 4.5 grams |
| Fat content per tablespoon: | 0.1 gram |

### Yogurt Cheese

Pour off surface whey from plain yogurt and place remaining solids in a cheese cloth bag. Hang the bag over the sink or a bowl and allow to drain overnight or until the cheese is of a spreading consistency. The older the yogurt, the sharper the cheese. Season with salt or add chopped fresh chives or herbs.

*Fat content of recipe:*
  *8-ounce carton, plain yogurt:*   3.6 grams

## Cheese Dishes

Some cheese dishes can be worked into the menu as substitutes for meat from time to time. They will add variety and will not increase the fat consumption too greatly if used in this way. Remember that the ratio of protein to fat is higher in meat than in cheese, and therefore cheese should not be substituted often.

The imitation pasteurized process cheese spreads are discussed on pages 153–154. In addition to these, there are processed cheddar cheese foods which are so labeled. Finally, there is pasteurized processed cheese. You will note from the list below that the imitation pasteurized process cheese spreads have, by far, the lowest fat content. In dishes calling for grated cheddar cheese, this would be the appropriate substitution.

158

*Fat content per ounce:*
*American pasteurized processed*
   *cheese:*                 9.0 grams
*American pasteurized process*
   *cheese spread:*        6.0 grams
*Chef's Delight® imitation*
   *pasteurized process cheese*
   *spread:*               1.4 grams
*Count Down® imitation*
   *pasteurized process skim*
   *milk cheese spread:*      0.3 gram

### Grated Cheese Topping

For dishes in which a topping of grated cheese is desired, sapsago cheese (see page 155) may be used. This is a hard green cheese made from skim milk and herbs and imported from Switzerland. It is sold both in solid cones and in grated form. Before grating, allow the cone to come to room temperature; it will then grate easily. You can store the ground-up cheese in the refrigerator in a jar with a tight-fitting top, ready for use when needed. Its fat content is low: approximately 0.3 gram per ounce.

### Cheese Toast

Toast one slice of rye bread on one side under broiler. On untoasted side place a 1-ounce slice of imitation pasteurized process cheese spread. Run this under the broiler until the cheese begins to brown and bubble up. Serve at once. For variety, add a slice of tomato placed on top of the cheese before broiling.

*Fat content of recipe:*
   *1 slice rye bread:*          trace

*1 ounce Chef's Delight®:*    1.4 grams
*1 ounce Count Down®:*    0.3 gram

## Mock Rarebit

**1 chicken bouillon cube**
**¼ cup hot water**
**3 tablespoons flour**
**1½ cups liquefied nonfat dry milk**
**½ teaspoon salt**
**¼ teaspoon dry mustard**
**¼ teaspoon pepper**
**1 teaspoon Worcestershire sauce**
**Paprika**
**1 cup freshly grated (coarse) imitation pasteurized process cheese spread, Chef's Delight® or Count Down®**

Dissolve bouillon cube in water in double boiler. Blend in flour and seasonings. Add milk slowly, stirring until blended. Add cheese and stir until cheese melts and rarebit thickens to desired consistency. Serve on toast.

*Fat content of recipe*
*(exclusive of toast):*    *4 servings*
*    bouillon cube:*    negligible
*    flour:*    negligible
*    milk:*    trace
*    cheese:*
*        Chef's Delight®:*    11.2 grams
*        Count Down®:*    2.4 grams
*    Total:*    2.4–11.2 grams
*Fat content per serving:*    0.6–2.8 grams

160

Any salad dressing made with oil is a source of large quantities of fat in the diet (one cup of salad oil contains 220 grams of fat) and as such is fair game for the cook searching out low-fat menus. For some time it was thought possible to get around this problem by substituting mineral oil for salad oil. This did not alter the taste of the dressings, and since mineral oil was not absorbed by the body the quantity of fat did not matter. However, mineral oil interferes with vitamin absorption and, as well, many people dislike the idea of eating it. The following recipes have been designed to retain the flavor and texture of conventional mayonnaise and French dressing and at the same time to eliminate the oil completely. Butter has been eliminated in the cooked dressing, and skim milk has been substituted for whole; otherwise it is similar to a standard cooked dressing. Some recipes in this chap-

**161**

ter call for low-fat cottage cheese. For information see the chapter on cheeses, pages 155–156.

Remember that, although you must control the content of your salad dressings, you have great latitude in the other ingredients you use. Fresh greens, fresh fruits (except avocado and coconut), shell fish, tuna fish not packed in oil, vegetables fresh or cooked without fat are all suitable. Such additions as dilly beans or pickles will add interest.

## Ready-Prepared Special Mayonnaises and Salad Dressings

There are available among "diet" foods certain special dressings of lowered fat and caloric content. Though their fat content is not as low as that of the recipes in this chapter, it is considerably below that of conventional dressings. Such special diet products usually carry a detailed analysis on the label; you will be able to determine the fat content of any particular brand by studying the label. You should then include this total in your calculation of the week's fat intake. The list below will be helpful.

*Fat per tablespoon, grams*

*Ann Page*®[1] *Low Calorie*
  *French Style Regular*                                   1.6

[1] Ann Page, The Great A & P Tea Co., Inc., New York, New York 10017;
Tillie Lewis Foods, Inc., Stockton, California 95201;
Thomas J. Lipton, Inc., 800 Sylvan Ave., Englewood Cliffs, New Jersey 07632;
T. Marzetti Co., Box 29163, Columbus, Ohio 43229;
Old Dutch Co., Division of Root Company, Daytona Beach, Fla. 32015;
Reese Finer Foods, Division of Pet Inc.:
  Lively Boulevard & Kirk, Elk Grove Village, Illinois 60007
  745 Army Street, San Francisco, Calif. 94124
  2150 East 10th Street, Los Angeles, Calif. 90021
  1325 Morris Park Ave., Bronx, New York 10461.

| | |
|---|---|
| French Style Chef | 0.7 |
| Italian | 0.7 |
| Blue Cheese | 0.9 |
| Thousand Island | 1.5 |
| Tillie Lewis® Diet Foods[1] | |
| Chefs | trace |
| Italian | trace |
| Cheese | 1.1 |
| French | trace |
| Whipped | 0.9 |
| May-Lo-Naise | 0.9 |
| Remoulade | 0.9 |
| Thomas J. Lipton®, Inc.[1] | |
| Wish-Bone® Low Calorie Dressings | |
| French Style | 1.0 |
| Italian | 0.2 |
| Russian | 0.6 |
| Thousand Island | 1.6 |
| Marzetti®[1] | |
| Marzetti® Low-Cal Dressings | |
| Low-Calorie Slaw Dressing | 1.8 |
| Low-Calorie French | trace |
| Low-Calorie Italian | 0.2 |
| Low-Calorie Thousand | |
| Island | 1.1 |
| Low-Calorie Blue Cheese | 1.4 |
| Frenchette® Low-Calorie Dressings | |
| Mayonette Gold | 2.8 |
| Frenchette French | trace |
| Frenchette Italianette | 0.2 |
| Frenchette Thousand Island | 1.1 |
| Frenchette Blue Cheese | 1.4 |
| Frenchette Caesar | 2.6 |
| Frenchette Gourmet | 1.3 |
| Frenchette Green Goddess | 1.5 |
| Frenchette Slaw Dressing | 1.8 |

Old-Dutch®[1]
 "Old-Dutch" Sweet-Sour
   Dressing     negligible
Reese®[1]
 Tropical Fruit, Oil Free  negligible

## Low-Fat Recipes for Dressings

### Special Mayonnaise

½ teaspoon plain gelatin
1½ cups evaporated skimmed milk, undiluted
2 egg yolks
2 tablespoons sugar
1½ teaspoons dry mustard
1 teaspoon salt
¼ cup mild vinegar

Soak gelatin in ¼ cup cold milk. Scald 1¼ cups milk in double boiler. Remove from fire and dissolve gelatin in it. Beat together egg yolks, sugar, dry mustard, and salt. Stir into this a little of the hot milk and gelatin mixture. Blend and add remainder of milk mixture. Return these ingredients to the double boiler and cook and stir over a very low flame until they begin to thicken (about 10 minutes). Remove from fire. Add vinegar slowly. This will still be a comparatively thin mixture. It thickens as it cools. If any lumps of gelatin remain, strain while pouring into jar for storage. Allow to cool, and then refrigerate. This dressing is fine on coleslaw. If you usually thin your mayonnaise with vinegar when using it on slaw, you can do so with this dressing.

*Fat content of recipe:*  *Yield: approximately 1 pint*
**164** *evaporated skimmed milk:*  0.8 gram

| eggs: | 12.0 grams |
| Total: | 12.8 grams |
| *Fat content per tablespoon:* | 0.4 gram |

### Cooked Salad Dressing

**1½ cups liquefied nonfat milk**
**2 tablespoons cornstarch**
**1 egg yolk**
**¼ cup vinegar**
**2 teaspoons prepared mustard**
**1 teaspoon salt**

Blend together in top of double boiler nonfat milk and cornstarch, adding milk gradually to make first a smooth paste and then a smooth liquid. In small mixing bowl beat together egg yolk, vinegar, mustard, and salt. Place double boiler top over hot water on low flame and cook milk and cornstarch, stirring constantly, until thick and clear-looking (When cornstarch is thoroughly cooked, you should not be able to taste it.) Add egg mixture and cook until egg has thickened completely. Pour in jar and refrigerate when cool.

| *Fat content of recipe:* | *Yield: approximately 1 pint* |
| *liquefied nonfat milk:* | trace |
| *cornstarch:* | negligible |
| *egg:* | 6.0 grams |
| *Total:* | 6.0 grams |
| *Fat content per tablespoon:* | 0.2 gram |

### French Dressing (with Pectin) I

**3 tablespoons lemon juice**
**2 tablespoons powdered pectin[2]**
**½ cup water**

[2]Powdered pectin may be purchased under the trade name Sure Jell®.

½ teaspoon salt
Pepper
Paprika
1–2 cloves of garlic, peeled

Place all ingredients in jar and shake well. Allow to stand so that some of garlic flavor will be absorbed into dressing.

*Fat content of recipe:*   0.0 gram

## French Dressing (with Pectin) II

2 tablespoons red wine vinegar (garlic flavored)
2 tablespoons powdered pectin[2]
½ cup water
½ teaspoon salt
¼ teaspoon paprika
⅛ teaspoon pepper
1–2 cloves of garlic, peeled

Place all ingredients in a jar and shake well. Allow to stand an hour or more so flavors will blend. This dressing can be varied by substituting tarragon vinegar for the red wine vinegar.

*Fat content of recipe:*   0.0 gram

## French Dressing III

1 cup consommé
1 tablespoon catsup
1 teaspoon onion juice
1 teaspoon Italian herbs (or your own mix of dried herbs)
½ teaspoon paprika

½ teaspoon salt
⅛ teaspoon pepper
1 tablespoon wine vinegar

Shake well. Refrigerate 30 minutes. Use over mixed greens.

*Fat content of recipe:* negligible

### French Dressing IV

1 clove garlic, mashed
1 cup red wine vinegar
1 cup tomato juice
1 teaspoon salt
½ teaspoon cracked pepper
¼ teaspoon dry mustard
1½ teaspoons sugar

Mix in jar; let stand at least 2 hours.

*Fat content of recipe:* negligible

### Good Seasons® Salad Dressings

There is available a group of salad dressings (dehydrated) packaged under the trade name "Good Seasons"®. These come in a variety of flavors:

| | |
|---|---|
| Mild Italian | Onion |
| Cheese Italian | Cheese Garlic |
| Bleu Cheese | Old Fashion French |
| Garlic | Riviera French |
| Italian | Low Calorie Italian |

Any one of these mixes may be used in the following recipe.

167

1 package Good Seasons® Salad
 Dressing mix
2 tablespoons powdered pectin (See
 footnote 2, page 165)
3 tablespoons lemon juice
¾ cup water

Place the ingredients in a bottle and shake well. (If, when you purchase your Good Seasons® Salad Dressing mix, you also purchase the kit containing the mixing bottle, you can place your mix, pectin, and lemon juice in the kit bottle and add water to the line marked "oil." Then shake well.)

*Fat content of recipe:*   negligible

## French Dressing (with Tomato Catsup)

½ cup sweet pickle vinegar
1 package Good Seasons® Salad Dressing mix, Old Fashion French or Riv-
 iera French flavor
½ cup catsup

Place all ingredients in jar and shake well. For variation 1 tablespoon of sherry may be added to dressing.

*Fat content of recipe:*   negligible    *Yield: 1 cup*

## Blue Cheese Dressing

Mix up any flavor Good Seasons® Salad Dressing according to preceding rule. To this add one ¾-ounce package of blue cheese, well crumbled. Although we have pointed out that care must be exercised in the use of cheese, the fact that blue cheese can be purchased in a ¾-ounce package makes it simple to provide accurate measurement for its use in this recipe. This quantity of dressing will be sufficient for a tossed salad to serve eight.

*Fat content of recipe:*
   *Good Seasons® Salad Dressing:*     negligible
   *¾ ounce blue cheese:*     6.8 grams
*Fat content per serving:*     0.9 gram

### Creamy Bleu Cheese Dressing

**1 12-ounce box dry or low-fat cottage cheese**
**1 teaspoon Good Seasons® Salad Dressing Mix, Bleu Cheese Flavor (dry)**
**¾ ounce blue cheese**

Put the cottage cheese and the dry salad dressing mix into the electric blender and blend until very smooth. Remove from the blender and stir in with a fork the crumbled blue cheese. Serve over lettuce.

| *Fat content of recipe:* | *5 servings* |
|---|---|
| *cottage cheese:* | 1.0–6.8 grams |
| *Good Seasons® Salad* | |
| *Dressing mix:* | negligible |
| *¾ ounce blue cheese:* | 6.8 grams |
| *Total:* | 7.8–13.6 grams |
| *Fat content per serving:* | 1.6–2.7 grams |

### Cottage Cheese Dressing

**½ 12-ounce box low-fat cottage cheese**
**¼ cup buttermilk**
**Generous shaking of Seasoned Salt**

Blend gently in blender. This will dress mixed greens for 6.

169

| Fat content of recipe: | 6 servings |
|---|---|
| cottage cheese: | 1.7–3.4 grams |
| buttermilk: | negligible |
| Total: | 1.7–3.4 grams |
| Fat content per serving: | 0.3–0.6 gram |

## Lawry's® Salad Dressings

These dehydrated salad dressing mixes can be made up in the same way as the Good Seasons® mixes (see recipe, page 168). The list below gives fat content for the variety of flavors.

| | Fat content | |
|---|---|---|
| | grams per package | grams per serving (6 to the package) |
| Bacon | 0.9 | 0.2 |
| Bleu | 5.0 | 1.0 |
| Caesar Garlic Cheese | 2.4 | 0.4 |
| Green Goddess | 0.9 | 0.2 |
| Italian | 0.1 | negligible |
| Italian with Cheese | 2.4 | 0.4 |
| Lemon Garlic | 0.2 | negligible |
| Old Fashioned French | negligible | negligible |
| Thousand Island | 0.2 | negligible |

## Shrimp Salad Dressing

Serve over chilled, cooked shrimp on lettuce.

**½ cup evaporated skimmed milk, undiluted**
**½ cup Special Mayonnaise (page 164)**
**3½ tablespoons chili sauce**

170

1½ teaspoons prepared horseradish
1 teaspoon Worcestershire sauce
1 tablespoon lemon juice
½ teaspoon salt
¼ teaspoon paprika

Beat the milk into the Special Mayonnaise. Blend in remaining ingredients.

*Fat content of recipe (excluding shrimp):*
| | |
|---|---|
| milk: | 0.3 gram |
| mayonnaise: | 3.2 grams |
| chili sauce: | negligible |
| Total: | 3.5 grams |

## Salads

### Coleslaw with Creamy Dressing

You may, if you wish, make your usual coleslaw, using the Special Mayonnaise. However, the following dressing is fresh-tasting and offers variety.

½ cup evaporated skimmed milk, undiluted
2 tablespoons lemon juice
½ teaspoon dry mustard
1½ teaspoons sugar
¾ teaspoon salt
   Dash pepper
¼ cup finely chopped onion
⅓ cup finely chopped parsley
¼ cup dry or low-fat cottage cheese

Chill the evaporated milk in refrigerator tray until icy cold. Chill small bowl and beater. Blend mustard with lemon juice. Whip evaporated skimmed milk until stiff, adding lemon juice after the milk has started to stiffen. Fold in remaining ingredients, blending well. Mix with 3 cups chilled, shredded cabbage and serve immediately.

| Fat content of recipe: | 5 servings |
|---|---|
| milk: | 0.3 gram |
| cottage cheese: | 0.3–1.7 grams |
| Total: | 0.6–2.0 grams |
| Fat content per serving: | 0.1–0.4 gram |

## Coleslaw

**4 cups grated cabbage**
**4 green onions, chopped**
**3 heaping tablespoons India relish**
**1 teaspoon sugar**
   **Salt**

Combine cabbage, onions, India relish and sugar. Salt lightly. Chill.

*Fat content of recipe:* negligible   *Yield: 4 cups*

## Marinated Cucumbers

Chill, peel, and slice cucumbers. Marinate them in either:

**French Dressing (with Pectin) I (page 165)**
   **or**
**Good Seasons® Salad Dressing, any flavor (page 167)**
   **or**
**Vinegar, salt, and pepper**

*Fat content of recipe:* negligible

### Wilted Cucumbers with Dill

2 medium-sized cucumbers
Salt
1 teaspoon sugar
⅓ cup vinegar
Water
Pepper
1 tablespoon fresh dill or ½ tablespoon dried dill

Peel and score cucumbers. Slice thin. Arrange in layers in a bowl, salting each layer generously. Cover and let wilt in the refrigerator for several hours. Then press out the salt water that forms. Add sugar. Dilute the vinegar with enough water to make ½ cup. Pepper the cucumbers and pour the diluted vinegar over them. Sprinkle with the dill. Let stand in the refrigerator about 1 hour to marinate.

*Fat content of recipe:*      negligible      *4 servings*

### Gelatin Cucumber Salad

2 cups boiling water
1 package lime-flavored gelatin
1 large cucumber
1 teaspoon onion juice
1 tablespoon vinegar
½ teaspoon salt

Dissolve gelatin in water. Grate cucumber on coarse side of grater. Press juice from pulp through cheesecloth. Onion juice may be extracted the same way. Add cucumber juice, onion juice, vinegar, and salt to dissolved gelatin. Place in mold and chill. Serve on lettuce with low-fat cottage cheese.

173

*Fat content of recipe:*                      *6 servings*
    *cottage cheese, per 12-ounce box:*   3.4–6.8 grams

## Sherry Gelatin with Black Bing Cherries

Prepare Wine Gelatin Dessert, Sherry flavor, according to directions on the package. When the gelatin is almost cold and just before it begins to jell, add 1 can (No. 303) black Bing cherries, pits removed.

This may be served as a salad on a salad green with Special Mayonnaise (page 164) or for dessert as it is.

*Fat content of recipe:*   negligible

## Congealed Fruit Salad

**1 jar mixed salad fruits, drained**
**1 package grape-flavored gelatin**
**Yogurt**

Place pieces of fruit in individual molds. Prepare gelatin according to instructions on package and pour over fruit. Refrigerate to congeal. Unmold onto lettuce leaves on individual salad plates. Top with a tablespoon of yogurt before serving. Using average-sized molds this recipe will yield about 6 servings.

*Fat content of recipe:*   negligible
*Fat content of yogurt topping, per 1 tablespoon*
    *serving:*                         0.3 gram

## Tomato Aspic

**2 tablespoons gelatin**
**½ cup cold tomato juice**
**3½ cups hot tomato juice**

Soak gelatin in cold tomato juice. Dissolve it in hot tomato juice. Tomato juice varies. Check the taste to see whether additional seasoning is needed. If further seasoning is needed, try lemon juice or a teaspoonful of dried basil. If you wish, you may add two cupfuls of solid ingredients, chopped, such as celery, green peppers, cabbage, carrots. Mold the aspic, chill, unmold, and serve as salad on lettuce.

*Fat content of recipe:*     negligible     *8 servings*

### Easy Tomato Aspic

**1 package (3 oz.) lemon Jello®
2 cups "V-8"® Cocktail Vegetable Juice**

Add 1 cup boiling "V-8"® juice to contents of gelatin package. Stir until dissolved. Add 1 cup cold "V-8"®. Chill until firm.

*Fat content of recipe:*     negligible     *4 servings*

### Fruited Lettuce

**1 head lettuce, torn in pieces
1 large grapefruit, sectioned
½ 12-ounce box low-fat cottage cheese**

Toss lettuce, grapefruit sections, and low-fat cottage cheese. Chill.

*Fat content of recipe:*                    *4 servings*
  cottage cheese:            1.7–3.4 grams
*Fat content per serving:*     0.4–0.9 gram

### Garden Salad

Cube fresh tomatoes and cucumbers. Serve with Low-Fat Sour Cream (page 199). Toss the vegetables gently with the dressing, so that the cubes will be well coated.

*Fat content of recipe:*
  *1 recipe Low-Fat Sour Cream:*   3.4–6.8 grams

## Imitation Bacon Bits

To vary the flavor of mixed green salads add bacon bits.

|  | Fat content grams per teaspoon |
|---|---|
| *Durkee Imitation Bacon Bits®* | 0.4 |
| *French's Imitation Bacon Crumbles®* | 0.3 |
| *McCormick Baconbits®* | 0.4 |

## Garlic Croutons

Toast three slices of white bread, and rub both sides with a large clove of garlic. The rough texture of the toast acts as a grater for the garlic. While the toast is still hot, remove crusts, cut into half-inch squares, and place in a low oven (200°) until all moisture is removed. Toss salad with dressing first, and when leaves are thoroughly coated, add croutons and toss a little more.

*Fat content of recipe:*
  *bread:*      3.0 grams

## Grapefruit Lobster–Crab Salad

**Fresh or canned lobster or crab meat**
**Catsup**
**Lemon juice**

**Horseradish**
**Grapefruit sections**
**Lettuce**

Season catsup to taste with lemon juice and horseradish. Serve over lobster or crab meat on lettuce bed with grapefruit sections.

*Fat content of ingredients for one average serving:*
  *lobster, 3 ounces canned:*          1.2 grams
  *crab, 3 ounces canned*
    *or cooked:*                        2.1 grams

**Dilled Mushroom Salad**

½ **pound fresh mushrooms**
½ **cup thinly sliced celery**
½ **cup diced green pepper**
3 **tablespoons finely chopped onion**
2 **tablespoons chopped fresh dill or 1
  teaspoon dry dill**
1 **tablespoon chopped fresh parsley**
1 **recipe Good Seasons® salad dressing,
  garlic flavor (page 167)**

Rinse, pat dry, and slice mushrooms. In a large bowl combine mushrooms, celery, and green pepper. Mix salad dressing and combine onions, dill, and parsley with it. Pour over mushroom mixture. Cover and refrigerate one or two hours. Pass pepper grinder, if desired, with salad.

*Fat content of recipe:*     negligible     *Yield: 1 quart*

**Green Bean Salad**

2 **cans (No. 303) Blue Lake green beans**
½ **stalk celery, chopped**

**1 bunch green onions, chopped**
**½ teaspoon dry mustard**
**1 8-ounce bottle Ann Page® Low Calorie**
**Italian dressing**

Mix ingredients together and chill in refrigerator for several hours.

| | |
|---|---|
| *Fat content of recipe:* | *8 servings* |
| salad dressing: | 11.0 grams |
| *Fat content per serving:* | 1.4 grams |

## Three Bean Salad I

**1 small purple onion**
**½ green pepper**
**1 1-pound can kidney beans**
**1 1-pound can wax beans**
**1 1-pound can green beans**
**¼ cup vinegar**
**¼ cup sugar**
**4 ounces Ann Page® Low Calorie Italian**
**dressing**

Slice onion and green pepper. Wash kidney beans and strain with other beans. Dissolve sugar in vinegar, add dressing. Stir and add other ingredients. Refrigerate, stirring occasionally.

| | |
|---|---|
| *Fat content of recipe:* | *6–8 servings* |
| kidney beans: | 1.8 grams |
| salad dressing: | 5.5 grams |
| Total: | 7.3 grams |

*Fat content per serving, based on 6 servings:*
1.2 grams
*Fat content per serving, based on 8 servings:*
0.9 gram

### Three Bean Salad II

Several companies market Three Bean Salad. Check label for ingredients. If no oil has been added, the fat content will be less than 1 gram per ½-cup serving.

### Bean Sprout Salad

**2 cups fresh or canned bean sprouts**
**2 green onions, chopped fine**
**1 clove garlic, crushed**
**2 teaspoons sesame seed**
**1 canned pimento chopped**
**2 tablespoons soy sauce**

Remove tails from fresh bean sprouts. Put into boiling water and boil until slightly soft, drain. Wash in cold water and drain. If using canned bean sprouts, drain thoroughly.

Mix together chopped green onions, crushed garlic, sesame seed, chopped pimento and soy sauce. Pour over bean sprouts. Toss lightly. Serve chilled.

*Fat content of recipe:*　　　　　　　　*4–6 servings*
　*sesame seed:*　　　　3.8 grams
　*soy sauce:*　　　　　trace
　*Total:*　　　　　　3.8 grams
*Fat content per serving, based on 4 servings:*
　　　　　　　　　　　　　　1.0 gram
*Fat content per serving, based on 6 servings:*
　　　　　　　　　　　　　　0.6 gram

### French Tomato Salad

**6 medium unpeeled tomatoes**
**½ cup minced parsley**
**2 minced shallots or green onions**

Cut tomatoes into very thin vertical slices. Place them so they overlap on a cold platter. Combine minced parsley and shallots or onions. Sprinkle over tomatoes.

*Fat content of recipe:*   negligible   *Yield: 6 servings*

### Mixed Vegetable Salad

**1 10-ounce package frozen mixed vegetables**
**Good Seasons® Dressing, garlic flavor**

Cook and drain the mixed vegetables. Prepare Good Seasons® dressing according to recipe page 167. Marinate vegetables in dressing for several hours in refrigerator. Serve on lettuce.

*Fat content of recipe:*   negligible.   *2–3 servings*

FAT INTAKE FOR THE WEEK

In many cases you will find that simply by using the Special Mayonnaise or Cooked Salad Dressing described on pages 164 and 165 you can make your usual sandwiches. It is necessary, of course, to take the sandwiches into account when calculating the fat intake for the week. The only absolute prohibition is peanut butter—1 tablespoon contains 8.0 grams of fat and does not cover enough territory to justify its use!

Check your grocery shelves for seasoned mustards—such as those with horseradish, onion, or spices—to vary flavor.

### Tongue and Horseradish

Chop canned tongue and blend with horseradish and Special Mayonnaise or Cooked Salad Dressing (pages 164–165).

181

*Fat content of recipe:*                    *Yield: 6 sandwiches*
   *mayonnaise or dressing:*          negligible
   *tongue (6-ounce can):*            34.5 grams
*Fat content per sandwich (excluding bread):*

                                      5.8 grams

### Mock Chicken

  **1 medium onion, minced**
  **½ pound ground beef, lean round without bone**
  **½ teaspoon poultry seasoning**
  **2 tablespoons flour**
  **½ cup liquefied nonfat milk**
  **Salt, pepper**
  **Special Mayonnaise or Cooked Salad Dressing**

Put in a skillet onion, beef, ½ cup water, and poultry seasoning. Simmer a few minutes. Mix flour and milk; stir into meat mixture. Cook until thickened. Add salt and pepper to taste. Cool; then chill. When ready to use, add enough Special Mayonnaise or Cooked Salad Dressing (pages 164–165) to make mixture of spreading consistency.

*Fat content of recipe:*                    *Yield: 10½*
                                    *generous sandwiches*
   *beef:*                            10.6 grams
   *flour:*                           negligible
   *milk:*                            trace
   *mayonnaise or dressing:*          negligible
   *Total:*                           10.6 grams
*Fat content per sandwich (excluding bread):* 1.0 gram

### Tuna or Chicken Salad Sandwiches

Flavor the tuna or chicken with chopped celery, green pepper, or pickle and blend with Special Mayonnaise or Cooked Salad Dressing (pages 164–165). If you add chopped hard-cooked egg to the mix, remember to include the fat content of the egg in the total.

*Fat content of ingredients (excluding bread):*

| | |
|---|---|
| water-pack tuna, white,<br>6½-ounce can: | 1.5 grams |
| dietetic-pack, Chicken<br>of the Sea® or Star<br>Kist® brands,<br>6½-ounce can: | 3.2 grams |
| chicken, 5-ounce can: | 16.7 grams |
| 1 egg: | 6.0 grams |
| mayonnaise or dressing,<br>1 tablespoon: | 0.4 or 0.2 gram |

Note that a sandwich made with water-pack, white tuna and with the egg omitted will have a very low fat content.

### St. Otho® Cheese on Pumpernickel or Rye

Slice St. Otho® Cheese (see chapter on cheeses, page 155) and spread bread with mustard on one slice, Special Mayonnaise (page 164) on the other.

*Fat content of ingredients:*

| | |
|---|---|
| St. Otho® cheese, 1 ounce: | 1.4 grams |
| pumpernickel or rye bread<br>1 pound loaf: | 5.0 grams |
| 1 slice: | trace |
| mayonnaise, 1 tablespoon: | 0.4 gram |

### Dried Beef and Tomato

If you wish to freeze this sandwich, omit the tomato. When ready to serve, the tomato slices can easily be slipped into the sandwich.

183

Spread 1 piece of bread with Special Mayonnaise or Cooked Salad Dressing (pages 164–165) and the other with mustard. Place pieces of dried beef and sliced tomato between slices and close sandwich.

*Fat content of recipe:*                    *Yield: 5 sandwiches*
  *1 jar dried beef*
    *(2½ ounces):*                              4.5 grams
  *mustard:*                                   negligible
  *mayonnaise or dressing:*                    negligible
*Fat content per sandwich (excluding bread):* 0.9 gram

## Herring on Rye or Pumpernickel

Herring fillets packed in wine or tomato sauce—avoid those in sour cream sauce—are tasty. They contain too much fat to be included among appetizers, for there you want to nibble freely. However, used in sandwiches and calculated in the week's fat intake, they provide a substantial lunch. Spread rye or pumpernickel bread with Special Mayonnaise (page 164) cover both slices of bread with lettuce to avoid soaking from the herring, and place herring fillets on the lettuce.

*Fat content of ingredients:*
  *herring, 1 fillet (1 ounce):*           3.9 grams
  *pumpernickel or rye bread:*
    *1 pound loaf:*                          5.0 grams
    *1 slice:*                               trace
  *mayonnaise, 1 tablespoon:*              0.4 gram

## Pimento Cheese Sandwich

An excellent sandwich can be made with the Pimento Cheese Spread of lowered fat content described in the chapter on Cheeses, recipe, page 157.

184

## Orange Bread

See page 308 for recipe.


## Cottage Cheese and Brown Bread

It is not recommended that this sandwich be stored in the refrigerator or frozen.

Spread slices of canned Boston brown bread with raisins with dry or low-fat cottage cheese.

*Fat content of recipe:*
*cottage cheese, 1 ounce:*      0.1–0.6 gram
*brown bread (1 slice,*
    *3 by ¾ inch):*      1.0 gram
*Fat content of sandwich, including bread, 2 slices:*
     2.1–2.6 grams


## Cottage Cheese with Holland Honey® Breads or Cakes

Cottage cheese may be used on Holland Honey Fruit Cake®, Holland Honey Raisin Date Loaf®, or Holland Premium Honey Cake® in the way described above for Cottage Cheese and Brown Bread. See chapter on desserts (pages 285–286) for description of Holland Honey products.

The following general information will help you devise other sandwich fillings:

Apple butter, 1 tablespoon, 0.1 gram fat
Special Mayonnaise, 1 level tablespoon, 0.4 gram fat
    (page 164)
Cooked Salad Dressing, 1 level tablespoon, 0.2 gram
    fat (page 165)

185

Mustard, 1 level tablespoon, 0.6–0.9 gram fat

Pickle relish or chopped pickles, fat per serving, negligible

Tomato catsup, 1 tablespoon, trace

Tomatoes: For sandwiches to be packed in lunches, it is suggested that sliced tomatoes be wrapped separately, to be inserted just before the sandwich is eaten. This will prevent soaking.

Eggs: If eggs are used, count one large egg as 6.0 grams fat.

Tuna fish: If you wish to use tuna fish in a spread, be sure to use either water-pack or dietetic-pack or to wash all the oil off under hot water.

This brief chart of the fat content of cheeses, meats, and breads will help you judge how much of your fat allowance you wish to invest in sandwiches. Not all of these foods are suitable for lowered fat menus, but are common ingredients in sandwiches. Table 3 includes a more complete listing.

## Cheeses

|  | FAT, grams |
| --- | --- |
| *American, pasteurized processed, 1 ounce* | 9.0 |
| *Blue or Roquefort type, 1 ounce* | 9.0 |
| *Camembert, 1 wedge (3 in 4-ounce pkg.)* | 9.0 |
| *Cheddar, 1 ounce* | 9.0 |
| *Cheese foods, pasteurized process, American, 1 ounce* | 6.1 |
| *Cheese spread, pasteurized process, American, 1 ounce* | 6.0 |
| *Chef's Delight®, imitation pasteurized process* | |

| | |
|---|---|
| cheese spread, 1 ounce | 1.4 |
| Cottage, from skim milk, uncreamed, 1 ounce | 0.1 |
| Count Down®, imitation pasteurized process skim milk cheese spread, 1 ounce | 0.3 |
| Cream cheese, 1 ounce | 10.7 |
| Limburger, 1 ounce | 7.5–8.4 |
| Parmesan, 1 ounce | 9.0 |
| St. Otho®, 1 ounce | 1.4 |
| Swiss, 1 ounce | 8.0 |
| Swiss, processed, 1 ounce | 8.0 |

## Meats

| | |
|---|---|
| Bacon, broiled or fried, drained, 1 slice | 4.0 |
| Bologna, all meat, 1 ounce | 6.5 |
| Bologna, with cereal, 1 ounce | 5.8 |
| Boned Chicken with Broth (Swanson®), 5-ounce can[1] | 11.0 |
| Boned Turkey with Broth (Swanson®), 5-ounce can[1] | 9.0 |
| Chicken Spread (Swanson®), 5-ounce can[1] | 21.0 |
| Corned beef, canned (medium-fat), 1 ounce | 3.4 |
| Dried beef, 1 jar (2½ ounces) | 4.5 |
| Frankfurter, 1 | 15.0 |
| Ham, boiled, 1 ounce | 4.8 |
| Liverwurst, smoked, 1 ounce | 7.8 |

[1]Fat content is manufacturer's estimate.

S
A
N
D
W
I
C
H
E
S

187

Luncheon meat, canned, spiced
or unspiced, 1 ounce                 7.1
Oscar Mayer® Products[1] (those low enough in fat to
be used):
Bar-B-Q Loaf, 1 ounce               2.3
Beef, Jellied, 1 ounce              1.2
Beef, Thin-Sliced, 1 ounce          1.1
Bologna, Lebanon, 1 ounce           3.0
Canadian Bacon, 1 ounce             1.9
Corned Beef Loaf, Jellied           1.0
Canned Ham, 1 ounce                 1.9
Cooked Ham (smoked),
1 ounce                             1.8
Ham, Thin-Sliced, 1 ounce           1.8
Honey Loaf, 1 ounce                 1.8
Luncheon Roll Sausage,
1 ounce                             1.3
Luxury Loaf, 1 ounce                1.6
Peppered Loaf, 1 ounce              2.4
Turkey Breast Meat,
1 ounce                             0.2
Vienna sausage, 1 sausage
(7 per 5-ounce can)                 3.0

## Breads

(The fat content of a slice of bread is not altered by
toasting.)
Boston brown bread, 1 slice
(3 by ¾ inch)                       1.0
Cracked wheat, 1 slice              1.0
English muffin, Wonder®[1],
1 muffin                            0.7
French or Vienna, 1-pound loaf      14.0

| | |
|---|---|
| Italian, 1-pound loaf | 4.0 |
| Orange bread, 1 loaf | |
| (page 308) | 9.5 |
| Pumpernickel, 1-pound loaf | 5.0 |
| Raisin, 1 slice | 1.0 |
| Raisin Rounds, Wonder®[1] | 1.0 |
| Rye, American, 1 slice | trace |
| White, 1 slice | 1.0 |
| Whole wheat, 1 slice | 1.0 |

**SANDWICHES**

189

**Chocolate Sauce I**

**1 package Royal Instant Chocolate Pudding® (4 ounces)**
**1 cup light corn syrup**
**¼ cup water**

Stir these ingredients together until blended. Do not cook. This makes a thick, rich sauce of good flavor.

*Fat content of recipe:*       *Yield: 1½ cups*
  *Royal Instant Chocolate*
      *Pudding®:*         3.2 grams
*Fat content per serving:*    negligible

**Chocolate Sauce II**

**½ cup cocoa**
**1 cup sugar**

191

⅛ teaspoon salt
1 cup water
2 teaspoons vanilla

Mix the cocoa, sugar, and salt in a saucepan. Stir in the water; boil for 5 minutes. Cool slightly; add vanilla. Pour into a glass jar with a tight-fitting cover. Store in refrigerator. This is a thinner sauce than the one above. It mixes very satisfactorily with milk for a chocolate milk drink or for quick hot cocoa.

| Fat content of recipe: | Yield: 1 pint |
|---|---|
| cocoa: | 13.6 grams |
| Fat content of 1 tablespoon: | 0.4 gram |

## Butterscotch Sauce

1 package Royal Instant Butterscotch
  Pudding® (3½ ounces)
1 cup light corn syrup
2 tablespoons water

Stir these ingredients together until blended. Do not cook. This makes a thick sauce of good flavor.

| Fat content of recipe: | Yield: 1¼ cups |
|---|---|
| Royal Instant Butterscotch | |
| Pudding®: | 1.6 grams |
| Fat content per serving: | negligible |

## Lemon Sauce

½ cup sugar
1 tablespoon cornstarch
1 cup boiling water
3 tablespoons lemon juice
½ teaspoon grated lemon rind
⅛ teaspoon salt

Add sugar and cornstarch to boiling water. Cook until clear and thick. Stir in lemon juice, lemon rind, and salt.

*Fat content of recipe:*  negligible   *Yield: about 1 cup*

### Fruit Sauce for Ice Cream

1 orange
1 lemon
½ cup sugar
1 No. 303 can cling peach halves, drained

Put an orange and a lemon through food chopper, using a fine knife, and combine in a saucepan with the sugar and peaches. Cover and simmer 10 minutes. Serve over ice cream—it has a very pleasant tang.

*Fat content of recipe:*  negligible

### Sauce Cockaigne

2 cups dried apricots
1¼ cups water
1½ cups sugar
5 cups canned crushed pineapple

Cook gently, in a wide-bottomed, covered pan, apricots and water, until the fruit is pulpy and disintegrates easily when stirred with a wire whisk. Add sugar. Stir until dissolved. Add pineapple. Bring the mixture to a boil. Pour into jars and cover. Keep under refrigeration. Serve over ice milk.

*Fat content of recipe:*  negligible     *Yield: 8 cups*

### Creole Sauce

1 can condensed Campbell® tomato soup (10¾ ounces)

193

**½ cup chopped green peppers, onion, celery, pickle relish**

Place ingredients in saucepan, stir together, and heat.

*Fat content of recipe:*
   *tomato soup:*   4.5 grams

## Barbecue Sauce

**12–14 ounces tomato catsup**
**½ cup white distilled vinegar**
**1 teaspoon sugar**
**Red and black pepper**
**⅛ teaspoon salt**

Combine ingredients and simmer for 15 minutes, stirring frequently.

*Fat content of recipe:*                    *Yield: 1½ cups*
   *tomato catsup:*   1.7 grams

## Prepared Barbecue Sauces

James River Barbeque and Meat Sauce®, manufactured by Smithfield Ham & Products Co., Inc., Smithfield, Va. 23430, contains tomato purée, pepper pulp, and seasonings. Its fat content is negligible.
   French's® Barbecue Sauces (Mild, Regular, or Smoky) are all of negligible fat content.

## Herb Sauce for Lamb

**1 small onion**
**3 cloves garlic**
**12 fresh mint leaves**
**2 sprigs rosemary or ⅛ teaspoon dried rosemary**

¼ cup white vinegar
½ cup water

Chop or grind onion very fine. Mince garlic. Crush or chop mint leaves and rosemary. Combine all ingredients. Let stand overnight. Use to brush on lamb before and during grilling. If you want to be really extravagant, use a small bunch of mint leaves as a brush.

| | | |
|---|---|---|
| *Fat content* | | *Yield:* |
| *of recipe:* | negligible | *approximately 1 cup* |

## Cheltenhouse® Sweet-and-Pungent Sauce

This sauce—prepared from peaches, apricots, pineapple, sugar, vinegar, salt, Worcestershire Sauce, and water—is manufactured by Cheltenhouse Products, Inc., Philadelphia, Pa. It can be used to baste poultry about fifteen minutes before cooking is completed or it can be served as a dipping sauce with the cooked poultry.

*Fat content of product:*   negligible

## Mock Hollandaise Sauce I

1 scant cup low-fat cottage cheese (see chapter on cheeses, pages 155–156)
3 tablespoons lemon juice
1 egg yolk
½ teaspoon Seasoned Salt
½ teaspoon salt
Dash of pepper
Dash of cayenne

Into an electric blender put the cottage cheese, seasonings, and lemon juice. Whip until the mixture is a

195

smooth cream. Remove from blender. Stir in egg yolk. Cook, stirring constantly with wire whisk, over low heat until just thick. Do not boil.

| Fat content | Yield: |
|---|---|
| of recipe: | approximately 1¼ cups |
| cottage cheese: | 2.3–4.6 grams |
| egg: | 6.0 grams |
| Total: | 8.3–10.6 grams |

### Mock Hollandaise Sauce II

**1 chicken bouillon cube**
**¼ cup hot water**
**2 tablespoons flour**
**Salt, pepper**
**¼ teaspoon dry mustard**
**½ cup water**
**Juice of 1 lemon**

Dissolve bouillon cube in hot water. Blend in flour, salt, pepper, and mustard. When blended to a smooth paste, slowly stir in remaining water, stirring continuously. Stir as it cooks and thickens. After the sauce has thickened, slowly stir in the lemon juice and continue cooking, stirring constantly, until sauce is of desired thickness.

| Fat content | | Yield: |
|---|---|---|
| of recipe: | negligible | approximately 1 cup |

### Mushroom Sauce

**1 chicken bouillon cube**
**¼ cup hot water**
**3 tablespoons flour**
**Salt, pepper, paprika**

1½ cups liquefied nonfat milk
1 teaspoon Worcestershire sauce
2 tablespoons tomato catsup
1 can mushrooms (4 ounces mush-
    rooms—plain, not broiled in butter,
    2¾ ounces broth)

Dissolve bouillon cube in hot water. Blend flour, salt, pepper, and paprika with bouillon to make a smooth paste. Slowly blend in milk, stirring constantly. Stir in Worcestershire sauce and catsup. Add mushrooms— solids and broth. Cook, stirring constantly until sauce is of desired thickness. May be stored, covered, in refrigerator. (This is excellent over green beans.)

*Fat content*                    *Yield:*
*of recipe:*    negligible    *approximately 1 pint*

### Mushroom Curry Sauce

2 chicken bouillon cubes
2 cups boiling water
1 4-ounce can sliced mushrooms, plain,
    not broiled in butter
⅛ teaspoon rosemary
⅛ teaspoon curry
2 tablespoons cornstarch
¼ teaspoon onion salt
½ teaspoon salt
2 tablespoons cold water

Dissolve bouillon cubes in boiling water in small saucepan. Drain mushrooms, add broth to bouillon, and bring to boil over moderate heat. Combine and add rosemary, curry, cornstarch, onion salt, salt, and water. Cook, stirring constantly until sauce is thick and clear. Add mushrooms and heat thoroughly. Remove from heat and pour into warm sauce bowl.

*Fat content of recipe:*   negligible   *Yield: 2 cups*

## Zippy Tomato Sauce

1 1-pound can tomatoes
1 8-ounce can tomato sauce
1 medium-sized onion, chopped
3 tablespoons cider vinegar
1 tablespoon Worcestershire sauce
1 tablespoon prepared mustard
1 teaspoon chili powder
¼ teaspoon salt

Combine ingredients; simmer 15 minutes, stirring occasionally. (This is fine over cold sliced meats or fowl.)

*Fat content of recipe:*   negligible   *Yield: 3 cups*

## Sauces or Dips for Shrimp

See Chapter on appetizers, pages 26–28.

## Basic White Sauce

1 chicken bouillon cube
¼ cup hot water
2 tablespoons flour
  Salt, pepper
1 cup liquefied nonfat milk

Dissolve bouillon cube in hot water. Blend flour, salt, and pepper with bouillon to make a smooth paste. Slowly blend in milk, stirring constantly. Cook, stirring, until desired thickness is achieved.

**198** *Fat content of recipe:*   negligible   *Yield: approximately 1 cup*

### Horseradish Sauce

Mix equal parts of prepared horseradish and mild cider vinegar. (Good passed at the table with spinach or any type of greens.)

*Fat content of recipe:*   negligible

### Low-Fat Sour Cream

**1 12-ounce box low-fat cottage cheese
(see chapter on cheeses, pages 155–156)
½ cup buttermilk
Salt to taste
Pinch of citric acid or a few drops of
lemon juice**

Place all ingredients in electric blender and blend until very smooth. Here are some gourmet suggestions for the use of Low-Fat Sour Cream:

over tiny new potatoes which have been boiled in their jackets;
on sliced cucumbers which may be served with a tomato aspic ring if desired;
over pickled herring as an appetizer.

*Fat content of recipe for Low-Fat Sour Cream:
cottage cheese:*   3.4–6.8 grams

### Yogurt

Yogurt is a tasty topping for salads, soups, vegetables or desserts. Lemon- and pineapple-flavored yogurts complement fruit salads and desserts. Soups and vegetables are enhanced by plain yogurt, passed at the table. Experiment with the other flavors according to individual preference.

*Fat content of skim milk yogurts:*

|  | per 8-ounce cup | per tablespoon |
|---|---|---|
| *plain:* | 3.6 grams | 0.2 gram |
| *vanilla, coffee:* | 3.2 grams | 0.2 gram |
| *banana, strawberry, pineapple–orange, prune whip, apricot, red raspberry, boysenberry, blueberry:* | 2.5 grams | 0.2 gram |

These figures are for Dannon® brand skim milk yogurts. Check labels on other skim milk yogurts, A&P® or Borden's®, and you will find them comparable.

## Cranberry–Orange Relish

**4 cups fresh cranberries**
**2 oranges**
**2 cups sugar**

Put cranberries and oranges (which have been quartered and seeds removed) through food chopper. Add sugar. Mix well and store in refrigerator several hours, for flavors to blend, before serving.

This relish is available, also, ready prepared.

*Fat content of recipe:* negligible

## Spiced Fruit

**1 1-pound 13-ounce jar fruits for salad, not the diced fruit**
**12 whole cloves**
**1 stick cinnamon**
**1 tablespoon vinegar**

Place in covered saucepan. Bring to boil. Simmer 5 minutes. Serve with meat or as a dessert.

*Fat content of recipe:* negligible

### Spicy Prunes

**1 pound dried prunes**
**Water to cover**
**¼ teaspoon salt**
**½ teaspoon ginger**
**½ teaspoon cloves**
**1 teaspoon cinnamon**
**¼ cup brown sugar**
**3 tablespoons lemon juice**

Combine prunes, water, salt, and spices. Simmer 30 to 50 minutes. Stir in sugar and lemon juice. Serve cold. A good accompaniment for meat or poultry.

*Fat content of recipe:* negligible

### Pickled Pumpkin

**6–7 pounds pumpkin, peeled, seeded,**
**and with membrane removed**
**4 cups cider vinegar**
**4 cups sugar**
**2 cups water**
**18 cinnamon sticks**

Cut pumpkin into 1-inch cubes. Place cubes in large saucepan and cover with water. Simmer until fork tender. Drain. Return pumpkin to saucepan. Add vinegar, sugar, and 2 cups water. Bring to a boil. Pack in sterilized pint-size jars, arranging three cinnamon sticks in each jar. Seal. Follow general instructions for processing, using water bath method. Process 30 minutes for quarts or pints.

*Fat content of recipe:* negligible *Yield: 6 pints*

When one first undertakes low-fat cooking, vegetables present a problem. Vegetables, in themselves, are of very low fat content; it is the method of cooking and seasoning that causes trouble. It is such standard procedure to season vegetables with salt, pepper, and butter—the more the better—that one is at a loss. Sauces help to a degree, but too many sauces become monotonous. Now comes a chance to join the ranks of the gourmets and experiment with herbs. If you will add a bouillon cube to the water in which you cook your vegetables (beef bouillon cubes are somewhat saltier than chicken—suit yourself), and then sprinkle the vegetables, before serving, with herbs to your taste, you will discover you have lost nothing and, indeed, have gained a whole series of new flavors. Various broths and seasoned stock bases may be used 203 in place of bouillon cubes. (See Soups, pages 31–32.) An herb chart is included in the Appendix.

Steaming vegetables is an excellent method for preserving the natural flavor, fresh taste and the nutritional values. It is possible to improvise a steamer by placing a colander in any pot with a tight-fitting lid. We believe, however, that you will find steaming such a superior method you will wish to use one of the perforated, folding steamers which adjust to fit pots of varying sizes. Have your water boiling before you place the steamer over it. Cover tightly. Allow a few more minutes than you would if cooking the vegetables directly in the water.

Steamed vegetables may be seasoned simply with one of the Seasoned Salts (fat content negligible), one of the butter-flavored salts (0.1–0.9 gram of fat per teaspoon), or with skim milk yogurt passed at the table (0.3 gram of fat per tablespoon).

Be sure to read the labels on all vegetables frozen or canned. The vegetables may be of negligible fat content, but ingredients added in processing may raise the fat content to 6 grams or more for a half-cup serving.

## Artichokes

### Artichoke Hearts with Mushrooms

1 9-ounce package frozen artichoke hearts
1 4-ounce can sliced mushrooms, plain not broiled in butter
1½ teaspoons cornstarch
2 tablespoons dry or medium sherry
½ teaspoon lemon juice

**Salt, onion salt, garlic salt, and pepper to taste
1 tablespoon chopped parsley**

Cook and drain artichoke hearts. Drain mushrooms, reserving liquid. Mix cornstarch and sherry in a saucepan, stirring until perfectly smooth; add mushroom liquid. Cook, stirring over medium heat until mixture is thickened and clear. Add remaining ingredients. Combine this sauce with the artichoke hearts and mushrooms. Heat gently before serving.

This recipe is equally satisfactory used with frozen lima beans or French-style green beans.

*Fat content of recipe:*     negligible     *3–4 servings*

# Beans

### Butter Beans (Lima Beans)

Steam or cook in water seasoned with a bouillon cube. Drain. Season with one of the Seasoned Salts and dried basil.

### Green Beans (String Beans)

Steam or cook in water seasoned with a bouillon cube. Drain. Season with one of the Seasoned Salts and dried basil.

### Marinated Green Beans

Steam or cook in water green beans and while they are still hot marinate them well in French Dressing with Pectin or in one of the Good Seasons® Salad Dressings.

205

Add chopped chives, chopped onion, or pearl onions. Chill the beans thoroughly and serve on lettuce, or simply as a cold vegetable. They keep well in the refrigerator if you wish to prepare them the day before they are to be used. Thin raw carrot slices may be added for variety.

## Green Beans with Mushroom Sauce

Steam or cook green beans in water seasoned with bouillon. Drain. Pour mushroom sauce over beans and serve. See page 196 for Mushroom Sauce.

*Fat content of mushroom sauce:* negligible

## Seasoned Green Beans

Add approximately ½ teaspoon of smoked hickory salt to a 10-ounce package of green beans (frozen) or equivalent amount of fresh or canned ones. This seasoning imparts a ham or bacon flavor.

*Fat content of ingredients:* negligible

## Green Beans with Water Chestnuts

Wash, remove ends, and French-cut 2 pounds young green beans. Put in pot with 1 cup boiling water; cook uncovered until tender, about 15 minutes; do not overcook. Two packages frozen French-cut green beans may be used. Follow package directions. Drain off most of the liquid, return to the pot and add 6–8 canned water chestnuts, sliced; ½ teaspoon salt; and a dash of pepper.

### Green Beans with Wine Vinegar

1 package frozen Frenched green beans
2 tablespoons red wine vinegar
1 tablespoon Worcestershire Sauce
¼ teaspoon mustard
1 drop hot pepper sauce

Cook beans as directed on package or steam. Drain. Combine remaining ingredients and pour over beans before serving.

### Italian Beans

1 tablespoon chopped onion
1 package frozen Italian beans
½ cup beef bouillon
½ clove garlic
1 teaspoon salt

Simmer the onion in 1 tablespoon of the beef bouillon. Add frozen beans. Cook 2 minutes. Add the remaining beef bouillon, garlic, and salt. Simmer, uncovered, until liquid is evaporated and beans are tender, about 6 minutes.

### Lima Bean Casserole

1 pound (2 cups) dried small lima beans
2 teaspoons salt
1 pint skim milk yogurt
⅓ cup brown sugar
1 small onion, finely chopped
½ teaspoon dry mustard

Soak beans in water to cover overnight unless the

VEGETABLES

package indicates that no soaking is necessary. Drain beans and place in a saucepan with about 2½ quarts of water and the salt. Bring to a boil, cover and simmer until tender, about 1 hour. Drain.

Preheat oven to 325°. Combine the yogurt, sugar, onion, and mustard and stir into the beans. Turn into an 8-inch square baking dish and bake uncovered 1¼ to 1½ hours.

| Fat content of recipe: | 4 servings |
|---|---|
| lima beans: | 14.6 grams |
| yogurt: | 7.2 grams |
| Total: | 21.8 grams |
| Fat content per serving: | 5.5 grams |

## Red Beans in Wine

**2 cans red kidney beans**
**2 teaspoons onion juice**
**1 bouillon cube dissolved in ¼ cup hot water**
**2 tablespoons cornstarch**
**1 teaspoon salt**
**Fresh ground black pepper**
**1 cup dry red wine**

Heat beans and keep warm. Combine in saucepan bouillon, onion juice, cornstarch, salt, and pepper. Stir until smooth. Add wine. Cook and stir over medium heat until thick and clear. Pour over beans.

| Fat content of recipe: | 6 servings |
|---|---|
| kidney beans: | 4.0 grams |
| Fat content per serving: | 0.7 gram |

# Beets

### Pickled Beets

¾ cup vinegar
½ cup water
2 teaspoons dry mustard
½ teaspoon salt
⅓ cup granulated sugar
½ teaspoon caraway seeds
2 cups sliced cooked beets (canned beets may be used)
1 medium-sized onion, chopped or sliced

Heat vinegar and water to boiling. Add mustard, salt, and sugar. Blend, then heat again to boiling. Pour over beets, caraway seeds, and onion. Cover and place in refrigerator to marinate overnight.

### Harvard Beets (Sour-Sweet)

Slice or dice:

**3 cups cooked beets**

Stir in a double boiler until smooth:

½ cup sugar
1 tablespoon cornstarch
½ teaspoon salt
½ cup mild vinegar or dry white wine

Cook and stir these ingredients until they are clear. Add the beets and place them over hot water for 30 minutes. Serve.

*Fat content of recipe:*     negligible     *6 servings*     209

## Congealed Beets

**1 can diced beets**
**¼ to ½ cup chopped celery**
**2 cups liquid, from beets and added water**
**1 package lemon jello**
**3 tablespoons vinegar**
**4 tablespoons horseradish**
**2 teaspoons onion juice**

Heat part of the liquid hot enough to dissolve the jello. Stir in the rest of the liquid and pour into mold which has been rinsed with cold water. Chill until it begins to thicken. Stir in remaining ingredients and chill until firm.

This may be topped with either Low-Fat Sour Cream (page 199) or skim milk yogurt on serving.

*Fat content of recipe:*    negligible
*Fat content of toppings:*
  *Low-Fat Sour Cream,*
     *1 ounce:*    0.3–0.6 gram
    *Yogurt, 1 tablespoon:*    0.3 gram

## Broccoli

Broccoli is another vegetable suitable for steaming (see page 204). Do not overcook. Season with one of the Seasoned Salts (fat content: negligible) or pass skim milk yogurt at the table (fat content: 1 tablespoon, 0.3 gram).

### Broccoli with Cheese Sauce I

**1 bunch fresh broccoli or 2 packages frozen broccoli**

⅓ cup buttermilk
⅓ cup grated imitation pasteurized process cheese spread (Count Down® or
Chef's Delight®)

Steam or cook broccoli in a small amount of boiling,
salted water. Be careful *not to overcook*. For frozen
broccoli follow time instructions on package. Drain.
Combine the buttermilk and cheese spread in a saucepan. Cook over low heat 5 minutes. Pour over drained
broccoli.

*Fat content of recipe:*
  *buttermilk:*              negligible
  *cheese spread:*       0.8–3.7 grams

### Broccoli with Cheese Sauce II    *Good*

    2 10-ounce packages frozen broccoli
       spears
    1 chicken bouillon cube dissolved in ¼
       cup water
    1 tablespoon minced onion
    2 tablespoons flour
    ~~½ teaspoon salt~~
       few grains black pepper
    ½ teaspoon dry mustard
    ⅛ teaspoon marjoram
    1½ cups nonfat milk
    ⅓ cup grated imitation pasteurized pro-
       cess cheese spread (Count Down® or
       Chef's Delight®)
    2 tablespoons grated cheese spread as
       above
       Paprika

Cook broccoli according to directions on package.    211

Drain. Meanwhile, heat bouillon in saucepan. Add onion and cook until soft. Remove from heat. Blend in a mixture of the flour, salt, pepper, mustard, and marjoram. Add milk gradually. Return to heat. Bring rapidly to boiling and continue stirring. Cook 1 or 2 minutes longer. Remove from heat. Add the ⅓ cup cheese spread and stir until melted.

Arrange cooked broccoli on a heat-resistant platter or in a shallow baking dish. Pour sauce over and sprinkle with remaining 2 tablespoons cheese spread and paprika. Broil about 3 inches from source of heat until cheese is melted and mixture is bubbly.

| *Fat content of recipe:* | *6 servings* |
|---|---|
| *nonfat milk:* | negligible |
| *Count Down®:* | 1.2 grams |
| *Chef's Delight®:* | 5.6 grams |
| *Total based on Count Down®:* | 1.2 grams |
| *Total based on Chef's Delight®:* | 5.6 grams |
| *Fat content per serving, based on Count Down®:* | 0.2 gram |
| *Fat content per serving, based on Chef's Delight®:* | 1.0 gram |

### Broccoli with Mock Hollandaise Sauce

Steam or cook broccoli in a small amount of boiling, lightly salted water. *Do not overcook.* For frozen broccoli follow exactly directions on package as to amount of water and cooking time. Pass at the table Mock Hollandaise Sauce I or II (pages 195–196).

## Brussels Sprouts

212  Steam or cook in boiling, lightly salted water. *Do not overcook.* For frozen brussels sprouts follow exactly

directions on package as to amount of water and cooking time. Omission of butter does not impair flavor.

## Cabbage

Cut cabbage in wedges. Soak in salted, cold water. Pour off all but ½ inch of the water. Cover tightly and cook. Drain and place in serving dish. Serve plain or pour over any one of the Good Seasons Salad Dressings® (see chapter on salads, page 167).

### Cabbage with Horseradish Dressing

Cook cabbage in salted water. Drain. To Basic White Sauce (see page 198) add:

**2 tablespoons horseradish**
**2 tablespoons lemon juice**

Blend with white sauce, heat, and pour over cabbage which has been placed in serving dish.

*Fat content of Basic White Sauce:* negligible

### Chinese Cabbage

Wash and slice Chinese cabbage diagonally into chunks. Cook gently, until tender, in chicken bouillon.

*Fat content of recipe:* negligible

### Red Cabbage

**1 small head red cabbage**
**4 tablespoons dehydrated onions**
**2 apples**

213

**1 teaspoon salt**
**½ cup red wine.**

Wash cabbage, peel off tough outer leaves, cut in quarters, remove core, shred and soak in cold water. Soak onions in water as directed on jar. Peel, core, and slice the apples very thin. Lift cabbage into covered dish allowing some water to adhere. Cover and simmer for 10 minutes. Watch carefully to avoid scorching. Add onions, apples, salt, and red wine. Simmer covered over very low heat for 1 to 1¼ hours.

*Fat content of recipe:* negligible

## Carrots

### Carrots in Consommé

**8 medium carrots**
**2 tablespoons chopped onion**
**1 tablespoon chopped parsley**
**1 can consommé**

In saucepan cook onion and parsley in 2 to 3 table-spoons of the consommé for 5 minutes. Add carrots cut in 1 to 1½-inch pieces and rest of can of consommé. Cover; cook over medium heat 25 minutes. Uncover, cook 20 minutes or until carrots are tender.

*Fat content of recipe:*            negligible       *4 servings*

## Cauliflower

### Cauliflower Casserole

**1 head of fresh cauliflower or frozen**
**    cauliflower**

Basic White Sauce, page 198
1 teaspoon dry mustard
Few grains cayenne pepper
Imitation pasteurized process cheddar
cheese spread (Count Down® or
Chef's Delight®)
¼ cup breadcrumbs

**VEGETABLES**

Break fresh cauliflower into florets. Boil until tender, about 15 minutes, in salted water. For frozen cauliflower, follow time instructions on package. Drain. Place in casserole. Pour over it Basic White Sauce, flavored with mustard and cayenne pepper. Place several strips of cheddar cheese spread on top. Sprinkle breadcrumbs on top. Bake in 350° oven until cheese is melted and crumbs lightly browned.

*Fat content of recipe:*

| | |
|---|---|
| *Basic White Sauce:* | negligible |
| *cheese spread, ½ inch from 2-pound block:* | 0.5–2.8 grams |
| *breadcrumbs:* | 1.3 grams |
| *Total:* | 1.8–4.1 grams |

### Cauliflower in Piquant Sauce

Steam or boil and drain cauliflower. Place in casserole. Pour over it the following sauce and brown in oven.

1 chicken bouillon cube
¼ cup hot water
2 tablespoons flour
Salt, pepper
1 cup liquefied nonfat milk
¼ teaspoon nutmeg
1 teaspoon A.1. Sauce®
2 tablespoons catsup

215

**1 tablespoon grated sapsago cheese (see Cheeses, page 155)**

Dissolve bouillon cube in hot water. Blend flour, salt, and pepper with bouillon to make a smooth paste. Slowly blend in milk, stirring constantly. Stir in nutmeg, A.1. Sauce®, catsup, and sapsago. Cook, stirring, until desired thickness is achieved.

*Fat content of recipe:*   negligible

## Corn

### Frozen Corn

Place contents of one package of frozen whole-kernel corn in top of double boiler with 1 chicken bouillon cube and one of the Seasoned Salts. Heat. It is not necessary to add any liquid.

### Green Giant® Shoe Peg Whole Kernel White or Whole Kernel Yellow Corn

Heat one 12-ounce can in double boiler. Season with Seasoned Salt and serve.

### Roasted Ears

Turn back the husks and strip off silk from ears of corn. Replace husks. Soak the husk-covered ears in cold water for several hours. Boil over outdoor fire 5 mins. Remove from water and place on grill over coals. Roast 10 minutes, turning frequently. The flavor from cooking over either charcoal or a wood fire makes further seasoning unnecessary.

# Eggplant

## Eggplant Creole

Medium-sized eggplant
1 chicken bouillon cube dissolved in 3
   tablespoons water
3 tablespoons flour
2 cups canned tomatoes
1 small green pepper, seeded and
   chopped
1 small onion, peeled and chopped
1 teaspoon salt
1 tablespoon brown sugar
½ bay leaf
2 cloves
¼ cup breadcrumbs
¼ cup grated imitation pasteurized process cheese spread (Count Down® or
   Chef's Delight®)

Peel and dice eggplant. Cook 10 minutes in boiling
water. Drain and place in casserole. In saucepan blend
flour with bouillon. Add remaining ingredients except
breadcrumbs and cheese. Cook 5 minutes. Pour over
eggplant. Top with breadcrumbs and grated cheese.
Bake at 350° for 30 minutes.

| Fat content of recipe: | 6 servings |
|---|---|
| breadcrumbs: | 1.3 grams |
| cheese | |
| Count Down®: | 0.6 gram |
| Chef's Delight®: | 2.8 grams |
| Total with Count Down®: | 1.9 grams |
| Total with Chef's Delight®: | 4.1 grams |
| Fat content per serving: | |
| with Count Down®: | 0.3 gram |
| with Chef's Delight®: | 0.7 gram |

VEGETABLES

217

### Eggplant Salad

    **Medium-sized eggplant**
**2 green onions, chopped (Use both**
    **green and white parts.)**
**3 medium-sized tomatoes, cubed**
  **¼ teaspoon basil**
  **½ cup Ann Page® Low Calorie Italian**
    **Dressing**

Preheat oven to 375°. Place eggplant on baking sheet and bake until tender, 30 to 45 minutes. When cool enough to handle, peel. Chill, then cut into cubes. Mix the eggplant cubes with the remaining ingredients and marinate several hours. This is a substantial salad which can be used as you would use potato or macaroni salad. If you wish to use some other low-fat content dressing, recalculate the fat content of the recipe.

| | |
|---|---|
| *Fat content of recipe:* | *4 servings* |
| *Ann Page® Low Calorie Italian* | |
| *Dressing:* | *7.1 grams* |
| *Fat content per serving:* | *1.8 grams* |

### Stuffed Eggplant

    **Medium-sized eggplant**
**1½ cups cooked rice**
  **¼ clove garlic, minced**
  **2 tablespoons chopped green pepper**
  **½ pound cooked, cleaned shrimp**
  **1 teaspoon grated onion**
  **¼ cup skim milk**
    **Salt**
218      **Paprika**

**¼ cup breadcrumbs**
**Sapsago cheese**

Cut the top from a medium-sized eggplant. Scoop out the pulp, drop it into a small quantity of boiling, salted water (1½ teaspoons of salt to the quart) and cook until it is tender. Drain well and mash. Combine with the other ingredients. Fill the eggplant shell. Cover the top with breadcrumbs. Sprinkle with sapsago cheese. Place the eggplant in a moderate oven and bake until the stuffing is well heated.

| *Fat content of recipe:* | *4 servings* |
|---|---|
| *rice:* | trace |
| *shrimp:* | 1.8 grams |
| *milk:* | negligible |
| *breadcrumbs:* | 1.3 grams |
| *sapsago cheese:* | negligible |
| *Total:* | 3.1 grams |
| *Fat content per serving:* | 0.8 gram |

## Lentils

### Lentils with Onions

**1 cup lentils**
**½ tablespoon salt**
**¾ cup dehydrated onions**

Soak lentils in cold water, in refrigerator, overnight. Next day drain, place in large kettle with cold water. Add salt and onions. Stir. Bring to boil. Reduce heat and simmer until tender—two hours or more.

| *Fat content of recipe:* | *4 servings* |
|---|---|
| *lentils:* | 2.5 grams |
| *Fat content per serving:* | 0.6 gram |

## Lima Beans

### Lima Beans with Mushrooms

1½ 10-ounce packages frozen lima beans,
   large Fordhook type
1 4-ounce can whole mushrooms (plain,
   not broiled in butter)
½ teaspoon salt
⅛ teaspoon pepper

Place frozen lima beans in 1½ quart casserole. Pour
mushrooms and juice over beans and add remaining
ingredients. Cover and bake at 350° for 1 hour.

*Fat content of recipe:*     negligible     *5–6 servings*


## Mushrooms

### Mushrooms with Herbs and Wine

12 ounces fresh mushrooms
1 chicken bouillon cube
1 cup hot water
1 tablespoon chopped parsley
1 tablespoon flour
1 tablespoon chopped fresh marjoram
½ clove garlic chopped fine or put
   through garlic press
1 small onion chopped
⅛ teaspoon nutmeg
¼ cup dry sherry
   Sapsago cheese, grated

220    Prepare mushrooms for cooking as follows: wipe well

with damp cloth, separate caps from stems, peel caps, and chop stems. Place in casserole. Dissolve chicken bouillon in the hot water. Pour about ¼ cup of this chicken bouillon into a small saucepan and in it simmer the parsley, garlic, onion, and marjoram for 3 minutes. Add flour and nutmeg and blend until smooth. Add remaining bouillon gradually, stirring until it thickens; stir in sherry. Pour over mushrooms. Sprinkle with grated sapsago cheese. Cover and bake 20 to 30 minutes in 350° oven.

*Fat content of recipe:*　　negligible　　*4 servings*

### Deviled Mushrooms

　½ **pound fresh whole mushrooms**
　1 **tablespoon flour**
　　**Chicken bouillon cube dissolved in 4**
　　**tablespoons water**
　½ **cup skim milk**
　1 **teaspoon Worcestershire Sauce**
　½ **teaspoon dry mustard**
　½ **teaspoon paprika**
　4 **slices bread, toasted**

Remove stems from four of the mushrooms; flute caps and set aside. Chop stems and remaining mushrooms; sprinkle with the flour. In a skillet cook the four fluted caps and the chopped mushrooms in the chicken bouillon until lightly browned; remove whole mushroom caps. Season mushrooms in skillet with a little salt and pepper. (Remember there is some salt in the chicken bouillon.) Stir in milk, Worcestershire, dry mustard, and paprika; heat through. Spoon over toast. Garnish each serving with a fluted mushroom cap. This is a tasty luncheon dish.

*Fat content of recipe:*                 *4 servings*
   *milk:*                   negligible
   *bread, per slice:*         1 gram

## Onions

### Onions with Parsley Flakes

Place contents, including liquid, of one can of small whole onions in double boiler with beef bouillon cube. Sprinkle with dried parsley flakes. Heat and serve. *3–4 servings*

### Small Onions Braised

**Small onions**
**Beef bouillon cube**
**Hot water**
**Salt, paprika**

Skin small onions. Pour over them, to a depth of ½ inch, boiling stock made from bouillon cube and water. Cook them, covered, over a slow fire. Permit them to absorb the liquid. When they are tender, season them with salt and paprika. Additional stock may be added as required. *4 servings*

## Blackeye Peas

Bush's Best Fresh Shelled Blackeye Peas, distributed by Bush Bros. & Co., Dandridge, Tenn. 37725, are packed with only water and salt. They may be heated in their own liquid, drained, and served without the addition

222

of further seasoning. There are a number of brands of canned blackeye peas which are packed with salt pork or other added fat. Be sure to get the water pack.

*Fat content of recipe:*     1.3 grams     *3–4 servings*

## Green Peas

### Green Peas with Basil

Cook in water seasoned with bouillon and one of the Seasoned Salts. Drain. Sprinkle with dried basil.

### Green Peas and Mushrooms

To water in which you will cook peas, add one of the Seasoned Salts and canned mushrooms. (These are plain mushrooms, not the broiled-in-butter type.) Cook together. Drain. Serve.

### Peas à la Bonne Femme

> 2 packages frozen green peas or fresh green peas
> 2 green onions minced (with green stalks)
> 1 teaspoon Accent®
> 2 tablespoons sugar
> 2 chicken bouillon cubes
> 1 teaspoon salt
> Freshly ground pepper
> ¼ head of lettuce broken into bite-size pieces

Bring water to boil in large covered pan. Add peas and     223 other ingredients. Cover, bring back to a boil and simmer for 25 minutes. *6–8 servings*

## Peas with Water Chestnuts

**1 package frozen green peas**
**½ 8-ounce can water chestnuts**
**Seasoned Salt**

Place peas in double boiler and cover closely with lettuce leaves as well as with top of double boiler. Steam till tender. Timing depends on the size of the peas. Slice water chestnuts. When peas are tender, remove lettuce leaves, season with Seasoned Salt, stir in water chestnut slices and heat till water chestnuts are heated through. *3–4 servings*

# Potatoes

## Canned White Potatoes

Place contents, including liquid, of one can of small whole white potatoes in top of double boiler. Add one beef bouillon cube and parsley flakes. Heat and serve. *3–4 servings*

## Baked Potatoes with Yogurt

Preheat oven to 425°. Wash, scrub and dry even-sized baking potatoes. Place on oven rack and bake 40 minutes to 1 hour depending on size. When potatoes are half-done, pull out rack and quickly puncture skin once with fork to permit steam to escape. When done, serve with skim-milk yogurt.

*Fat content of recipe:*
  *yogurt, 1 tablespoon:*   0.3 gram

### Potato Boats

**Baking potatoes**
**Liquefied nonfat milk**
**Sapsago cheese, grated (see Cheeses, page 155)**

Bake potatoes. Cut in halves and remove pulp from shell. Beat together, until smooth, potato pulp and enough milk to moisten. Return whipped pulp to shells and sprinkle with grated sapsago cheese. Place under low flame in broiler until lightly browned on top.

### Mashed Potatoes

**6 medium-sized old potatoes**
**4 cups boiling water**
**½ teaspoon salt**
**⅓ cup hot liquefied nonfat milk**

Pare potatoes. Cook them covered from 20 to 40 minutes in boiling water. When they are done, drain them well. Mash the potatoes with a fork or a potato masher, or put them in an electric blender or mixer. Add salt and hot liquefied nonfat milk. Chopped parsley, chives, and watercress are all good additions to mashed potatoes.

*Fat content of recipe:*      negligible      *6 servings*

### Polish Potatoes

Boil little new potatoes in their jackets in salted water until tender. At the table pass Low-Fat Sour Cream, recipe page 199, or skim-milk yogurt.

225

### Scalloped White Potatoes I

Place alternate layers of sliced raw potatoes and onions in baking dish. Sprinkle each layer with flour and Seasoned Salt. Dissolve chicken bouillon cubes in hot water and pour over vegetables to cover. The quantity of bouillon needed will depend on the quantity of vegetables. Use one chicken bouillon cube for each cup of hot water. Bake at 350° for 1½ hours.

### Scalloped White Potatoes II

Place alternate layers of sliced potatoes and sliced onions in baking dish, seasoning with salt and pepper. Sprinkle flour over top. Pour over all 1½ cups Mushroom Sauce (see page 196). Add about ¾ cup liquefied nonfat milk or to cover. Sprinkle with grated sapsago cheese (see Cheeses, page 155). Bake in moderate oven about 1 hour.

*Fat content of recipe:*
| | |
|---|---|
| *mushroom sauce:* | negligible |
| *nonfat milk:* | trace |
| *sapsago cheese:* | negligible |
| *Total:* | negligible |

## Sweet Potatoes

### Mashed Sweet Potatoes

Boil, peel, and mash sweet potatoes. Moisten with orange juice. Stir in a handful of plumped raisins. Season with sugar, nutmeg, and a pinch of salt. Place in casserole and heat in oven. Instead of heating in a casserole, you may fill orange shells with the potatoes and heat.

### Baked Sweet Potatoes

Preheat oven to 425°. Wash, scrub and dry even-sized sweet potatoes. Cut small slice from each end to prevent bursting in oven. Place on oven rack and bake 40 minutes to 1 hour depending on size. Flavorful sweet potatoes need no further seasoning.

### Sweet Potatoes Baked in Foil

Cut gash lengthwise in sweet potato. Submerge in liquefied nonfat milk to prevent discoloration. Drain. Fill gash with 1 orange section, raisins. Sprinkle with salt, brown sugar, nutmeg. Wrap individually in aluminum foil. A tight wrap is important to prevent leakage. Bake 1 hour in barbecue oven or stove (375°).

## Rice

### Baked Rice

1 medium onion, diced
1 beef bouillon cube
1 can consommé
1 can water
1 cup uncooked rice
1 small can mushrooms (plain, not
  broiled in butter)
1 bay leaf
  Parsley
  Salt and pepper to taste
  Dash of Worcestershire sauce

Crumble bouillon cube well. Combine all ingredients in covered casserole and bake one hour in 350° oven.

VEGETABLES

227

### Creole Rice

½ cup chopped green pepper
½ cup chopped onion
1 medium firm, ripe tomato, peeled
   and chopped or 1 can (10-ounce) tomatoes, drained
3 tablespoons chopped parsley
1 bay leaf, crushed
1 teaspoon chili powder
1½ teaspoons salt
⅛ teaspoon pepper
5 cups cooked rice (boil or steam without added fat)
2 medium tomatoes, sliced
½ cup grated imitation pasteurized process cheese spread, Count Down® or
   Chef's Delight®

Quick-cook green pepper and onion in Teflon®-coated
pan or one treated with Pam®, Lean-Fry® or Pan Pal®,
just until soft. Add chopped tomato, parsley, bay leaf,
chili powder, salt, and pepper. Simmer three minutes;
add rice. Turn into 1½-quart Teflon® or treated casserole. Top with sliced tomatoes; sprinkle with cheese.
Bake in 375° oven 20 to 30 minutes or until cheese melts
and browns.

| | |
|---|---|
| *Fat content of recipe:* | *6 servings* |
| *rice:* | 1.3 grams |
| *cheese:* | |
| *Count Down®:* | 1.1 grams |
| *Chef's Delight®:* | 5.6 grams |

228

*Total:*
    *with Count Down®:*        2.4 grams
    *with Chef's Delight®:*     6.9 grams
*Fat content per serving:*    0.4–1.2 grams

## Rice in Consommé

For a different-tasting boiled rice omit the salt and boil the rice in canned consommé (undiluted) instead of water. This adds both color and flavor to the rice. Never add fat when cooking rice.

## Curried Rice

**1 teaspoon curry powder**
**2 cups Swanson® Chicken Broth**
**1 cup uncooked rice**

In a saucepan dissolve curry powder in a little of the chicken broth; add remaining broth; heat to boiling. Slowly sprinkle in rice, stir well, cover. Simmer gently 25 minutes or until rice is tender and broth is absorbed.

| *Fat content of recipe:* | | *4 servings* |
|---|---|---|
| *chicken broth:* | 3.2 grams | |
| *rice:* | 1.0 gram | |
| *Total:* | 4.2 grams | |
| *Fat content per serving:* | 1.1 grams | |

## Rice with Oysters and Tomatoes

**½ cup raw rice**
**1 cup canned tomatoes**
**1 medium onion, chopped**

229

1 cup oysters, drained
1 teaspoon salt
Fresh ground pepper
Cracker crumbs from saltine crackers

Cook rice. Combine rice and remaining ingredients in casserole. Top with cracker crumbs. Bake in 350° to 400° oven about 30 minutes.

| Fat content of recipe: | 5 servings |
|---|---|
| rice: | 0.5 gram |
| oysters: | 4.0 grams |
| cracker crumbs, 4 saltines (yield: ¼ cup): | 1.0 gram |
| Total: | 5.5 grams |
| Fat content per serving: | 1.1 grams |

## Yellow Rice

Yellow Rice Mix® packed by R. M. Quigg, Inc., Miami, Florida 33155, contains rice, monosodium glutamate, and dehydrated onion and garlic, turmeric, dextrose, and saffron. The instructions on the package suggest the addition of 1 tablespoon butter. The authors find this can be omitted without impairing the flavor.

Pour contents of package (5 ounces) into 2 cups boiling water; add 1 teaspoon salt. Boil 1 minute, cover tightly and reduce to very low heat for 20 minutes. Stir once.

| Fat content of recipe: | 3–4 servings |
|---|---|
| rice: | 0.6 gram |
| Fat content per serving: | 0.2 gram |

# Pasta

## Pasta with Sapsago Cheese

Spaghetti, macaroni, or noodles
Sapsago cheese, grated (see Cheeses, page 155)

230

**Consommé, undiluted**
**Salt**

Cook spaghetti, macaroni, or noodles in boiling salted water according to directions on package. Drain in colander and rinse with hot water. Sprinkle grated sapsago cheese between layers. Heat consommé until very hot and pour over top. Serve immediately.

*Fat content of ingredients:*
| | |
|---|---|
| *spaghetti, 8 ounces dry:* | 2.7 grams |
| *or* | |
| *macaroni, 8 ounces dry:* | 2.7 grams |
| *or* | |
| *noodles, 8 ounces dry* | |
| *(containing egg):* | 10.5 grams |
| *sapsago cheese:* | negligible |
| *consommé:* | negligible |

## Spinach

### Spinach I

Fresh spinach has excellent flavor when steamed (See page 204). Season with one of the Seasoned Salts or pass horseradish sauce (page 199) at the table. If you prefer, you may cook the spinach in boiling, salted water, but steaming produces a more flavorful dish.

### Spinach II

**1 box frozen leaf spinach or 1 pound
   fresh spinach
1 tablespoon chopped onion
   Seasoned Salt
   Evaporated skimmed milk, undiluted**

To use frozen spinach, thaw and drain. Brown the

chopped onion in a Teflon®-coated pan or one treated with Pam®, Lean-Fry®, or Pan Pal®. Add spinach, seasoning and evaporated skimmed milk as needed to moisten. Simmer, stirring gently to prevent scorching, till heated through.

With fresh spinach, wash and drain and cook as above. The fresh spinach yields a more tasty dish than the frozen variety.

*Fat content of recipe:*                 *2–3 servings*
   *evaporated skimmed milk, 1 cup:*    0.5 gram

## Squash

### Baked Acorn Squash

To bake acorn squash, wash and rub shell with bacon grease. Since you will not eat the shell, this will not add to the fat content of the finished dish. Place the squash in a 300° oven and bake about an hour depending upon the size of the squash. When no longer firm to the touch, remove from oven, cut in half, remove seeds, and sprinkle squash with one of the seasoned salts and basil. One squash yields 2 servings.

### Filled Acorn Squash

**3 acorn squash**
**½ cup crushed pineapple**
**2 tablespoons brown sugar**
**¼ teaspoon ground nutmeg**
**¼ teaspoon salt**

Bake acorn squash as in preceding recipe. Combine other ingredients. When squash is cooked and cut and the seeds removed, fill centers with pineapple mixture.

Return to oven for a few minutes to heat through.

### Yellow Squash (Summer or Crookneck)

**Yellow squash**
**Evaporated skimmed milk, undiluted**
**Seasoned Salt**

Scrub squash with a vegetable brush. Slice into saucepan. Cook with a small amount of boiling water until tender. (Squash has a great deal of water in it, so a large amount of added water is not needed, and the squash will cook down to about half its original volume.) Remove from heat, drain off any excess water, and mash. Add some evaporated skimmed milk and return to fire. Simmer over low heat until squash reaches a smooth consistency, adding evaporated skimmed milk as needed to maintain moisture. This needs 45 minutes to 1 hour. Flavor with one of the Seasoned Salts.

*Fat content of recipe:*
  *evaporated skimmed milk, 1 cup:*   0.5 gram

## Succotash

### Frozen Succotash

Cook in boiling, lightly salted and sugared water as directed on package. Drain and sprinkle with Seasoned Salt. Omission of butter does not impair flavor.

## Tomatoes

### Baked Tomatoes I

Cut off top of tomato and pare strip of skin off about one-third of tomato. Sprinkle cut top generously with Seasoned Salt. Sprinkle with cracker crumbs. Place in a

**VEGETABLES**

233

pan with a small amount of water. Bake in a moderate oven (350°) for about 20 minutes until tomatoes are tender but will still hold their shape. Brown crumbs under broiler. Chopped green peppers and chopped onions may also be added to top before baking, for variety.

### Baked Tomatoes II

This rule, although very similar to the one above, is a pleasing variation in flavor.

Cut off the tops of 4 medium-sized tomatoes. Scoop out a small part of the center pulp. Mix together ¼ teaspoon salt, ½ teaspoon sugar, ¼ teaspoon onion powder, ⅛ teaspoon basil, ⅛ teaspoon oregano, and a dash of pepper. Sprinkle the tops of the tomatoes with this mixture. Top with cracker crumbs. Bake in a moderate oven (350°) for 20 to 30 minutes or until the tomatoes are tender.

### Broiled Tomato Slices

Slice fresh tomatoes about ⅜ inch thick. Sprinkle liberally with Seasoned Salt. Run under broiler until edges begin to brown. Serve at once.

### Tomatoes in Foil

**2 large tomatoes**
**Salt**
**Freshly ground pepper**
**2 tablespoons chopped parsley**
**3 tablespoons chopped green onion, including tops**
**½ teaspoon basil, crushed**

½ teaspoon tarragon, crushed
½ clove garlic, crushed in garlic press

Cut tomatoes in halves crosswise. Sprinkle cut surface of each tomato half generously with salt and pepper. Mix remaining ingredients and mound one-fourth of the mixture on each tomato half. Set tomatoes on a large piece of heavy-duty aluminum foil; wrap and seal tightly. Grill 3 inches from coals about 10 minutes or until just tender.

### Baked Stewed Tomatoes

Combine canned tomatoes and Pepperidge Farm® Herb Seasoned Stuffing. Adjust proportions for desired thickness and number of servings. Bake in 375° oven until bubbly.

*Fat content of recipe:*
  *1 cup Pepperidge Farm® Herb Seasoned Stuffing:*
  0.8 gram

## Zucchini

### Zucchini Creole

  1 cup green pepper strips
  1 cup sliced onion
1½ pounds zucchini, sliced
  3 medium-sized, firm, ripe tomatoes, peeled and chopped or 1 can (1 lb. 4 oz.) Italian plum tomatoes
  ¾ teaspoon basil
  1 teaspoon salt
  Dash of pepper

235

**1 tablespoon cornstarch**
**1 tablespoon water**

Quick-cook until soft green pepper and onion in Teflon®-coated pan or one treated with Pam®, Lean-Fry®, or Pan Pal®. Add zucchini, tomatoes, basil, salt, and pepper. Cover; simmer 15 minutes. Blend cornstarch and water to a smooth paste; stir into mixture in skillet. Cook until thickened.

This can be prepared ahead of time and reheated in a casserole in the oven.

*Fat content of recipe:*     negligible      *5 servings*

## LOW-FAT DESSERTS

There are a few delicacies which cannot be included in a low-fat menu: "short" piecrust; cakes requiring considerable amounts of shortening; nuts (except litchi nuts, which are, in fact, a fruit) by themselves or as ingredients in your baking; and, of course, whipped-cream toppings. But there are so many delicious desserts of relatively low fat content that no problem really exists in this area. In recipes calling for greased pans, the quantity of fat incorporated in the product is negligible. Mineral oil can be substituted for greasing if desired. Teflon®-lined pans or use of the preparations Pam®, Lean-Fry®, and Pan Pal®, described in the chapter on meats (page 45) can eliminate the need for greasing.

You will find as you read the recipes below that a considerable number of egg whites are used in low-fat 237 desserts. This leaves a surplus of egg yolks, the use of which, in any quantity, is incompatible with low-fat cookery. Using powdered egg whites provides a solution to this problem. The authors have been unable to purchase powdered egg white on the retail market, but it is available in large quantities for commercial bakeries and the like. You might, therefore, be able to purchase small quantities through your local bakery.

To give your desserts a "party look" or an extra touch of flavor there are a number of suitable low-fat toppings:

a sprinkling of cinnamon or nutmeg
a sprig of mint
a maraschino cherry
grated lemon or orange rind
fresh berries
slices of fresh or canned fruit
jelly
ginger marmalade
marshmallow sauce (marshmallow creme)

Several whipped toppings are available which can be used as a substitute for whipped cream. This is not an extremely low-fat product but does have a lower fat content than that of whipping cream. It is decorative and palatable, and you may wish to invest a portion of your fat intake in this topping. One heaping tablespoon of the whipped product contains approximately 1.0 to 1.5 grams of fat.

Skim-milk yogurts, fruit flavored (2.5–3.2 grams of fat per 8-ounce carton) and plain (3.6–4.0 grams of fat), may be used as dessert toppings.

## Ice Creams and Sherbets

Any of the commercially produced fruit sherbets may be used.

The so-called low-calorie ice creams or "ice milks" are low-fat as well as low-calorie and can be used. They have the further advantage of being considerably less expensive than regular ice cream. See Appendix, Table 3, for the fat content of ice cream, ice milk, and ices.

### Cranberry Sherbet

    2 cups cranberries
1¼ cups water
    1 cup sugar
    1 teaspoon unflavored gelatin
    ¼ cup cold water
       Juice of 1 lemon or 2 tablespoons lemon juice

Cook cranberries in 1¼ cups water until skins pop. Press through sieve. Add sugar and cook until sugar dissolves. Add gelatin softened in cold water; cool. Add lemon juice. Freeze in automatic refrigerator tray 2 to 3 hours, stirring twice.

*Fat content of recipe:*      negligible      *5 servings*

### Grape Juice Sherbet

    ½ package lemon Jello®
    2 lemons
    ½ cup sugar
    1 cup grape juice
    1 cup boiling water
    1 egg white

Squeeze lemons. Dissolve Jello® in one-half cup boiling water. Add lemon juice, sugar, grape juice, and the rest of the water. Freeze. When partly frozen, stir and fold in beaten egg white. Continue to freeze, beating

239

two or three more times to maintain smooth blend and consistency.

*Fat content of recipe:* negligible

## Grapefruit Sherbet

    **2 cups sugar**
    **1 cup water**
    **2 egg whites**
    **2 tablespoons sugar**
   **1¾ cups grapefruit juice**
    **¼ cup lemon juice**
    **1 tablespoon grated grapefruit rind**

In a saucepan combine the 2 cups sugar and the water; bring to a boil over moderate heat and cook 5 minutes. Remove the syrup from the heat and let it cool slightly. In an electric mixer beat egg whites until they hold soft peaks; add the 2 tablespoons sugar and beat until the whites hold firm peaks. Beat in the syrup in a thin stream. Add grapefruit juice, lemon juice, and grapefruit rind. Beat the mixture until it is well combined and add more lemon juice if desired. Transfer the mixture to refrigerator trays and freeze until set around the edges. Stir thoroughly and freeze, stirring thoroughly every hour, for 5 hours or more.

*Fat content of recipe:*     negligible    *Yield: 4 cups*

## Raspberry–Pineapple Sherbet

   **1 10-ounce package frozen raspberries**
   **1 13½-ounce package frozen pineapple**

Break frozen fruit apart with fork. Put in electric blender a small quantity at a time and blend after each addition. When smooth and of sherbet consistency serve at once. If you prefer a firmer sherbet, you may store for a short time in freezing tray of refrigerator. This sherbet is good served in meringue shells because its tangy flavor contrasts with the sweetness of the meringue.

*Fat content of recipe:*  negligible  *4 servings*

**Four-Fruit Sherbet**

> 2 cups mashed bananas (3 medium ba-
>   nanas)
> ¼ cup lemon juice
> ⅓ cup orange juice
> ½ cup white Karo® syrup
> ⅛ teaspoon salt
> 1 egg white
> ⅓ cup sugar
> 1 cup whole milk
> ¼ cup maraschino cherry juice
> ½ cup coarsley chopped maraschino
>   cherries
> 1 teaspoon grated orange rind

Mash bananas thoroughly with lemon juice. Add orange juice, Karo® syrup, and salt. Beat egg whites until stiff but not dry; gradually beat in sugar. Fold into banana mixture. Add milk, stirring slowly. Add maraschino cherry juice, chopped cherries, and orange rind. Pour into freezing tray. Freeze with cold control set for fast freezing until mixture is almost firm. Turn into chilled bowl and beat with rotary beater. Return to freezing tray and freeze until firm, beating mixture once with spoon. Set cold control midway between fast freezing and normal for storage. If sherbet gets icy during storage, beat with rotary beater to restore creamy consistency.

| Fat content of recipe: | Yield: 1 quart; 6 servings |
| milk: | 9.0 grams |
| Fat content per serving: | 1.5 grams |

## Ice Milk Whip

**1 package flavored gelatin dessert**
**1 pint low-calorie ice milk**

Make up gelatin dessert according to directions on the package. Chill until slightly thickened. Add ice milk. Beat together quickly. Pour into mold. Chill until set.

| Fat content of recipe: | 5 servings |
| low-calorie ice milk, 1 pint: | 13.3 grams |
| Fat content per serving: | 2.7 grams |

## Cherries Jubilee

**1 10-ounce jar currant jelly**
**1 tablespoon orange marmalade**
**2 cups (1 1-pound 14-ounce can) pitted**
  **Bing cherries, drained**
**Vanilla ice milk**

Melt jelly and marmalade over low heat. Add cherries; heat to simmering. Serve over vanilla ice milk. This sauce will dress 8 servings of ice milk.

*Fat content of recipe:*
  *jelly, marmalade and cherries:*  negligible
  *ice milk, 1 pint:*  13.3 grams

## Cinnamon Mocha Bounce

**¾ cup double-strength coffee**
**1 cup skim milk**

**¼ cup sugar**
**⅓ cup chocolate syrup, thin type**
**2 scoops chocolate ice milk**
**2 scoops vanilla ice milk**
**½ teaspoon cinnamon**

Place all ingredients in blender; cover, blend well.

| *Fat content of recipe:* | *Yield: 2 servings* |
|---|---|
| *skim milk:* | trace |
| *chocolate syrup:* | 2.7 grams |
| *4 scoops ice milk (1 cup):* | 7.0 grams |
| *Total:* | 9.7 grams |
| *Fat content per serving:* | 4.9 grams |

### Flaming Sundaes

Top scoops of ice milk with a marshmallow. Place on the marshmallow a small sugar cube dipped in lemon extract. Light the sugar lump. The flame will toast the marshmallow. These delight children.

*Fat content of recipe:*
   *ice milk, 1 pint:*      13.3 grams

## Cookies

### Meringue Kisses

**1 cup sugar**
**2 egg whites**
**⅛ teaspoon salt**
**½ teaspoon vanilla**

Whip until stiff the egg whites and salt. (In mixer, use speed for eggs and candy.) Continue beating, at same speed, adding sugar very slowly. When last of sugar

243

**DESSERTS**

has been added, add vanilla. Drop by teaspoon on cooky sheet. Bake in very slow oven (225°) until firm and lightly brown.

*Fat content of recipe:*   0.0 grams

### Fruited Meringue Kisses

**1 cup sugar**
**2 egg whites**
**⅛ teaspoon salt**
**½ teaspoon vanilla**
**¾ cup ready-cut glazed fruits and peels**

Whip until stiff the egg whites and salt. (In mixer, use speed for eggs and candy.) Continue beating, at same speed, adding sugar very slowly. When last of sugar has been added, add vanilla. Then gently fold in fruit. Drop by teaspoon on cooky sheet. Bake in very slow oven (225°) until firm and lightly brown. This makes a more substantial meringue than the preceding recipe. It is quite chewy. For variety substitute raisins for the glazed fruit.

*Fat content of recipe:*   negligible

### Cocoa Kisses

**1 cup sugar**
**3 egg whites**
**⅛ teaspoon salt**
**2 teaspoons water**
**1 teaspoon vanilla**
**3 tablespoons cocoa**

Sift the sugar. Whip the egg whites and salt until stiff, not dry. Gradually add ½ of the sugar. Combine water and vanilla. Add the liquid, a few drops at a time, alternately with the remaining sugar. Whip constantly.

Fold in the cocoa. Drop by teaspoon on wax paper on cooky sheet. Bake in a very slow oven (250°) until they are partly dry and will retain their shape, approximately 30 minutes. Remove from the wax paper while hot so they will not stick to the paper.

|  | Yield: approximately |
|---|---|
| Fat content of recipe: | 40 1-inch meringues |
| cocoa: | 5.1 grams |
| Fat content per meringue: | 0.1 gram |

## Cookies and Bars

### Mincemeat Cookies

½ package *dry* mincemeat (Borden's Nonesuch® or A & P®, 9-ounce package)
1 egg
½ cup sugar
1½ cups flour
1½ teaspoons baking powder
¼ cup *dry* skimmed milk powder
3 tablespoons water

Cut up mincemeat and blend in mixer with egg. Sift together and add to above the sugar, flour, baking powder, and dry milk powder. Add water. Drop by teaspoon on cooky sheet. Bake at 350° for 10–12 minutes.

| Fat content | Yield: approximately |
|---|---|
| of recipe: | 50 cookies |
| mincemeat: | 0.8 gram |
| egg: | 6.0 grams |
| flour: | negligible |
| milk: | negligible |

245

| Total: | 6.8 grams |
| Fat content per cooky: | 0.1 gram |

### Dry-Cereal Cookies

**1 cup cornflakes**
**1 cup Rice Krispies®**
**1 cup marshmallow sauce**
**½ cup raisins**

Heat marshmallow sauce in top of double boiler until syrupy. Pour over cereal and raisins. Mix well. Dip out by teaspoonfuls on aluminum foil. Chill. These cookies have two advantages: they require no baking, and they may be frozen without loss of crispness.

| Fat content | Yield: approximately |
| of recipe: | 1½ dozen cookies |
| cornflakes: | trace |
| Rice Krispies®: | 0.4 gram |
| marshmallow sauce: | negligible |
| Total: | 0.4 gram |
| Fat content per cooky: | negligible |

### Banana Oatmeal Cookies

**1 cup sugar**
**½ cup nonfat milk, liquefied**
**3 medium eggs**
**1 teaspoon vanilla**
**½ teaspoon lemon extract**
**3 mashed bananas**
**1½ cups quick-cooking rolled oats**
**2 cups sifted all-purpose flour**
**½ teaspoon baking soda**
**1 teaspoon baking powder**
**1 teaspoon salt**

Beat eggs. Add sugar, vanilla, lemon extract, and mashed bananas. Beat well. Sift and measure flour. Resift with salt, soda, and baking powder. To the banana mixture add alternately the dry ingredients and the milk. Stir in rolled oats. Drop by teaspoon onto Teflon® or treated baking sheet. Bake at 375° or 400° until done (approximately 15–18 minutes). This is a wet batter.

| Fat content | Yield: 5 dozen |
|---|---|
| of recipe: | 2-inch cookies |
| milk: | negligible |
| eggs: | 18.0 grams |
| oats: | 8.9 grams |
| flour: | 2.0 grams |
| Total: | 28.9 grams |
| Fat content per cooky: | 0.5 gram |

## Pablum® Spiced Drop Cookies

½ cup sugar
¼ teaspoon each clove, nutmeg, allspice, and cinnamon
2 medium eggs
½ teaspoon vanilla
½ cup all-purpose flour
2 teaspoons baking powder
Pinch of salt
1 tablespoon of liquefied nonfat milk, if needed
1 cup Pablum®

Beat eggs. Add sugar, vanilla, and spices. Sift flour with baking powder and salt and add to batter. Stir in cereal. If dry, add the tablespoon of liquefied nonfat milk. Drop from teaspoon onto Teflon® or treated cooky sheet. Bake at 325° for 15 minutes or until done.

247

| Fat content of recipe: | Yield: 35 2-inch cookies |
|---|---|
| eggs: | 12.0 grams |
| flour: | 0.5 gram |
| milk: | negligible |
| Pablum®: | 1.1 grams |
| Total: | 13.6 grams |
| Fat content per cooky: | 0.4 gram |

## Raisin Drop Cookies I

3 egg yolks
¼ cup liquefied nonfat milk
¾ cup sugar
½ teaspoon cream of tartar
1½ cups flour
3 teaspoons baking powder
Scant ½ teaspoon salt
Spice lightly with shake or two each of nutmeg, cinnamon, cloves, allspice, and mace
1 teaspoon vanilla
¼ cup raisins

Beat together egg yolks, milk, sugar, and cream of tartar. Mix and sift together flour, baking powder, salt, and spices. Stir into egg-yolk mixture. Add vanilla and raisins. Drop by teaspoonful on Teflon® or treated cooky sheet. Bake at 375° for 10 minutes.

| Fat content of recipe: | Yield: approximately 4 dozen |
|---|---|
| egg yolks: | 18.0 grams |
| milk: | negligible |
| flour: | 1.5 grams |
| Total: | 19.5 grams |
| Fat content per cooky: | 0.4 gram |

### Raisin Drop Cookies II

    3 egg whites
    ¾ cup sugar
    ½ teaspoon cream of tartar
    1½ cups flour
      3 teaspoons baking powder
        Scant ½ teaspoon salt
        Spice lightly with shake or two each
        of nutmeg, cinnamon, cloves, all-
        spice, and mace
      1 teaspoon vanilla
      ¼ cup raisins

Beat together, though not necessarily stiff, the egg whites, sugar, and cream of tartar. Into the beaten mixture, fold dry ingredients which have been mixed and sifted. Add vanilla and raisins. Drop by teaspoon-ful on Teflon® or treated cooky sheet. Bake at 375° for 10 minutes.

| | |
|---|---|
| *Fat content* | *Yield:* |
| *of recipe:* | *approximately 3 dozen* |
| *flour:* | 1.5 grams |
| *Fat content of 2 cookies:* | 0.1 gram |

### Raisin "Shortbread"

    2 eggs
    ½ cup sugar
    ¼ teaspoon cream of tartar
    2 cups flour
    3 teaspoons baking powder
      Scant ½ teaspoon salt
      Spice lightly with a shake or two each
      of nutmeg, cinnamon, cloves, allspice,
      and mace

1 teaspoon vanilla
¼ cup raisins

Beat together the eggs, sugar, and cream of tartar. To the beaten mixture add dry ingredients, which have been mixed and sifted. Add vanilla and raisins. On lightly floured board, roll dough to ⅜-inch thickness. Cut into 2-inch squares. Bake on Teflon® or treated cooky sheet at 375° for 10 minutes.

| Fat content | Yield: |
|---|---|
| of recipe: | approximately 3 dozen |
| eggs: | 12.0 grams |
| flour: | 2.0 grams |
| Total: | 14.0 grams |
| Fat content per cooky: | 0.4 gram |

## Butterless Drop Cookies

**1 cup sugar**
**3 eggs**
**1 teaspoon vanilla**
**2 cups all-purpose flour**
**1 teaspoon double-acting baking powder**
**1 teaspoon grated lemon rind or 2 teaspoons grated orange rind**

Sift sugar. Beat eggs until light and add sugar gradually. Beat 3 to 5 minutes on medium speed with an electric beater, somewhat longer if beating by hand. Add vanilla. Sift flour before measuring. Resift with baking powder. Combine flour and baking powder with sugar and egg mixture. Add grated fruit rind. Beat the batter about 5 minutes. Drop ½ teaspoon at a time, well apart, on Teflon® or treated cooky sheet. Bake about 12 minutes in 325° oven.

| Fat content | Yield: 50 |
|---|---|
| of recipe: | 1½–2-inch cookies |

| | |
|---|---|
| *eggs:* | 18.0 grams |
| *flour:* | 2.0 grams |
| *Total:* | 20.0 grams |
| *Fat content per cooky:* | 0.4 gram |

### Applesauce Cookies

1½ cups flour
½ cup brown sugar
½ teaspoon cloves
½ teaspoon cinnamon
 2 eggs
½ teaspoon baking soda
1½ teaspoons baking powder
¼ teaspoon salt
½ cup raisins
¼ cup applesauce

Beat eggs until thick. Add sugar. Continue beating until well mixed. Add flour that has been sifted with soda, salt, spices, and baking powder. Mix well. Add raisins and applesauce. Stir until well blended. Drop on a Teflon® or treated cooky sheet and bake at 375° until done (approximately 10 minutes).

| *Fat content of recipe:* | *Yield: 45 cookies* |
|---|---|
| *flour:* | 1.5 grams |
| *eggs:* | 12.0 grams |
| *applesauce:* | negligible |
| *Total:* | 13.5 grams |
| *Fat content per cooky:* | 0.3 gram |

### Gingerbread

Two gingerbread mixes can be prepared with water only:

*Dromedary®*
 *1 piece, 2" × 2", plain*      2.2 grams fat

*1 package mix (16 servings)* 35.2 grams fat
*Pillsbury®*
  *1 piece, 3" × 3", plain*     4.0 grams fat
  *1 package mix (9 servings)*  36.0 grams fat

## Ginger Cookies

**1 package Dromedary® or Pillsbury®
  Gingerbread mix
½ cup water
Handful of raisins**

Mix ingredients and store in refrigerator overnight. Drop by teaspoonful onto Teflon® or treated cooky sheet. Bake in 375° oven 10 minutes.

| *Fat content of recipe:* | *Yield: 50 cookies* |
|---|---|
| *gingerbread mix:* | 35.2–36.0 grams |
| *Fat content per cooky:* | 0.7 gram |

## Date Bars

**1 cup sugar
3 eggs
2 cups chopped dates
1 cup chopped candied fruit (mixed)
1 scant cup all-purpose flour
1 teaspoon baking powder
⅛ teaspoon salt
¼ teaspoon cloves
¼ teaspoon cinnamon
1 teaspoon vanilla
  Confectioners' sugar**

252    Sift sugar; beat eggs until light. Add the sugar gradually to the beaten eggs. Blend these ingredients until they are very light. Add chopped dates and chopped fruit.

Sift flour before measuring; resift with baking powder and salt; add spices. Add the sifted ingredients to the egg mixture with 1 teaspoon vanilla. Beat the batter until the ingredients are well blended. Pour it into a lightly greased and floured 9- by 13-inch pan. Bake it in a moderate oven (325°) for about 25 minutes. When the cake is cool cut it into bars. Sprinkle with confectioners' sugar.

| Fat content | Yield: 42 |
|---|---|
| of recipe: | 2½- by 1-inch bars |
| eggs: | 18.0 grams |
| flour: | 1.0 gram |
| Total: | 19.0 grams |
| Fat content per bar: | 0.5 gram |

### Molasses Squares

   ½ cup sugar
   ½ cup molasses
   ¼ teaspoon salt
 1½ teaspoons baking powder
   ½ cup liquefied nonfat milk
   1 cup mixed chopped figs, dates, and
      raisins
   2 eggs
   2 cups bread flour
   ¼ teaspoon soda

Beat eggs until well mixed. Add sugar, beating until light and creamy. Beat in molasses. Sift flour and resift with salt, soda, and baking powder. Add sifted ingredients in three parts to egg mixture, alternating with thirds of the milk. Beat batter after each addition until it is smooth. Stir in chopped fruit. Bake in a lightly greased 9- by 13-inch pan until done (15–20 minutes). Cut into squares.

253

| | |
|---|---|
| *Fat content* | *Yield: two dozen* |
| *of recipe:* | *2-inch squares* |
| *eggs:* | 12.0 grams |
| *milk:* | negligible |
| *flour:* | 2.0 grams |
| *Total:* | 14.0 grams |
| *Fat content per square:* | 0.6 gram |

## Gumdrop Bars

**1 cup sifted bread flour**
**¼ teaspoon salt**
**½ teaspoon cinnamon**
**¾ cups diced gumdrops (omit licorice flavor)**
**2 eggs**
**½ tablespoon water**
**1 cup light brown sugar**

Combine, then sift, the flour, salt, and cinnamon. Sprinkle one-fourth of the flour mixture over the diced gumdrops. Beat until light the eggs and water. Add the sugar gradually. When the sugar is well blended, stir in the flour mixture and, last, the gumdrops. Spread the batter in a lightly greased 9- by 12-inch pan. Bake in a moderate oven (350°) for about ½ hour. Cut into bars while warm and remove from the pan. (This recipe is a favorite with children.)

| | |
|---|---|
| *Fat content of recipe:* | *Yield: about 18 bars* |
| *flour:* | 1.0 gram |
| *eggs:* | 12.0 grams |
| *Total:* | 13.0 grams |
| *Fat content per bar:* | 0.7 gram |

## Christmas Fruit Cookies

**1 egg**
**¾ cup brown sugar**

½ cup honey
½ cup dark molasses
3 cups sifted flour
1¼ teaspoon cinnamon
1¼ teaspoon nutmeg
½ teaspoon cloves
½ teaspoon allspice
½ teaspoon soda
2 teaspoons baking powder
½ cup chopped mixed candied fruits
and peels or ½ cup raisins

Beat egg; add brown sugar and beat until light and fluffy. Stir in honey and molasses. Sift together dry ingredients; add to first mixture; mix well. Stir in fruits and peels or raisins. Chill dough several hours or overnight. On lightly floured board, roll to ⅛ inch; cut in rectangles about 3½ by 2 inches. Bake on Teflon® or treated cooky sheet about 12 minutes at 350°; cool slightly before removing from pan. This is a rather hard, brittle cooky—good dunked in milk. To mellow, store airtight with apple.

| Fat content | Yield: approximately |
|---|---|
| of recipe: | 4 dozen cookies |
| egg: | 6.0 grams |
| flour: | 3.0 grams |
| Total: | 9.0 grams |
| Fat content per cooky: | 0.2 gram |

### Leckerli

½ cup sugar
½ cup honey
¼ cup each chopped candied orange
and lemon peels
2¼ cups sifted flour
1½ teaspoons cloves

255

1½ teaspoons nutmeg
1 tablespoon cinnamon
Few grains salt
1 teaspoon soda
Grated rind ½ lemon
2 tablespoons orange juice
Glaze

Heat sugar and honey to boiling. Remove from heat. Add candied peels, sifted dry ingredients, lemon rind, and orange juice. Knead until well blended. Roll dough to ½-inch thickness, using as little flour as possible. Lift carefully onto lightly greased waxed paper on cooky sheet. Bake in moderate oven (325°) about 25 minutes. Turn out on rack, and remove paper at once. Turn right side up, and spread with glaze. Cool; cut in small diamonds. To soften and mellow cookies, store with apple in airtight container at least 1 week before using. These cookies can be frozen. They will ship well if airtight. *Glaze:* Cook ½ cup sugar and ¼ cup water until mixture spins a thread.

| | |
|---|---|
| *Fat content* | *Yield: approximately* |
| *of recipe:* | *5 dozen cookies* |
| *flour:* | 2.3 grams |
| *Fat content per cooky:* | negligible |

## Pfeffernüsse

5 eggs
2 cups brown sugar, packed
Grated rind 1 lemon
3 tablespoons strong coffee
5½ cups sifted flour
2 teaspoons baking powder
½ teaspoon salt
½ teaspoon pepper

½ teaspoon mace
½ teaspoon nutmeg
1 teaspoon ground cloves
1 teaspoon allspice
1 tablespoon cinnamon
⅛ teaspoon ground cardamon
½ cup chopped citron
¼ teaspoon anise seed
Apricot brandy

Beat eggs until thick. Gradually beat in sugar. Add remaining ingredients, except brandy; mix well. Chill. Shape in rolls 1 inch in diameter. Cut slices ½-inch thick. Let stand in cool place to dry overnight. Turn cookies over and put a drop of brandy on each to make cookies pop and become rounded. Bake on Teflon® or treated cooky sheet in 300° oven about 20 minutes. Store airtight with apple. They will ship well.

| Fat content | Yield: approximately |
|---|---|
| of recipe: | 80 cookies |
| eggs: | 30.0 grams |
| flour: | 5.5 grams |
| Total: | 35.5 grams |
| Fat content per cooky: | 0.4 grams |

## Springerle

4 eggs
4 cups (1 pound box) sifted
   confectioners' sugar
20 drops anise oil
4 cups sifted flour
1 teaspoon soda
Crushed anise seed

Beat eggs until light. Gradually add the sugar and continue beating until it is like a soft meringue. Add

257

anise oil. Sift together flour and soda; blend into egg mixture. Cover bowl tightly and let stand about 15 minutes. Divide dough into thirds. On lightly floured board, roll each piece in an 8-inch square about ¼ inch thick. Let stand 1 minute. Dust springerle rolling pin or springerle board lightly with flour. Roll or press just enough to make a clear design. With a sharp knife, cut cookies apart. Place on a lightly floured surface; cover with a towel and let stand overnight. Lightly grease baking sheets and sprinkle with 1½ to 2 teaspoons crushed anise seed. Brush excess flour from cookies; with finger, rub underside very lightly with cold water and place on baking sheets. Bake in a slow oven (300°) about 20 minutes, or until straw color. Store for several days in tightly covered containers before eating. If these cakes become too hard, keep an apple in the cooky jar.

| Fat content of recipe: | Yield: 6 dozen cookies |
|---|---|
| eggs: | 24.0 grams |
| flour: | 4.0 grams |
| Total: | 28.0 grams |
| Fat content per cooky: | 0.4 gram |

## Pies

Although you cannot include in a low-fat menu a piecrust made in the usual way (with a considerable amount of shortening), you can still have pie—and a very good pie. The recipe which follows makes a tender crust. The dough requires some pressure to roll but is easily handled because it does not crumble or tear. Do roll it thin. If you are making fresh apple or peach pie, add to the dough a shake or two of several spices: allspice, cinnamon, nutmeg, cloves, mace. If

258

you use a filling of low fat content, you can use the entire recipe and make a two-crust pie. If you are using a filling with a higher fat content (e.g., lemon, which requires two eggs), use one crust and top with a meringue. Still another method is to make one and one-half times the recipe; make two lower crusts and reserve the extra half recipe for strips across the top. The fat content of these various methods is noted at the end of the recipe.

**D**
**E**
**S**
**S**
**E**
**R**
**T**
**S**

### Piecrust

  2 eggs
  ¼ cup sugar
  ¼ teaspoon cream of tartar
1¾ cups flour
  3 teaspoons baking powder
  Scant ½ teaspoon salt

Beat together eggs, sugar, and cream of tartar. Mix and sift flour, baking powder, and salt. Stir dry ingredients into egg mixture. Roll on lightly floured board to ⅛-inch thickness. Bake at 350° to 375° until lightly browned. A shell will bake in 10 to 15 minutes. Time for filled pies will vary according to the filling, as in other pie-crusts.

| Fat content of recipe: | Yield: 2 single 9-inch crusts or 1 double crust | Per serving (6 per crust) |
|---|---|---|
| eggs: | 12.0 grams | |
| flour: | 1.8 grams | |
| Total: | 13.8 grams | |
| Fat content of 1 crust: | 6.9 grams | 1.2 grams |
| Fat content of double crust: | 13.8 grams | 2.3 grams |

259

### Fruit Batter Pie

**½ cup sugar**
**1 cup flour**
**1½ teaspoons baking powder**
**½ cup liquefied nonfat milk**

Lightly grease bottom and sides of Pyrex® baking dish.
(A larger surface is preferable to a deep dish.) Pour
batter into dish. Add fruit with approximately ¾ cup
sugar for each pint of raw fruit. Add small amount of
water if fruit is not juicy. Bake at 375° until brown on
bottom. Suggested fruits: apples, peaches, blueberries, blackberries, tart cherries.

   Fruits may be fresh, frozen, or canned. Additional
seasonings, such as cinnamon to apples, nutmeg to
peaches, may be used for added flavor. Addition of
lemon juice gives a new spark to canned fruits. Pie may
be topped with low-fat ice milk if desired.

*Fat content of batter:*
   *flour:*          1.0 gram
   *milk:*           negligible
   *Total:*          1.0 gram
*Fat content of fruits is not significant.*

   A reasonable topping of low-fat ice milk would not
be likely to exceed 3 grams of fat per serving.

### Meringue Pie

**1 cup granulated sugar**
**¼ teaspoon cream of tartar**
**4 egg whites**

This may be frozen successfully. Heat oven to 275°. To make meringue, sift sugar with cream of tartar; beat egg whites until stiff; gradually add sifted sugar and continue beating until glossy. Grease two 9-inch pie plates; spread meringue on bottoms and sides of pie plates, swirling it up at edges and keeping it off the rims of plates. Bake 1 hour. Cool. To freeze, simply wrap carefully and place in freezer. When ready to use, thaw for 15 minutes at room temperature. To serve, fill with spoonfuls of low-fat vanilla ice milk. Allow 1 quart per pie. Top with fresh or barely thawed fruit: peaches, strawberries, or raspberries.

| Fat content of recipe: | Yield: 2 pie shells |
|---|---|
| meringue shell: | 0.0 grams |
| fruit: | negligible |
| low-fat ice milk: | 26.5 grams per quart |

### Strawberry Meringue Pie

Make the meringue pie shell described above and fill with this frozen strawberry filling:

> 1 package frozen strawberries
> ¼ cup sugar
> ⅓ cup frozen lemonade concentrate (½ can)
> 1½ cups nonfat milk liquefied
> Red food coloring if desired
> 1 egg white
> 2 tablespoons sugar
> Fresh strawberries and mint for garnish

Combine frozen strawberries and ¼ cup sugar. Heat until the sugar is dissolved. Cool and add lemonade concentrate. Pour nonfat milk into freezing tray and freeze until edges are mushy. Pour into a cold bowl

261

and beat until the consistency of whipped cream. Add a few drops of red coloring. Beat egg white until frothy. Add 2 tablespoons sugar, slowly, beating well after each addition. Fold into whipped milk. Add strawberry mixture. Pour into 3 freezing trays and freeze partially. Place in a chilled bowl and beat again. Return to the freezer and continue freezing overnight. The next day rebeat until the consistency of ice cream. Freeze until set. Scoop out into pie shell. Garnish with fresh berries and mint.

*Fat content of recipe:*
  *nonfat milk:* trace
*Fat content per serving:* negligible

### Packaged Pie Fillings

If you use one of the packaged pie fillings, make a meringue shell or follow piecrust recipe (page 259).

## Puddings

Many of the packaged pudding or pie filling mixes may be used in low-fat menus. A teaspoon of ginger marmalade added to vanilla or butterscotch pudding will perk up these desserts without adding to their fat content. To help you choose those best suited to your taste, a brief chart of their fat content follows:

| *Royal® Pudding, Regular (3–4 oz. package)* (prepared with skim milk plus 2 eggs) | *Fat content per serving (⅙ recipe)* |
|---|---|
| *Key Lime Pie Filling* | 3.0 grams |
| *Lemon Pie Filling* | 3.0 grams |

| (prepared with skim milk) | Fat content per ½ cup serving | **DESSERTS** |
|---|---|---|
| Banana Cream | 0.1 gram | |
| Butterscotch | 0.2 gram | |
| Chocolate | 1.0 gram | |
| Chocolate Tapioca | 0.8 gram | |
| Custard Flavor Dessert | 0.1 gram | |
| Dark 'N' Sweet | 1.3 grams | |
| Vanilla | 0.1 gram | |
| Vanilla Tapioca | 0.1 gram | |

Royal® Pudding, Instant (3½–4½ oz. package)
(prepared with skim milk)

| Banana Cream | 0.4 gram |
|---|---|
| Butterscotch | 0.4 gram |
| Caramel Nut | 1.6 grams |
| Chocolate | 0.8 gram |
| Dark 'N' Sweet | 0.8 gram |
| Lemon | 0.7 gram |
| Mocha Nut | 1.8 grams |
| Pistachio Nut | 0.9 gram |
| Toasted Coconut | 1.9 grams |
| Vanilla | 0.4 gram |

Royal® Gelatin Desserts (3-oz. package)
(prepared as directed with water)

| All flavors | 0.0 grams |
|---|---|

Jell-O® Golden Egg Custard
(prepared with skim milk,
no egg yolk)

| | 1.4 grams |
|---|---|

Jell-O® Puddings and Pie Fillings
(prepared with skim milk)

| Banana | 0.2 gram |
|---|---|
| Butterscotch | 0.2 gram |
| Chocolate | 0.6 gram |
| Chocolate Fudge | 0.6 gram |
| Coconut Cream | 1.6 grams |

263

| | |
|---|---|
| French Vanilla | 0.2 gram |
| Milk Chocolate | 0.6 gram |
| Vanilla | 0.2 gram |
| Jell-O® Lemon Pudding and Pie Filling | |
| (prepared with | |
| 2 egg yolks) | 2.0 grams |
| (prepared with | |
| 1 whole egg) | 1.0 gram |
| Jell-O® Tapioca Puddings | |
| (prepared with skim milk) | |
| All flavors | 0.1 gram |
| Jell-O® Soft Swirl Dessert | |
| (prepared with skim milk) | |
| Chocolate | 5.1 grams |
| Peach | 2.9 grams |
| Strawberry | 2.9 grams |
| Vanilla | 2.9 grams |
| Jell-O® Gelatin | |
| (prepared as directed with water) | |
| All flavors | 0.0 grams |

## Junket® Puddings

Danish Dessert®. This is a fruit-flavored pudding which comes in three flavors: cherry–plum, currant–raspberry, and strawberry. It is made with water, and can be served with or without topping.

*Fat content of mix:* negligible

Rennet® Tablets. Milk must be used to make this dessert, and skim milk is satisfactory. The fat content of the tablets themselves is negligible.

## Lemon Lady Fingers

**1 package of lady fingers (8 pieces, net weight: 4 ounces)**

**1 package lemon pudding and pie filling (Jell-O® or Royal®)**
**Eggs or skim milk as indicated in package directions**

Line a loaf pan with wax paper. Separate each lady finger into two parts. Arrange around sides and bottom of pan. Make lemon filling according to directions on package. Beat stiff the remaining egg whites and slowly beat in the sugar. Fold this into the pudding mixture. Pour carefully into loaf pan and chill dessert in refrigerator until firm. To serve lift from pan to plate and slice.

*Fat content of recipe:*                    *6 servings*
  *lady fingers:*          8.9 grams
  *mix:*                   negligible
  *milk:*                  negligible
  *eggs, per egg:*         6.0 grams


### Baked Custard

**3 cups liquefied nonfat dry milk or skimmed milk**
**3 whole eggs**
**⅝ cup maple syrup**
**⅛ teaspoon salt**

Scald milk and salt. Stir in maple syrup. Beat eggs and slowly pour milk, salt and syrup mixture over them. Beat the custard until it is well blended. Pour into baking dish or individual molds. This quantity will fill eight small custard cups. Place molds in pan of hot water in moderate oven (325°) for about ¾ hour or until firm. To test, insert silver knife. If custard does not adhere to knife, it is done.

*Fat content of recipe:*                    *6–8 servings*
  *skimmed milk:*         0.8 gram
  *eggs:*                 18.0 grams

265

| Total: | 18.8 grams |
| Fat content per serving: | |
| 6 servings: | 3.1 grams |
| 8 servings: | 2.4 grams |

## Apple Snow

**Dash nutmeg**
**Pinch salt**
**1 teaspoon vanilla**
**1⅔ cups unsweetened applesauce**
**2 egg whites**
**¼ cup granulated sugar**

Add the nutmeg, salt, and vanilla to the applesauce. Beat the egg whites until quite stiff and then add the sugar gradually, continuing to beat constantly. Fold in applesauce. Chill and serve.

*Fat content of recipe:*     negligible     *5 servings*

## Pineapple Sponge

**2 tablespoons unflavored gelatin**
**¼ cup cold water**
**½ cup boiling water**
**½ cup sugar**
**¼ teaspoon salt**
**1 cup crushed pineapple**
**2 tablespoons lemon juice**
**2 egg whites**
**⅛ teaspoon salt**

Soak gelatin in cold water; dissolve in boiling water; add remaining ingredients. Cool until nearly set. Beat with a wire whisk until frothy. Whip egg whites and salt until stiff and fold them lightly into the gelatin mixture. Chill until firm.

### Scandinavian Pudding

**1 cup strained fruit (suggested fruits: apricots, prunes, peaches)**
**¾ cup water**
**1 teaspoon grated lemon rind**
**1 tablespoon lemon juice**
**⅛ teaspoon allspice**
**⅛ teaspoon cinnamon**
**2 tablespoons sugar**
**⅛ teaspoon salt**
**2 tablespoons cornstarch**

Combine all above ingredients. Cook, stirring until thickened. Pour into four sherbet glasses. Refrigerate. To serve, top each dessert with 1 tablespoon ice milk.

| *Fat content of recipe:* | | *4 servings* |
|---|---|---|
| *pudding:* | negligible | |
| *topping (per serving):* | 0.4 gram | |

### Cottage Cheese Dish

This may be served as a dessert or as an accompaniment to a meat course.

Beat in electric mixer at heavy-batter speed 1 12-ounce box of dry or low-fat cottage cheese. Sweeten it as desired with sugar and vanilla. Place it in a bowl. Sprinkle the top with cinnamon. Chill.

Serve the mixture very cold with fresh Cranberry Relish (page 200), or with stewed cranberries, stewed cherries, crushed and sweetened strawberries, etc. If you wish to use this as an accompaniment to a meat course (turkey, chicken, veal, etc.), serve the cheese and fruit side by side in small dishes.

**Cherry Whip**

1 teaspoon unflavored gelatin
¼ cup cold water
1 No. 303 can pie cherries (dark red, pitted)
⅞ cup sugar
2 egg whites
Pinch of salt

Soak gelatin in cold water. Combine and heat to the boiling point the contents of the can of cherries. Add sugar and stir until dissolved. Drain the cherries, reserving the fruit and juice. Dissolve the gelatin in the hot juice. Chill this mixture over cracked ice. When it begins to thicken, fold in cherries, salt, and egg whites beaten until stiff. Chill.

*Fat content of recipe:*       negligible       *5 servings*

**Steamed Holiday Cranberry Pudding**

1 cup raw cranberries, coarsely chopped
1 cup finely diced, drained canned pineapple slices or chunks
⅓ cup finely diced citron or mixed candied fruits
½ cup molasses
¼ teaspoon cinnamon
¼ teaspoon powdered cloves
1½ cups sifted all-purpose flour
¼ teaspoon nutmeg
½ teaspoon salt

**1 teaspoon baking soda
2 tablespoons cold water**

Combine fruits, molasses, and spices. Add sifted flour and salt. Dissolve soda in cold water, add, and blend well. Turn the batter into a greased or oiled 1½-quart pudding mold, cover with greased lid or double parchment paper tied on tightly. If a pudding mold is not available, a coffee can may be used. Place covered mold in pot or skillet on a rack. Add hot water so that at least half the mold is immersed at all times. Steam 2 hours. Puddings may also be successfully steamed in greased or oiled double boiler.

This pudding may be served without sauce, or it may be topped with the following fluffy hard sauce or lemon yogurt. Since the fat content of the pudding is so low (entire recipe less than 2 grams), the use of the fluffy hard sauce or yogurt is possible without making the fat content per serving of dessert unduly high.

### Fluffy Hard Sauce

**1 cup sugar
1 tablespoon butter
3 tablespoons whipping cream
3 egg whites
⅛ teaspoon salt
1 teaspoon or more vanilla, rum, or
sherry**

Sift sugar. Beat butter until soft and gradually add sugar. Add 1 tablespoon of the cream. Beat these ingredients until they are well blended. Whip the egg whites and salt until stiff. Fold them into the sugar mixture. Add the remaining 2 tablespoons of cream and the flavoring. Beat the sauce well. Pile it in a dish. Chill it thoroughly.

269

| Fat content of pudding recipe: | | 5 servings |
|---|---|---|
| flour: | 1.5 grams | |
| Fat content of sauce recipe: | | 10 servings |
| butter: | 12.0 grams | |
| cream: | 15.0 grams | |
| Total: | 27.0 grams | |
| Fat content of yogurt: | | |
| per tablespoon: | 0.3 gram | |
| Fat content per serving of complete dessert: | | |
| pudding: | 0.3 gram | |
| sauce: | 2.7 grams | |
| yogurt: | 0.3 gram | |
| Total: | 0.6 or 3.0 grams | |

### Steamed Cranberry Pudding

2 cups coarsely chopped raw
  cranberries
1⅓ cups flour
½ teaspoon salt
1 teaspoon soda
¼ teaspoon cinnamon
¼ teaspoon cloves
¼ teaspoon mace
⅓ cup hot water
½ cup molasses

Add cranberries to sifted dry ingredients. Add water
and molasses; mix well. Fill greased 1-pound coffee
can, pudding mold, or individual custard cups two-
thirds full. Cover mold tightly. Steam 2 hours as
instructed in Steamed Holiday Cranberry Pudding,
pages 268–269. This pudding freezes satisfactorily but it
should be reheated before serving. Suggest using
Fluffy Hard Sauce, page 269, lemon yogurt, or brandy
(ignited) over pudding.

*Fat content of recipe:*             *6 servings*
   *flour:*   1.3 grams
*Fat content per serving, without topping:*     0.2 gram

### Black Pudding

> **1 cup dark molasses**
> **1 beaten egg**
> **⅔ cup boiling water**
> **1 teaspoon ginger**
> **1 teaspoon soda**
> **1½ cups flour**
> **¾ teaspoon baking powder**

Mix egg and molasses. Add dry ingredients and boiling water. Put in pan approximately 8 inches in diameter and 2½ to 3 inches deep. Steam 1 to 1½ hours. (The steamer is covered, but not the mold which contains the pudding.) Serve hot with Fluffy Hard Sauce, page 269, or lemon yogurt.

*Fat content of recipe:*             *6 servings*
   *egg:*        6.0 grams
   *flour:*      1.5 grams
   *Total:*      7.5 grams
*Fat content per serving, without topping:*    1.3 grams

### Prepared Plum Puddings

Two prepared plum puddings of suitable fat content are:

|  | *Per 4-ounce serving* |
|---|---|
| *Nestlé Crosse and* | |
| *Blackwell® Plum Pudding* | 1.0 gram  fat |
| *R & R® Plum Pudding* | 1.2 grams fat |

271

## Jellies

### Wine Jelly

    2 tablespoons gelatin
    ¼ cup cold water
    ¾ cup boiling water
    ½ cup sugar
1¾ cups orange juice
    6 tablespoons lemon juice
    1 cup well-flavored wine

Soak gelatin in ¼ cup cold water. Dissolve it in ¾ cup boiling water. This makes a soft jelly of a very good consistency to serve in sherbet glasses or from a bowl. If a stiff jelly is desired for molds, increase the gelatin to 3 tablespoonfuls. Stir in ½ cup or more sugar until dissolved. One-half cupful is sufficient if both the oranges and wine are sweet. Cool these ingredients. Add the orange juice, lemon juice, and wine. Add a little red coloring if the mixture is not a good color. Chill.

*Fat content of recipe:*    negligible    *8 servings*

## Fruit Desserts

Fruits are of negligible fat content. The two exceptions are avocado and coconut. Avocado should be omitted entirely. If coconut is used, it must be calculated in the total fat content of the menu. Otherwise fruits may be eaten as desired. See Table 3, page 354.

### Broiled Grapefruit

Remove seeds and cut around sections of grapefruit halves. Place scoop of low-calorie vanilla ice milk on top of each grapefruit half. Cover entire top of grape-fruit half with meringue topping. Brown under broiler. Serve immediately.

*Fat content of recipe:*
  *½ medium grapefruit:*          negligible
*Fat content per serving:*
  The total fat content per serving is, of course, dependent upon the size of the scoop of ice milk. The following figures will serve as a guide:
  *low-calorie ice milk, fat content:*
    *per pint:*              13.3 grams
    *per tablespoon:*        0.4 gram

### Orange Compote

Cut the yellow rind off four oranges. Cut rind into thin slices, add to it and boil for 20 minutes:

**2 cups water**
**1½ cups sugar**
**⅛ teaspoon salt**

Skin and remove the membrane from the four oranges and five additional oranges. Place the sections in a serving bowl or in individual sherbet dishes. Pour the hot syrup and rind over them. Chill the compote. Before serving you may add to the total recipe 2 tablespoons rum or liqueur, or a suitable portion of this amount if served in individual dishes.

*Fat content of recipe:*     negligible     *5 servings*

### Tropical Compote with Wine Sauce

**1 package frozen pineapple cubes**
**2 sliced bananas**
**1 large grapefruit in sections**
**1 cup seeded Malaga grapes**

273

½ cup sugar
⅓ cup sherry
2 tablespoons Madeira wine

Prepare fruit. Add sugar and wine. Chill in refrigerator.

*Fat content of recipe:*     negligible     *6 servings*


## Pear Cardinal

5 to 6 Anjou pears
2 cups water
1½ cups sugar
2 teaspoons vanilla
¼ teaspoon salt
1 cup red jelly
1 tablespoon lemon juice
3 tablespoons grenadine syrup

Peel pears, leaving stem on. In shallow pan, mix together water, sugar, vanilla, and salt. Heat to boiling; add whole pears and simmer 20 to 25 minutes, or until pears are tender. Turn pears occasionally. Remove from heat and let pears cool in syrup. Chill. Prepare sauce by heating jelly, lemon juice, and grenadine syrup in top of double boiler over boiling water. Heat until smooth, stirring occasionally. Remove from heat and chill. To serve, place one pear upright in each dessert dish and spoon sauce over top.

*Fat content of recipe:*     negligible     *5–6 servings*


## Festive Pineapple

Hollow out two halves of a large fresh pineapple; refill with the pineapple fruit, diced, and lemon sherbet; top with meringue and brown quickly under the broiler.

274

Fat content of recipe:
  pineapple:                    negligible
  sherbet:
    milk sherbet, 1 pint:       5.5 grams
    fruit ice, 1 pint:          trace

## Cakes

### Angel Food Cake

Your favorite recipe for angel food will do as well as any other. Its fat content is negligible. If you wish to use a packaged mix or commercially baked angel food, you may. There are numerous ways in which this delicious cake can be used.

### Angel Cake Bars or Balls

Bake angel cake in bread pans. Cut into 1-inch slices, then into bars 1 inch thick and about 2 inches long. Spread the bars with any approved icing.

To make balls, bake the batter in deep muffin tins. Shape the cakes, while warm, into balls. Ice with any approved icing.

If the icing is rather soft, it will be easier to spread on these light cakes.

### Angel Food Layers

Slice an angel food cake crosswise into three layers. Fill between layers with fruit sherbet. If you use two different kinds of sherbet, the contrasting colors and flavors give a party air to this dessert.

Fat content of recipe:
  angel food cake:              negligible
  milk sherbet, 1 pint:         5.5 grams

275

## Cherry Angel Jubilees

Prepare sauce for Cherries Jubilee (page 242). Keep warm.

Bake mounds of angel food batter (about ¼ cup each) on ungreased baking sheet at 375° for 10 to 15 minutes until a light golden brown. (Remaining batter may stand while cakes are baking.) Remove from baking sheet at once. Place in chafing dish or on large serving plate. Spoon sauce over cakes. Just before serving top each with a small sugar cube soaked in lemon extract. Light.

*Fat content of recipe:*     negligible     *Yield: 3 dozen*


## Daffodil Cake

**1 package angel food cake mix**
**4 egg yolks**
**3 tablespoons orange juice**
**2 tablespoons sugar**
**½ teaspoon vanilla**

Mix angel food cake according to the directions on the package; omit vanilla until later. Set aside. Beat egg yolks, orange juice, and sugar until very thick and light. Fold in one-third of angel food cake mixture, using fifteen fold-over strokes. Fold vanilla into remaining two-thirds cake mixture. Place alternate yellow and white mixtures in a 10-inch ungreased tube pan to make a marble effect. Cut through the batter twice with a knife to break large air bubbles. Bake in preheated 375° oven 35–40 minutes. Invert pan. Do not remove cake until thoroughly cooled, about 1 hour. Frost with Marshmallow Orange Icing.

*Fat content of recipe:*                    *12 servings*

| | |
|---|---|
| *angel food cake mix:* | negligible |
| *egg yolks:* | 24.0 grams |
| *Total:* | 24.0 grams |
| *Fat content per serving:* | 2.0 grams |

## Marshmallow Orange Icing

**2 egg whites**
**1 cup sugar**
**4 tablespoons orange juice**
**16 marshmallows**

Place unbeaten egg whites, sugar, and orange juice in saucepan; beat with egg beater until mixed thoroughly. Cook on low heat, beating constantly with rotary beater until frosting will stand in peaks. Remove from stove and beat until thick enough to spread. Fold in marshmallows which have been cut in quarters. Spread on top and sides of cake.

*Fat content of recipe:* negligible

## Lemon Angel Cake

**1 angel cake**
**1 package lemon pudding and pie filling mix (Jell-O® or Royal®)**

Slice angel cake crosswise into three layers. Make up pudding mix according to instructions on package for pie filling. Cool. Spread the cooled filling between the layers and over the top. Put layers together and chill in refrigerator for several hours.

*Fat content of recipe:*
| | |
|---|---|
| *angel food:* | negligible |
| *mix:* | negligible |

277

milk:                          negligible
eggs, per egg:                 6.0 grams

## Confetti, Lemon Custard, or Strawberry Angel Food Cake Mixes (Betty Crocker®)

The fat content of these mixes is negligible.

## Mocha Angel Cake

Ice an angel cake with the Mocha Icing on page 287.

Fat content of                              8 servings
  Mocha Icing:        10.2 grams
Fat content per
  serving:            1.3 grams

## Baked Alaska

**1 layer angel food cake**
**1 quart low-calorie ice milk (brick)**
**5 stiffly beaten egg whites**
**⅔ cup sugar**

Trim layer of angel food cake 1 inch bigger on all sides than brick of low-calorie ice milk. Place on a wooden cutting board covered with heavy paper. To make meringue, gradually add two-thirds cup sugar to five stiffly beaten egg whites; beat until meringue forms peaks. After making meringue, place 1 quart brick ice milk on cake. Spread meringue over ice milk and cake; seal carefully to edges of cake. Sprinkle top with granulated sugar for a snowy effect. Bake in very hot oven (450°) until golden brown—about 5 minutes. To serve, slide from board to plate.

*Fat content of recipe:*                        *6 servings*
  *1 quart low-calorie ice milk:*           26.5 grams
*Fat content per serving:*                    4.4 grams

## Chocolate Icebox Angel Food Dessert

**1 bar angel food cake**
**1 package instant chocolate pudding
(Royal®)**

Mix chocolate pudding as directed on package, using liquefied nonfat milk. Slice crosswise through angel food, so that you have three layers. When pudding has set for five minutes or more, spread layers and cover outside of cake. Place in refrigerator and allow to chill for 2 hours. Slice and serve.

*Fat content of recipe:*                        *8 servings*
  *filling (including skim milk):*            3.2 grams
*Fat content per slice:*                        0.4 gram

## English Sponge Cake

**1 cup sifted confectioners' sugar**
**⅔ cup sifted cornstarch**
**3 eggs, separated**
**⅛ teaspoon cream of tartar**
**2 tablespoons water**
**½ teaspoon vanilla**

Preheat oven to 350°.

Sift together one-half cup of the sugar and the cornstarch three times. Set aside. Beat egg whites, cream of tartar, and water in a large bowl with a rotary beater or electric mixer until the mixture stands in soft peaks. Gradually beat in the remaining one-half cup sugar, a little at a time, continuing to beat until stiff

279

peaks form when the beater is raised. Add the egg yolks and vanilla; beat only until well blended. Fold in the sugar-cornstarch mixture, a little at a time, until it is all added and is well blended.

Pour the batter into two ungreased eight-inch cake pans and bake until the cake rebounds to the touch when pressed lightly in the center, about 30 minutes. Place on wire racks to cool. Cut around the edge of the cakes before removing from the pans.

Spread strawberry or raspberry jam between the sponge layers. Sprinkle the top with confectioners' sugar. Cut into wedges to serve.

| | |
|---|---|
| *Fat content of recipe:* | *8 servings* |
| *eggs:* | 18.0 grams |
| *Fat content per serving:* | 2.3 grams |

### Hot Milk Sponge Cake

1½ cups sugar
3 eggs
1½ cups cake flour, sifted before measuring (⅞ cup bread flour equals 1 cup cake flour)
1½ teaspoons any baking powder
½ teaspoon salt
¾ cup liquefied nonfat milk
1 teaspoon vanilla or ½ teaspoon grated lemon rind

Sift sugar. Beat eggs until very light. Add sugar to eggs very slowly, beating constantly. Beat for 5 minutes by hand or 2½ minutes in mixer. Sift the flour before measuring and then resift with baking powder and salt. Fold these ingredients quickly and briefly, all at one time, into the egg mixture. Heat but do not boil the milk and add it rapidly all at one time; fold mixture again briefly. Add vanilla or lemon rind. Bake the batter in ungreased 9-inch tube pan in a moderate oven (325°) for 1 hour.

Note: The uncooked Lemon Icing on page 287 is excellent on this cake.

| *Fat content of recipe:* | *10 servings* |
|---|---|
| *milk:* | negligible |
| *eggs:* | 18.0 grams |
| *flour:* | 1.5 grams |
| *Total:* | 19.5 grams |
| *Fat content per serving:* | 2.0 grams |

### Lazy Daisy Cake

This is a good cake when you need a quick family dessert.

> **2 eggs**
> **1 tablespoon shortening**
> **1 cup sugar**
> **1 teaspoon vanilla**
> **1 cup flour**
> **1 teaspoon baking powder**
> **¼ teaspoon salt**
> **½ cup hot liquefied nonfat milk**

Sift together three times the flour, baking powder, and salt. Put shortening in milk and heat to boiling point. Shortening will then be melted. Beat eggs; gradually add sugar. Mix dry ingredients together. Add dry ingredients and milk to egg mixture, stirring until blended. Add vanilla. Bake 30 minutes at 350° in tube pan.

| *Fat content of recipe:* | *8 servings* |
|---|---|
| *eggs:* | 12.0 grams |
| *shortening:* | 13.0 grams |

| milk: | negligible |
|---|---|
| *Total:* | 25.0 grams |
| *Fat content per serving:* | 3.1 grams |

## Gingerbread

See pages 251–252.

## Spice Cake

 **2 cups all-purpose flour**
½ **teaspoon salt**
 **1 teaspoon cinnamon**
½ **teaspoon each nutmeg and cloves**
 **1 teaspoon soda**
 **1 cup sugar**
 **2 tablespoons butter**
 **1 can Campbell® tomato soup (10¾ ounces)**
 **1 cup raisins**

Preheat oven to 350°.

Sift the flour before measuring. Resift with the salt, cinnamon, nutmeg, cloves, and soda. Sift sugar. Cream butter until soft. Add the sifted sugar gradually and cream these ingredients well. Stir the flour mixture in about three parts into the sugar mixture, alternating with thirds of the tomato soup. Stir the batter until smooth after each addition. Fold in raisins. Bake in 9-inch tube pan, treated with Pam®, Lean-Fry®, or Pan Pal®, for about 45 minutes.

| *Fat content of recipe:* | *Yield: 10 wedges* |
|---|---|
| *flour:* | 2.0 grams |
| *butter:* | 24.0 grams |
| *soup:* | 4.5 grams |

### War Cake

This cake which has good flavor and texture is appreciably lower in fat content than the preceding recipe, and it will be particularly helpful in diets with a considerable degree of restriction.

> **2 cups brown sugar**
> **2 cups hot water**
> **2 teaspoons corn oil**
> **1 package raisins**
> **1 teaspoon salt**
> **1 teaspoon cinnamon**
> **1 teaspoon cloves**
> **3 cups flour**
> **1 teaspoon soda dissolved in 2 teaspoons hot water**

Boil together for five minutes after the mixture begins to bubble the brown sugar, hot water, corn oil, raisins, salt, cinnamon, and cloves. Cool. (Be sure the mixture is cold before proceeding.) Add the flour and dissolved soda. Bake in Teflon®-lined tube pan or one treated with Pam®, Lean-Fry®, or Pan Pal® for one hour at 375°.

Serve topped with lemon yogurt, if desired.

| | |
|---|---|
| *Fat content of recipe:* | *Yield: 10 wedges* |
| corn oil: | 9.3 grams |
| flour: | 3.0 grams |
| Total: | 12.3 grams |
| *Fat content per serving:* | 1.2 grams |
| *Fat content of yogurt* | |
| *(8-ounce carton):* | 3.0–4.0 grams |

### Pain d'Epice

1½ cups water
1 teaspoon anise seed
1 cup honey
1¼ cups sugar
1 tablespoon baking soda
4½ cups sifted flour
¼ teaspoon salt
1 teaspoon cinnamon
½ teaspoon nutmeg
6 tablespoons mixed chopped candied fruit

Bring water with anise to a boil. Remove from heat. Add honey and sugar and stir until the sugar is dissolved. Add soda. Sift together flour, salt, cinnamon, and nutmeg. Add candied fruits and mix. Add honey mixture to dry ingredients and stir until smooth.

Turn into two 8½ × 4½ × 2¾ inch loaf pans which are Teflon®-coated or treated with Pam®, Lean-Fry®, or Pan Pal®. Bake in a 350° oven for about one hour.

These loaves freeze well. They also retain their freshness for a considerable period in the refrigerator.

*Fat content of recipe:*                    *Yield: 2 loaves*
  *flour:* 4.5 grams


### Fruit Cake (Unbaked)

¾ cup evaporated skimmed milk (undiluted)
2 dozen finely cut regular marshmallows or 2½ cups miniature marshmallows (approximately 6¼ ounces)
⅓ cup bourbon

284

6 dozen 2½-inch-square graham crackers
½ rounded teaspoon cinnamon
½ rounded teaspoon nutmeg
¼ rounded teaspoon cloves
1½ cups seedless raisins (preferably half
golden, half dark)
¾ cup finely cut dates
1¼ cups candied fruit, cut-up

Put the milk, marshmallows, and bourbon in a bowl
and let stand until needed. Roll the graham crackers
into fine crumbs. If rolled in a plastic bag, the crumbs
will not scatter. Put the crumbs, spices, raisins, and
dates into a large bowl and add the candied fruit. Add
milk mixture. Mix with a spoon, then with the hands,
until crumbs are moistened. Press firmly into a tube or
loaf pan. Top with additional fruit if desired. Cover
tightly. Chill two days before slicing. Keep in a cool
place. The fat content per serving will vary according to
the size slice served.

*Fat content of recipe:*
  *evaporated skimmed milk:*      0.4 gram
  *graham crackers:*              54.0 grams
  *Total:*                        54.4 grams


## Holland Honey Loaves

The Holland Honey Cake Company of Holland, Michi-
gan, makes three loaves of dark cake with varied
seasonings and fruit. They are all of low fat content.

*Premium Honey Cake®:*          1.5 grams per
                                13-ounce loaf
*Honey Fruit Cake®:*            1.9 grams per
                                13-ounce loaf

285

*Raisin Dake Loaf®:*       1.1 grams per
13-ounce loaf

Thus a half-inch thick slice of any one of the three would contain approximately 0.1 gram of fat.

All three products are made with honey, rye flour, buttermilk, spices, and leavening. The Honey Fruit Cake® contains, also, mixed fruits, and raisins. The Raisin Date Loaf® has raisins and dates added to the batter.

## Icings

### Seven-Minute White Icing

Sufficient to cover the tops and sides of two 9-inch layers. One-half this amount will make a light icing for a 9-inch loaf cake. Use the full amount for a heavy icing.

> **2 unbeaten egg whites**
> **1½ cups sugar**
> **5 tablespoons cold water**
> **¼ teaspoon cream of tartar**
> **1½ teaspoons light corn syrup (optional)**
> **1 teaspoon vanilla**

Place in top of double boiler and beat until thoroughly blended all ingredients except vanilla. Place over rapidly boiling water and beat constantly with a rotary beater or with a wire whisk for 7 minutes. Remove the icing from the fire. Add vanilla. Continue beating until the icing is the right consistency to spread.

Note: Nearly all boiled white icings are fat free. Composed as they are of sugar and egg white, they have no fat content. Use your favorite recipe for this type of icing if you wish.

### Lemon Icing (Uncooked)

This is sufficient for an average angel food or sponge cake cooked in 9-inch tube pan.

Place two egg whites in mixer; beat and, when they begin to stiffen, gradually add confectioners' sugar, beating constantly, until this is the right consistency to spread. Flavor to your taste with lemon juice and grated lemon rind.

*Fat content of recipe:* negligible

### Marshmallow Orange Icing

See page 277.

### Mocha Icing (Uncooked)

This covers generously twenty-four medium cupcakes or an average sponge cake or angel food cake.

> **1¼ cups confectioners' sugar**
> **6 level tablespoons cocoa**
> **¼ cup very strong instant coffee (liquid)**
> **1 teaspoon vanilla**

Stir ingredients together.

*Fat content of recipe:*
  *cocoa:* 10.2 grams

### Party Icing (uncooked)

This is sufficient for an average two-layer cake.

> **1 egg white**
> **1 glass tart red jelly (12 ounces)**
> **1 pinch salt**

287

Put unbeaten egg white in a bowl. Add jelly and salt. Beat until mixture stands in peaks. This icing never gets hard.

*Fat content of recipe:* negligible

## Candies

The following candies are compatible with low-fat eating when calories are not restricted. They have negligible fat content for an average serving.

Candied fruits as apricots, cherries, citron, figs, ginger root, grapefruit, lemon, orange peel, and pineapple
Divinity, plain
Fondant
Gumdrops
Hard candy
Jelly beans
Lollipops
Marshmallows, plain
Mints, plain
Sea foam, plain

### Royal Round-ups

**4 cups Kellogg's Sugar Frosted Flakes®**
**1 package Royal Instant Chocolate Pudding®**
**½ cup light corn syrup**

Measure 2½ cups Sugar Frosted Flakes® into a large wide bowl. Crush remaining Sugar Frosted Flakes® slightly. Set aside. Add pudding mix to corn syrup, stirring until well blended; pour over Sugar Frosted

Flakes®, mixing lightly until well coated. Drop by teaspoonfuls into crushed flakes, rolling until coated. Press lightly together. Arrange on platter and let stand until hardened. (These do not need refrigeration.)

| Fat content | Yield: approximately |
|---|---|
| of recipe: | thirty 1-inch candies |
| Frosted Flakes®: | 1.6 grams |
| Royal Pudding®: | 3.2 grams |
| Total: | 4.8 grams |
| Fat content per candy: | 0.2 gram |

DESSERTS

In low-fat menus, we are concerned with actual fat content of the foods and not with calories per se. Beverages, therefore, like other foods, are considered for their fat content.

Certain beverages are either fat-free or of negligible fat content:

Fruit juices and vegetable juices
Tea
Coffee
Ginger ale
Other carbonated beverages, including cola-type
Alcoholic beverages: beer, wines, and liquor

Nonetheless, for those readers who are using a lowered fat diet for weight control, it is important to realize that alcoholic beverages and carbonated bever-

291

ages have a high enough *calorie content* that free use will interfere with weight reduction. The following table gives the caloric values of such beverages.

| | |
|---|---|
| beer, 12 fl. oz. | 150 calories |
| gin, rum, vodka, whiskey, | |
| 1½ fl. oz. | |
| 80 proof | 100 calories |
| 86 proof | 105 calories |
| 90 proof | 110 calories |
| 94 proof | 115 calories |
| 100 proof | 125 calories |
| wines, 3½ fl. oz. | |
| dessert | 140 calories |
| table | 85 calories |
| carbonated water, 12 fl. oz. | |
| sweetened (quinine sodas) | 115 calories |
| unsweetened (club sodas) | 0 calories |
| cola type, 12 fl. oz. | 145 calories |
| fruit-flavored sodas and | |
| Tom Collins mixes, | |
| 12 fl. oz. | 170 calories |
| ginger ale, 12 fl. oz. | 115 calories |
| root beer, 12 fl. oz. | 150 calories |

Milk does contain fat, and its fat content must be considered in menu planning.

| Fat content: | grams per cup | grams per quart |
|---|---|---|
| Whole milk | 9.0 | 36.0 |
| Partly skimmed (2%) | 5.0 | 20.0 |
| Skim | trace | 1.0 |
| Buttermilk (skim) | trace | 1.0 |
| Evaporated, unsweetened | 20.0 | 80.0 |
| Condensed, sweetened | 27.0 | 108.0 |
| Evaporated skimmed milk, undiluted | 0.5 | 2.0 |

| | | |
|---|---|---|
| *Evaporated skimmed milk,* | | |
| *diluted* | 0.3 | 1.0 |

In the recipes in this book wherever "nonfat dry milk, liquefied," is used, skim milk from the dairy may be substituted. You will note in the list above that there is some difference between evaporated skimmed milk and skim milk. When evaporated skimmed milk is used in a recipe, it is so stated. Evaporated skimmed milk is a canned product in which part of the water has been evaporated from skim milk. Do not confuse evaporated *skimmed* milk with evaporated (whole) milk.

Some dairy skim milk is now fortified with Vitamin A and Vitamin D.

Most commercial buttermilk is made from skimmed milk. However, some dairies label whole lactic acid milk as buttermilk. Such milk would have the same fat content as whole milk. If there is any doubt in your mind, check with your local dairy.

## Milk or Cream Substitutes

The authors cannot recommend the use of these substances in cooking, because they simply put back into the food some of the fat which low-fat cookery removes. For persons on a relatively liberal fat allowance (e.g., 50 grams per day), such substitutes might be used in place of coffee cream. The following table gives comparable figures from manufacturers analyses.

| | | |
|---|---|---|
| *Pream®* | *1 teaspoon* | 0.7 gram fat |
| *Pream®* | *1 teaspoon dry* | 0.7 gram fat |
| | *recommended for* | |
| | *1 cup coffee* | |

293

| | | |
|---|---|---|
| Coffee Rich®, powdered | 1 tablespoon reconstituted | 1.0 gram fat |
| Coffee Rich Liquid® | 1 tablespoon | 1.9 grams fat |
| light coffee or table cream | 1 tablespoon | 3.0 grams fat |
| half and half | 1 tablespoon | 2.0 grams fat |

## Cocoa Beverage I

**1 cup skim milk**
**1 tablespoon cocoa powder**
**½ to 1 tablespoon sugar**
**Pinch of salt**

Combine ingredients and cook over direct heat until blended. Continue cooking in double boiler. Beverage may be covered and allowed to sit over the hot water, if desired.

| *Fat content of recipe:* | | *Yield: 1 cup* |
|---|---|---|
| *milk:* | trace | |
| *cocoa:* | 1.7 grams | |
| *Total per cup:* | 1.7 grams | |

## Cocoa Beverage II

**1 cup skim milk**
**2 tablespoons Chocolate Sauce II (pages 191–192)**

Stir sauce into milk and heat in saucepan.

| *Fat content of recipe:* | | *Yield: 1 cup* |
|---|---|---|
| *milk:* | trace | |
| *sauce:* | 0.8 gram | |
| *Total per cup:* | 0.8 gram | |

## Spiced Tea

1 cup sugar
1 cup water
2 teaspoons black tea
2 sprigs fresh mint or 2 teaspoons dried
  mint
½ teaspoon allspice
6 tablespoons lemon juice
¾ cup orange juice
2 quarts boiling water

Boil together the sugar and one cup water for 5 minutes. Add the tea, mint and allspice. Cover and simmer ten minutes. Strain. Add the remaining ingredients and serve hot immediately or chill and serve cold.

| *Fat content* | | *Yield:* |
|---|---|---|
| *of recipe:* | negligible | *12 servings* |

In general, you can divide breakfast eaters into two groups: (a) those who eat a very light meal (orange juice, toast, and coffee, for example) and (b) those who believe in starting the day with a "good, substantial meal" under their belts. If you belong to the first group and decide to experiment with low-fat cooking, you will find that your breakfast habits are your ally. If you are willing to substitute marmalade or jelly for butter on your toast and take your coffee black (or with double-strength skim milk or evaporated skimmed milk), you can have nearly your whole fat allowance for your other two meals. If, however, you belong in the second group and believe in ham and eggs (or breakfast bacon, or a good, tangy sausage), you will have to give the matter more thought. For the ham-and-eggers, here is a summary of common breakfast foods

297

and some suggestions for other dishes that will provide interest and variety without using all your fat allowance first thing in the morning!

*Fat content:*

*Bread (fat content is unaltered by toasting):*

| | |
|---|---|
| Boston brown bread,<br> 1 slice<br> (3 by ¾ inch) | 1.0 gram |
| Cracked wheat, 1 slice | 1.0 gram |
| Holland Rusk®, 1 piece | 0.6 gram |
| Raisin, 1 slice | 1.0 gram |
| Rye, American, 1 slice | trace |
| White, 1 slice | 1.0 gram |
| Whole wheat, 1 slice | 1.0 gram |
| Wonder®: | |
| English Muffin,<br> 1 muffin | 1.0 gram |
| Raisin Round,<br> 1 round | 1.5 grams |
| Scones, 1 scone | 1.3 grams |

*Bread, 1-pound loaf (fat content is unaltered by toasting):*

| | |
|---|---|
| French or Vienna | 14.0 grams |
| Italian | 4.0 grams |
| Pumpernickel | 5.0 grams |

*Cereals, dry and cooked (low in fat content—in general less than 1 gram of fat per average serving)*

*Some varieties:*

| | |
|---|---|
| Bran flakes (40% bran),<br> 1 cup | 1.0 gram |
| Corn flakes, 1 cup | trace |
| Cream of Wheat®, ¾<br> cup cooked | 0.3 gram |
| Farina®, 1 cup cooked | 0.2 gram |
| Grape Nuts®, ¼ cup | 0.1 gram |

| | |
|---|---|
| Grape Nuts Flakes®, ⅔ cup | 0.3 gram |
| Grits, 1 cup cooked | trace |
| Oatmeal, 1 cup cooked | 2.0 grams |
| Puffed Rice®, 1 cup | 0.3 gram |
| Puffed Wheat®, 1 cup | 0.5 gram |
| Rice, 1 cup cooked | trace |
| Rice Krispies®, 1 cup | 0.4 gram |
| Shredded Wheat Miniatures®, ¾ cup | 0.4 gram |
| Special K®, 1¼ cups | 0.3 gram |
| Cereals, "Natural" (containing ingredients not present in other dry cereals such as nuts, vegetable oil, coconut, and therefore, markedly higher in fat content): depending upon brand, 1 serving (¼–⅓ cup) | 4.0–7.0 grams |
| Butter or margarine, ½ tablespoon[1] (approximately equal to standard pat, 7 grams) | 6.0 grams |
| Egg, 1 large-size | 6.0 grams |
| Bacon, broiled or fried, and drained, 2 slices (15 grams) | 8.0 grams |
| Canadian bacon, raw, 4 ounces | 16.3 grams |
| Ham, cured, 1 pound as purchased, without bone | 159.0 grams |
| Country-style sausage, link, smoked, 1 pound | 141.1 grams |
| Pork sausage, links or bulk, raw, 1 pound as purchased | 230.4 grams |

B
R
E
A
K
F
A
S
T

[1]With a product of such high fat content as butter or margarine, reasonable accuracy in handling is important.

299

| | |
|---|---|
| *Jam, jelly, marmalade (unless it contains nuts), and syrups (no butter added)* | 0.0 grams |
| *Cottage cheese, 1 cup:* | |
| *uncreamed* | 1.0 gram |
| *low-fat* | 3.4–6.8 grams |
| *Fruits, fruit juices, vegetable juices* | negligible |
| *Coffee* | 0.0 grams |
| *Tea* | 0.0 grams |
| *Milk, 1 cup:* | |
| *whole* | 9.0 grams |
| *partly skimmed (2%)* | 5.0 grams |
| *skimmed* | trace |
| *buttermilk* | trace |
| *evaporated skimmed, undiluted* | 0.5 gram |
| *evaporated skimmed, diluted* | 0.3 gram |
| *Cocoa, using 1 tablespoon cocoa powder (1.7 g. fat) and 1 cup skimmed milk to yield 1 cup cocoa beverage* | 1.7 grams |
| *Cream, 1 tablespoon:* | |
| *half and half* | 2.0 grams |
| *light or coffee* | 3.0 grams |
| *heavy or whipping* | 6.0 grams |
| *Milk or cream substitutes, per serving (See Beverage chapter, pages 293–294):* | 0.7–1.9 grams |

From this summary you will see that you can eat with

freedom:

jams, jellies, marmalade (without nuts), syrups (no
    butter added)
fruits, fruit juices, vegetable juices
tea, coffee, skim milk, buttermilk
dry cottage cheese (uncreamed)

You can have reasonable freedom with the following
items, although they should be counted in the fat
content of the diet:

breads, plain or toasted
cereals (except "Natural" cereals)
cocoa as a beverage
low-fat cottage cheese

You must exercise care in your use of
  eggs
and even more care with
  Canadian bacon
and use seldom or not at all:
  sausage
  bacon
  ham
  butter or oleomargarine
  cream

## Cereals

When fresh fruits are in season: peaches, strawberries,
blueberries, raspberries; a bowl of cereal and skim
milk topped with one of these fruits is a light and
appetizing breakfast. Bananas, available year-round,
are a pleasing addition, also.

Remember that the so-called "Natural" cereals may
contain vegetable oils, nuts, coconut, and are, therefore, markedly higher in fat content than the standard

**BREAKFAST**

301

dry cereals. Ingredients and fat content are listed on the package labels of these cereals.

## Eggs

There are a number of fresh egg substitutes now on the market. Some have lowered cholesterol, fat, and calorie content and are suitable for use in low-fat menus. Others have emulsifiers—usually unsaturated vegetable oils—added to replace the emulsifiers present in egg yolk. These vegetable oils are fats and, therefore, this group of egg substitutes *cannot* be included in lowered-fat menus. Read labels on such products with care. The table below will give you comparative figures for one product which is suitable:

*Fat content:*
    *1 large fresh egg*                6.0 grams
    *Tillie Lewis Tasti Diet Eggstra®*
        *(Tillie Lewis Foods Inc.*
        *Stockton, California 95201)*
        *½ package equals*
        *1 large egg*               1.2 grams

If you decide to have an egg for breakfast, use one of the following methods of cooking:

poach
soft cook
hard cook
scramble, without added butter (You can do this by
      scrambling the egg in a double boiler, if you
      wish; this will produce a delicate, creamy tex-
      ture, but is a slower method than using a skillet;

if you use a skillet, it should be Teflon®-lined or treated [see page 45].)

**Poached Egg Supreme**

**½ ounce smoked sliced beef**
**1 egg, poached**
**½ English muffin, toasted**

Crisp the smoked sliced beef in skillet. It will not be necessary to add fat to do this. Poach egg and toast English muffin. Place the meat on the toasted muffin half. Top with poached egg.

*Fat content of recipe:*
| | |
|---|---|
| *½ ounce smoked sliced beef:* | 1.0 gram |
| *½ English muffin:* | 0.5 gram |
| *egg:* | 6.0 grams |
| *Fat content per serving:* | 7.5 grams |

On a warm morning an eggnog is appetizing. Follow this recipe:

**Eggnog**

**1 egg**
**1 cup liquefied nonfat milk**
**To your taste: cinnamon, nutmeg, sugar, vanilla**

Place all ingredients in bowl and beat with egg beater until thoroughly mixed and somewhat frothy. Pour into glass.

*Fat content of recipe:*
| | |
|---|---|
| *nonfat milk:* | trace |
| *egg:* | 6.0 grams |
| *Total:* | 6.0 grams |

303

## Pancakes and Waffles

Pancakes or waffles should be cooked on a Teflon®-coated griddle or waffle iron, or on utensils treated with Pam®, Lean-Fry® or Pan Pal®.

You can use syrup, jam, jelly, or sugar on the pancakes, but not butter. Soft maple sugar, sometimes called maple butter, and honey spread, which is pure honey finely crystallized, are both delicious on pancakes or on the hot biscuit described on page 305. For variety you can add to the liquid ingredients of the pancake batter either:

> **1 large ripe banana, thinly sliced *or***
> **1 cup fresh or frozen blueberries *or***
> **1 tart juicy apple, thinly sliced**

### Buttermilk Pancakes

> **1 egg**
> **1 cup buttermilk**
> **1 teaspoon soda**
> **¾ cup flour**
> **¼ teaspoon salt**

Beat egg; stir soda into buttermilk and add to egg. Stir in flour and salt. Brown on a Teflon®-coated griddle or skillet.

| *Fat content of recipe:* | *Yield: 12 pancakes* |
|---|---|
| *egg:* | 6.0 grams |
| *buttermilk:* | trace |
| *flour:* | 0.8 gram |
| *Total:* | 6.8 grams |
| *Fat content per pancake:* | 0.6 gram |

## Pancake Mixes

Tillie Lewis Tasti Diet Low Calorie Pancake Mix® is available in 4-ounce packages which yield 8 to 10 4-inch pancakes or 4 5 × 5-inch waffles. Only water is added to the packaged mix.

*Fat content of recipe, analysis on package:*
| | |
|---|---|
| *1 4-inch pancake:* | 0.2 gram |
| *1 5 × 5-inch waffle:* | 0.5 gram |

## Hot Breads

If you like hot bread for breakfast, try these biscuits or muffins with honey or jam. You will see that the fat content of one or two of the biscuits or muffins is approximately equal to that of a slice of bread.

### Baking Powder Biscuit

1¾ cups flour
1 teaspoon salt
2 teaspoons baking powder
¼ teaspoon cream of tartar
1 teaspoon sugar
2 eggs
⅜ cup skim milk

Sift and measure flour. Resift with salt, baking powder, cream of tartar, and sugar. Beat eggs until thick and foamy. Add milk. Beat well. Mix with dry ingredients. Handling very little, put on lightly floured board and press out with hand. Cut with biscuit cutter. Like all biscuits, these are best eaten fresh and hot. Bake for 10 minutes in 425° oven.

| Fat content of recipe: | Yield: 24 2-inch biscuits |
|---|---|
| flour: | 1.8 grams |
| eggs: | 12.0 grams |
| milk: | trace |
| Total: | 13.8 grams |
| Fat content per biscuit: | 0.6 gram |

## Drop Biscuit

**2 egg yolks**
**¾ cup liquefied nonfat milk**
**1 cup flour**
**2 teaspoons baking powder**
**1 teaspoon salt**

Beat together egg yolks and salt. Stir in ¼ cup milk. Sift together flour and baking powder. Stir dry ingredients into milk and egg mixture. Add remaining milk and stir until batter is well blended. Drop by teaspoonful onto Teflon® or treated cooky sheet. Bake for 12 to 15 minutes in 375° oven.

| Fat content of recipe: | 20 biscuits |
|---|---|
| eggs: | 12.0 grams |
| milk: | trace |
| flour: | 1.0 gram |
| Total: | 13.0 grams |
| Fat content per biscuit: | 0.7 gram |

## Molasses Bran Muffins

**2 cups whole bran cereal**
**½ cup molasses**
**1½ cups skim milk**
**1 egg, beaten**
**1 cup sifted all-purpose flour**

½ teaspoon salt
1 teaspoon soda

Soften whole bran cereal in molasses and milk (5 to 15 minutes). Add egg to flour mixture. Mix all ingredients together. Fill Teflon® or treated muffin pans ⅔ full and bake in hot oven (400°) about 20 minutes.

| *Fat content of recipe:* | *Yield: 24 2-inch muffins* |
|---|---|
| *bran cereal:* | 2.8 grams |
| *molasses:* | negligible |
| *milk:* | trace |
| *egg:* | 6.0 grams |
| *flour:* | 1.0 gram |
| *Total:* | 9.8 grams |
| *Fat content per muffin:* | 0.4 gram |

### Crumb Muffins

1 cup dry breadcrumbs
⅓ cup raisins
¾ cup skim milk
½ cup bread flour, sifted before measuring
2 teaspoons baking powder
½ teaspoon salt
½ tablespoon margarine, melted
1 egg

Soak bread in milk for 10 minutes. Sift together the flour, baking powder, and salt. Add to crumbs. Beat egg with melted margarine and add to flour mixture. Blend with a few swift strokes. Fold in raisins. Partly fill Teflon® or treated muffin tins. Bake in 425° oven for 20 minutes.

*Fat content of recipe:*      *Yield: 20 1¾-inch muffins*      307

| | |
|---|---|
| *breadcrumbs:* | 5.0 grams |
| *milk:* | trace |
| *flour:* | 0.5 gram |
| *margarine:* | 6.0 grams |
| *egg:* | 6.0 grams |
| *Total:* | 17.5 grams |
| *Fat content per muffin:* | 0.9 gram |

## Orange Bread

**2 navel oranges**
**1 cup orange juice**
**1 cup sugar**
**½ cup water**
**1 cup skimmed evaporated milk, un-**
**diluted**
**1 egg, beaten light**
**3 cups flour, sifted**
**3 teaspoons baking powder**

Squeeze oranges. Grind the orange peel and cook in orange juice until tender. Add sugar and water and cook until it is a thick syrup. Pour into a bowl and cool. Add milk, egg, flour, and baking powder. Pour into greased bread pan. Bake 45 to 60 minutes in 350° oven. One cup of chopped dates may be added for variety, additional sugar for a sweeter bread.

| | |
|---|---|
| *Fat content of recipe:* | *Yield: 1 loaf* |
| *skimmed evaporated milk:* | 0.5 gram |
| *egg:* | 6.0 grams |
| *flour:* | 3.0 grams |
| *Total:* | 9.5 grams |

## Batter Bread

**2½ cups flour, unsifted**
**2 tablespoons sugar**

1 teaspoon salt
1 package yeast, active dry
1 cup skim milk
2 tablespoons margarine
1 egg

Thoroughly mix the flour, sugar, salt, and yeast in a large bowl. Heat milk and margarine until warm (margarine does not need to melt). Add egg to flour mixture. Stir in milk. Beat very hard for 300 strokes or until batter leaves the sides of the bowl.

Scrape batter down from sides of bowl, cover, and let rise in warm place until double in size (half an hour to an hour).

Stir batter down until almost its original size. Bake in 9 × 5 × 2½-inch loaf pan, Teflon®-coated or treated with Pam®, Lean-Fry®, or Pan Pal®, in 350° oven for 40 minutes or until lightly browned. Remove bread from pan immediately and cool on rack.

| Fat content of recipe: | Yield: 1 loaf, 16 slices |
|---|---|
| flour: | 2.5 grams |
| margarine: | 24.0 grams |
| egg: | 6.0 grams |
| Total: | 32.5 grams |
| Fat content per slice: | 2.0 grams |

## Variety in Your Toast

As a variant for toast and jam, you might try this cinnamon toast.

### Cinnamon Toast

8 slices bread
1 egg white

309

**2 tablespoons sugar**
**¾ teaspoon cinnamon**

Toast the bread in the toaster. Beat together the egg white, sugar, and cinnamon until smooth and creamy. Brush generously the tops of the toasted bread with this mixture. Run under broiler until lightly browned. Serve at once.

*Fat content of recipe:*
  *only the fat content of the bread:*   1.0 gram per slice

## Holland Honey® Breads and Cakes

These products are described in the chapter on desserts, pages 285–286. They are delicious plain, with jelly, or toasted.

Another variation for your toast is:

### Milk Toast

This recipe serves one.

**1 slice bread**
**½ tablespoon butter**
  **Salt**
**1 cup liquefied nonfat milk, hot**

Toast the bread lightly on both sides. Spread lightly with butter. Sprinkle with salt. Place in a bowl and pour the hot milk over it.

*Fat content of recipe:*
  *butter:*               6.0 grams
  *nonfat milk:*          negligible
  *bread:*          1.0 gram per slice
  *Total:*                7.0 grams

### Cheese Toast

See recipe, pages 159–160.

## Variety Dishes

### Dried (or Chipped) Beef, Pan-Browned

In a Teflon® or treated skillet place pieces of dried beef. Pan-brown meat over medium flame until thoroughly heated. Stir with fork to prevent scorching. This crisp dried beef complements the bland flavor of your breakfast egg much as bacon or sausage would. Personal preference will determine the quantity used.

*Fat content of ingredients:*
  *dried beef, 2 ounces:*  4.0 grams

### Smoked Sliced Beef

Wherever dried or chipped beef is used, smoked sliced beef may be substituted. Its tangy, smoked flavor makes it an ideal substitute for bacon or ham at breakfast.

In the chapter on meats you will find four dishes suitable for use in breakfast menus:

### Creamed Dried Beef

See page 69.

### Smoked Sliced Beef, Creamed

See page 69.

## Baked Beans and Brown Bread

See page 91.

## Tomatoes with Chicken Livers

See pages 82–83.

## Codfish and Finnan Haddie

Even though you may have spent some childhood hours dreading cod-liver oil, you will find that codfish is good and entirely suitable for use in low-fat menus. So, if you come from Boston or 'round about, you can put back on the breakfast list codfish cakes and creamed fish flakes made with Basic White Sauce (page 198).

Finnan haddie is another tasty breakfast possibility. It, also, can be prepared with Basic White Sauce (page 198).

*Fat content, 1 pound, flesh only:*
   *cod:*                                       1.4 grams
   *finnan haddie (smoked haddock):*     1.8 grams

# APPENDIX

## Table 1. Sample Weekly Menu
### Average 25 grams fat per day

| Monday | fat grams | | fat grams | | fat grams |
|---|---|---|---|---|---|
| fat grams 20.7–21.8 | | | | | |
| V-8 juice | | Grapefruit–crab salad on lettuce | (4 oz. crab) 2.8 | Broiled beef liver | (1/3 lb.) 5.7 |
| 1 scrambled egg (without butter) | 6.0 | 4 saltine crackers | 1.0 | Harvard beets | |
| Whole wheat toast, 2 slices | 2.0 | Low-fat cottage cheese | (4 oz.) 1.1–2.2 | Butter beans, steamed, herb seasoned | |
| Jelly | trace | Skim milk or buttermilk | trace | Lettuce, sliced tomato, yogurt with chives | (2 Tbsp.) 0.6 |
| Skim milk | trace | 3 coca kisses | 0.3 | Scandinavian pudding, topped with vanilla ice milk | (3 Tbsp.) 1.2 |
| *Coffee | | *Tea or coffee | | *Coffee | |
| | 8.0 | | 5.2–6.3 | | 7.5 |

## Tuesday

**fat grams 7.6–8.1**

| | |
|---|---|
| Orange juice | 0.4 |
| Shredded wheat with fresh strawberries, skim milk, sugar | trace |
| *Coffee | |
| | ___ |
| | 0.4 |

| | |
|---|---|
| Lipton® Onion Soup | 0.8 |
| Smoked sliced beef sandwich with lettuce and tomato on rye; | (2 oz. beef) 4.0 |
| 1 tsp. mustard, 1 tsp. Special Mayonnaise | 0.3–0.4 |
| 4 mincemeat cookies | 0.4 |
| Apple | |
| Skim milk or buttermilk | trace |
| *Tea or coffee | |
| | ___ |
| | 5.5–5.6 |

| | |
|---|---|
| Sweet-sour tuna | 0.7–1.1 |
| Rice | |
| Green beans, herb seasoned | |
| Bean sprout salad | |
| Wine jelly | 1.0 |
| *Coffee | |
| | ___ |
| | 1.7–2.1 |

# APPENDIX

*If used in coffee or tea, 1 tablespoon half-and-half adds 2.0 grams fat. If sugar is used, this adds no fat, but does contain 15 calories per teaspoon.

315

# Table 1. Sample Weekly Menu (cont.)
### Average 25 grams fat per day

| Wednesday | fat grams | | fat grams | | fat grams |
|---|---|---|---|---|---|
| fat grams 24.3–24.7 | | Homemade gazpacho soup | | Tomato juice | |
| Grapefruit | | Westphalian rye or pumpernickel, 3 slices | 0.4 | Beef stew I or II | 12.6 |
| Eggnog | 6.0 | Harzer hand cheese (Harzkäse) ¼ 6½-ounce pkg. | 0.5–0.9 | Coleslaw | |
| 3 molasses bran muffins | 1.2 | Whole orange | | 6 baking powder biscuits | 3.6 |
| Jelly | trace | Skim milk or buttermilk | trace | Lime sherbet, pain d'epice | trace |
| *Coffee | | *Tea or coffee | 0.9–1.3 | *Coffee | 16.2 |
| | 7.2 | | | | |

**Thursday**

| | fat grams | | fat grams | | fat grams |
|---|---|---|---|---|---|
| Sliced banana | 35.0 | Campbell® Chicken Gumbo Soup | 1.3 | Chops and rice (3/8 lb. chop, 1/4 cup rice) | 13.4 |
| 1 scrambled egg (without butter) | 6.0 | 10 oyster crackers | 0.8 | Green salad, garlic-flavor Good Seasons® dressing with pectin | |
| Canadian bacon, 2 slices (1½ oz.) | 6.1 | Deviled egg (2 halves, 1 Tbsp. Special Mayonnaise) | 6.0 | | |
| Rye toast, 2 slices | trace | Fresh pineapple | 0.4 | Lemon sherbet, pain d'epice | 1.0 |
| Jelly | trace | Skim milk or buttermilk | trace | *Coffee | trace |
| Skim milk | trace | *Tea or coffee | | | |
| *Coffee | | | | | |
| | 12.1 | | 8.5 | | 14.4 |

*If used in coffee or tea, 1 tablespoon half-and-half adds 2.0 grams fat. If sugar is used, this adds no fat, but does contain 15 calories per teaspoon.

317

# Table 1. Sample Weekly Menu (cont.)
### Average 25 grams fat per day

| Friday | fat grams | | fat grams | | fat grams |
|---|---|---|---|---|---|
| fat grams 13.9–14.8 | | Orange juice | | Tomato–orange blossom soup | | Baked fish fillets I, with mushroom sauce | 0.2 |
| | 0.2 | Farina® (add raisins, if desired), skim milk, sugar | 2.3 (⅓ can tuna, 2 Tbsp. Special Mayonnaise) | Tuna fish salad sandwich on white bread (white, water pack or dietetic tuna) | 0.2 | Yellow squash (summer or crookneck) |
| | trace | | 1.3–1.9 | | 0.5 | Spinach with horseradish sauce |
| | 6.0 | 1 poached egg | 2.0 | | | Creamy coleslaw |
| | 1.0 | Whole wheat toast, 1 slice | | Seedless white grapes | 0.1–0.4 | Cherry fruit batter pie |
| | | *Coffee | | Iced tea | 0.3 | Skim milk or buttermilk |
| | 7.2 | | 5.6–6.2 | | trace | *Coffee |
| | | | | | 1.1–1.4 | |

# APPENDIX

**Saturday**

| | | fat grams | | | fat grams | | fat grams |
|---|---|---|---|---|---|---|---|
| fat grams 19.7–21.7 | Grapefruit juice | | Jellied consommé | | | Beef kabob | 10.7 |
| | Creamed dried beef on whole wheat toast, 2 slices | 1.2 | Tomatoes with chicken livers (1 tomato) | 2.9 | | Italian bread, ¼ loaf, with chive cheese | 1.0 |
| | | | Melba toast | trace | | Wilted cucumbers with dill | 0.3–2.3 |
| | Skim milk | 2.0 | Fresh pear | | | Tropical fruit compote, pain d'epice | |
| | *Coffee | trace | 4 butterless drop cookies | 1.6 | | *Coffee | trace |
| | | 3.2 | Skim milk or buttermilk | trace | | | 12.0–14.0 |
| | | | *Tea or coffee | | | | |
| | | | | 4.5 | | | |

*If used in coffee or tea, 1 tablespoon half-and-half adds 2.0 grams fat. If sugar is used, this adds no fat, but does contain 15 calories per teaspoon.

319

## Table 1. Sample Weekly Menu (cont.)
### Average 25 grams fat per day

| Sunday | fat grams | | fat grams | | fat grams |
|---|---|---|---|---|---|
| fat grams 22.7–23.2 | | | | | |
| ½ cantaloupe | | Chili, home-made | 4.3 | Chicken Divan (with broccoli) (¼ of 3 lb. fryer) | 11.4 |
| 5 buttermilk pancakes, syrup | 3.0 | 6 saltines | 1.8 | Rice | 0.3 |
| *Coffee | | Apple | | Fruited let-tuce | 0.4–0.9 |
| | | Skim milk or buttermilk | trace | Lemon Angel | 1.5 |
| | | *Tea or coffee | | *Coffee | |
| | 3.0 | | 6.1 | | 13.6–14.1 |

*If used in coffee or tea, 1 tablespoon half-and-half adds 2.0 grams fat. If sugar is used, this adds no fat, but does contain 15 calories per teaspoon.

*Fat content of menus:*
*Total for week:* 143.9–149.3 grams
*Daily average:* 20.6– 21.3 grams

All foods included in these menus have been prepared by the methods or recipes described in this book. The estimate of fat content is based on these methods and recipes. The menus have been used in the Stead household. The *average* of this particular week's menu is less than 25 grams of fat per day. For purposes of simplification, in this sample menu all foods to be included were incorporated in the regular three-meals-a-day schedule. Some persons may wish to modify the menus to use some of their fat allowance for between-meal snacks. This can be done without altering either fat or calorie intake, simply by using some of the milk, cookies, or crackers already listed, between meals instead of at mealtime.

In these sample menus a "substantial" breakfast is planned for each day. If you prefer to have juice, toast with jelly, and black coffee at breakfast, you can have a more liberal fat allowance at luncheon and dinner. This plan is followed in the Stead household, where those members who prefer a light breakfast have larger portions at lunch and dinner. Because the average in this group of menus is less than 25 grams of fat per day, a tablespoon of half-and-half could be added to the breakfast coffee without exceeding the 25 gram average.

For persons who are not restricted in calories but are concerned with fat intake (i.e., thin persons who for one reason or another wish to decrease the fat content of their food), between-meal snacks of low fat content can be *added* to this 25-gram menu. The average daily fat intake of these menus is 20.6 to 21.3 grams. There is, therefore, 3 to 4 grams leeway for addition of snacks. Any of the following foods will alter the fat content of the week's menu very little.

*Fat content:*
   *Skim milk, 1 cup*                          trace

| | |
|---|---|
| Buttermilk, 1 cup | trace |
| Tea with lemon | 0.0 grams |
| Coffee (sugar if desired; no cream) | 0.0 grams |
| Fruit or vegetable juices | negligible |
| Carbonated beverages | negligible |
| Saltines, 1 cracker | 0.3 gram |
| Oyster crackers, 10 crackers | 0.8 gram |
| Water crackers | 0.0 grams |
| Melba Toast, 1 slice | trace |
| Jam | trace |
| Jelly | trace |
| Apple butter, 1 tablespoon | 0.1 gram |
| Pickles | negligible |
| Fruits | negligible |
| Dry cottage cheese dips | negligible |
| Meringues, plain or fruited | negligible |
| Angel food cake | negligible |
| Raisin Drop Cookies, II 2 cookies | 0.1 gram |
| Candies | See list under Desserts, page 288. |

The Food and Nutrition Board of the National Academy of Sciences–National Research Council recommends Daily Dietary Allowances based on age and sex. These recommended daily food values are intended to provide for individual variations and to take into account the fact that foods, both fresh and processed, vary from season to season and locale to locale. The sample menus for a 25-gram fat average daily intake have been analyzed and they meet or exceed the recommended daily requirements for all groups of individuals listed except in calories. With these menus the average daily intake is 1705 calories. This points up the fact that low-fat cookery can be used to provide healthful and interesting meals and still

322

accomplish caloric reduction. Again, as noted earlier, if less calorie reduction is desired, it is a simple matter to add calories with foods which have no fat content. The fact that the menus already exceed dietary requirements makes it unimportant if the added calories do not add nutritional value.

* * *

Table 2 (p. 324) aims at an average of 50 grams fat per day. It is included as a guide for persons who wish to lose a moderate amount of weight. The menus have been used in the Stead household. A menu averaging 50 grams fat per day is considerably below the fat content of the average American diet. A person eating his accustomed quantity of food but following such a menu using low-fat cookery will lose weight. All foods included in these sample menus have been prepared by the methods or recipes described in this book. If you modify your cooking to use lowered-fat methods, you will find you restrict your fat intake with no loss of taste or variety.

In these sample menus, as in the 25-gram menus, a "substantial" breakfast is planned for each day. If you prefer to have juice, toast with jelly, and black coffee at breakfast, you can have a more liberal fat allowance at luncheon and dinner. This is the plan followed in the Stead household, where members who prefer a light breakfast have larger portions at lunch and dinner.

In general, the same rules for between-meal eating apply to this menu as to the 25-gram menu. If you are watching both calories and fat intake but enjoy be-·tween-meal eating, use some of the foods included in the three-meal-a-day schedule for your between-meal snacks. If, on the other hand, you are concerned with

(continued on page 331) 323

## Table 2. Sample Weekly Menu
### Average 50 grams fat per day

**Monday** — fat grams 23.9–25.0

| | fat grams | | fat grams | | fat grams |
|---|---|---|---|---|---|
| Orange juice | | Crosse & Blackwell® black bean soup (Add at serving 1 Tbsp. sherry, 1 slice lemon, 1 slice hard-cooked egg) | 0.6 | Chops and rice | (⅜ lb. chop, ¼ cup rice) 13.4 |
| 1 poached egg | 6.0 | | | | |
| Whole wheat toast, 2 slices | 2.0 | Cheese toast, topped with tomato, 1 slice | 0.3–1.4 | Green salad, garlic-flavor Good Seasons® dressing with pectin | |
| Skim milk or buttermilk | trace | Fresh pear | | | |
| Jelly | trace | Skim milk or buttermilk | trace | Lemon sherbet pain d'epice | 1.0 |
| *Coffee | | *Tea or coffee | | *Coffee | trace |
| | 8.0 | | 1.5–2.6 | | 14.4 |

**Tuesday**

| fat grams 26.2–26.6 | | | | | |
|---|---|---|---|---|---|
| Baked apple (with cinnamon, brown sugar, lemon juice) | | Chilled cucumber soup | 2.5 | Grilled flank steak | (½ lb.) 13.0 |
| Oatmeal, skim milk, sugar | 2.0 | Westphalian rye or pumpernickel, 3 slices | 0.4 | Baked acorn squash | |
| 1 scrambled egg (no added butter) | trace 6.0 | Harzer Hand cheese (Harzkäse) ¼ 6½-ounce pkg. | 0.5–0.9 | Peas with water chestnuts | |
| *Coffee | | Skim milk or buttermilk | trace | Cherry tomatoes | |
| | | ½ cantaloupe | | Cherry pie with 1 crust and strips | 1.8 |
| | | Espresso, black | | *Coffee | |
| | 8.0 | | 3.4–3.8 | | 14.8 |

*If used in coffee or tea, 1 tablespoon half-and-half adds 2.0 grams fat. If sugar is used, this adds no fat, but does contain 15 calories per teaspoon.

**APPENDIX**

## Table 2. Sample Weekly Menu (cont.)
### Average 50 grams fat per day

| Wednesday | fat grams | | fat grams | | fat grams |
|---|---|---|---|---|---|
| fat grams 41.3 | | | | | |
| Orange juice | | Pea soup, garnished | 1.7 | Spit-cooked fryer | (½ of 2-lb. fryer) 15.1 |
| 5 buttermilk pancakes, syrup | 3.0 | Deviled egg (2 halves, 1 Tbsp. Special Mayonnaise) | 6.0 | Zucchini Creole | |
| 2 slices Canadian bacon (1½ ounces) | 6.1 | 4 Cheese Ritz® crackers | 0.4 | Vienna rolls, 2 | 4.0 |
| Skim milk | trace | Grapefruit half | 4.0 | Wilted cucumber with dill | |
| *Coffee | | Skim milk or buttermilk | trace | Date bars, 2 | 1.0 |
| | | *Tea or coffee | | *Coffee | |
| | 9.1 | | 12.1 | | 20.1 |

**Thursday**

| | | |
|---|---|---|
| fat grams 34.2–39.4 | | |
| Applesauce | | |
| Puffed wheat, skim milk | 0.5 | |
| Soft-cooked egg, ½ | trace | |
| Tbsp. butter | 6.0 | |
| *Coffee | 6.0 | |
| | 12.5 | |
| Deviled mushrooms on white toast | 1.0 | |
| 2 slices Canadian bacon (1½ oz) | 6.1 | |
| Sliced tomato | | |
| Seedless white grapes, pain d'epice | trace | |
| Skim milk or buttermilk | trace | |
| Espresso, black | | |
| | 7.1 | |
| Beef stew with red wine | | 12.6–16.8 |
| Noodles | | 2.0–3.0 |
| French tomato salad | | |
| Orange compote, pain d'epice | | trace |
| *Coffee | | |
| | | 14.6–19.8 |

*If used in coffee or tea, 1 tablespoon half-and-half adds 2.0 grams fat. If sugar is used, this adds no fat, but does contain 15 calories per teaspoon.

## Table 2. Sample Weekly Menu (cont.)
### Average 50 grams fat per day

| Friday | fat grams | | fat grams | | fat grams |
|---|---|---|---|---|---|
| fat grams 43.1 | | | | | (3 wings) |
| Whole orange | | Scallops broiled in blankets, 6 pieces | 1.2 | Chicken wings with oyster sauce | 8.3 |
| 1 scrambled egg (no added butter) | | Pumpernickel, 3 slices, with yogurt cheese (4 ounces) | 0.8 | Sweet-sour pork | 12.9 |
| Whole wheat toast, 2 slices | 6.0 | Holland Honey Fruit Cake® | 1.8 | Beef with green peppers | 8.6 |
| Jam | 2.0 | Skim milk or buttermilk | 0.1 | Bean sprout salad | 1.0 |
| *Coffee | trace | *Tea or coffee | trace | Rice | 0.4 |
| | | | | Chinese tea | |
| | 8.0 | | 3.9 | | 31.2 |

**Saturday**

| fat grams 22.3–22.6 | | | | | |
|---|---|---|---|---|---|
| Tomato juice | | | | | |
| Poached egg supreme | 7.5 | | | | |
| Skim milk | trace | Minestrone soup | 0.5 | Shrimp fondue | 1.8 |
| *Coffee | | Rye bread, 2 slices | trace | Three bean salad I | 0.9–1.2 |
| | 7.5 | Wedge of St. Otho® cheese (3 ounces) | 4.2 | Vienna rolls, 2 | 4.0 |
| | | Apple | | Meringue pie, fresh peaches, vanilla ice milk topping | 3.0 |
| | | 4 mincemeat cookies | 0.4 | *Coffee | |
| | | Skim milk or buttermilk | trace | | |
| | | *Tea or coffee | | | 9.7–10.0 |
| | | | 5.1 | | |

# APPENDIX

*If used in coffee or tea, 1 tablespoon half-and-half adds 2.0 grams fat. If sugar is used, this adds no fat, but does contain 15 calories per teaspoon.

329

# Table 2. Sample Weekly Menu (cont.)
## Average 50 grams fat per day

**Sunday** — fat grams 115.6–115.8

| Sunday | fat grams | | fat grams | | fat grams |
|---|---|---|---|---|---|
| ½ cantaloupe | | Tomato case filled with crab salad (3 oz. crab, 2 Tbsp. Special Mayonnaise) | 2.1 | †Duck à l'orange | (¼ of 4 lb. duck) 106.4 |
| Orange bread, 3 ½-inch slices | | | | Yellow rice | |
| Marmalade | 1.6 | Melba toast, white, 4 pieces | 0.8 | Broccoli, steamed, yogurt topping (2 Tbsp.) | 0.6 |
| Skim milk or buttermilk | trace | Grapefruit sherbet, pain d'epice | 0.4 | Pickled pumpkin | |
| *Coffee | trace | Espresso, black | trace | Green salad, Good Seasons® dressing with pectin | |
| | 1.6 | | 3.3 | Plum pudding, Nestlé Crosse & Blackwell® or R&R® | 1.0–1.2 |
| | | | | Fluffy hard sauce topping | 2.7 |
| | | | | *Coffee | |
| | | | | | 110.7–110.9 |

*Fat content of menus:*
*Total for week:* 306.6–313.8 grams    *Daily average:* 43.8–44.8 grams

*If used in coffee or tea, 1 tablespoon half-and-half adds 2.0 grams fat. If sugar is used, this adds no fat, but does contain 15 calories per teaspoon.

†This figure for duck is for the raw, ready-to-cook fowl. Note in analysis of recipe, page 147, comment on fat content and the fact that not eating the skin reduces the figure appreciably.

fat intake but not with calories *per se*, you can add snacks if their fat content is low. (In this particular menu, though it aims at an average of 50 grams fat per day, the actual daily average is 44 to 45 grams, so you have a margin here of 5 to 6 grams fat daily for snacks.) The between-meal snacks suggested with the 25-gram menu may be used with this menu also. We have intentionally suggested snacks of low or negligible fat content, because we believe snacks should not have to be counted bite by bite!

As in the 25-gram menus, these menus have been analyzed and checked against the Recommended Daily Dietary Allowances published by the Food and Nutrition Board of the National Academy of Sciences–National Research Council. They exceed these recommended allowances for all groups of persons except in calories. The average daily intake is 2094 calories. Again we see that with low-fat cookery it is possible to have nutritious and tempting food without excess calories. For less caloric reduction add foods with no fat content. Nutritional value of these added foods is unimportant since dietary requirements have already been met.

# TABLE 3. FAT CONTENT OF FOODS[1]

Common Household Units or 1 Pound as Purchased

*The foods are listed under the following major classifications:*

Beverages
Breads, Pasta, Crackers
Cereals, Flour, Grains
Chocolate, Chocolate
    Products
Condiments
Dairy Products
Eggs
Fats, Lards, Margarine,
    Oils, Salad Dressing
    and Mayonnaise
Fish, Frog Legs, Shellfish,
    Turtle
Fruits and Fruit Juices
Gelatin

Ice Creams, Ice Milks,
    Sherbets, Ices
Jams, Jellies, Preserves,
    Spreads
Legumes
Meats
Nuts
Pickles
Poultry
Soups
Starches
Sugars
Syrups
Vegetables and Vegetable
    Juices

## Key

## Beverages

Beverages, alcoholic. See Beverages chapter, p. 291.
Beverages, carbonated. See Beverages chapter, p. 291.
Milk. See DAIRY PRODUCTS

---

[1] Adapted from *Composition of Foods, Raw, Processed, Prepared,* U.S. Department of Agriculture, Agriculture Handbook No. 8. Washington, D.C., revised December 1963, and Nutritive Value of

# Breads[2], Pasta, Crackers

## Breads

*Fat grams*

| | |
|---|---|
| Bagel, 3-inch diameter: | |
|   Egg *or* Water, 1 bagel (55 g.) | 2.0 |
| *Biscuits, baking powder, | |
|   1 biscuit (2-in. diameter, 28 g.) | 5.0 |
| *Biscuits, baking powder from mix, 1 biscuit | |
|   (2-inch diameter, 28 g.) | 3.0 |
| Breads: | |
|   Boston brown bread, 1 slice (3 by ¾ in., 48 g.) | 1.0 |
|   Cracked wheat bread, | |
|     1 slice, 18 slices per loaf (25 g.) | 1.0 |
|   French or Vienna breads, 1 pound | |
|     (average loaf), (454 g.) | 14.0 |
|   Italian bread, 1 pound (454 g.) | 4.0 |
|   Raisin bread, 1 slice, 18 slices per loaf (25 g.) | 1.0 |
|   Rye bread, American (⅓ rye, ⅔ wheat), | |
|     1 slice, 18 slices per loaf, (25 g.) | trace |
|   Rye bread, pumpernickel, loaf, 1 pound (454 g.) | 5.0 |
|   White bread, soft-crumb and firm-crumb type, | |
|     1 slice | 1.0 |
|   Whole wheat bread, soft-crumb and firm-crumb | |
|     type, 1 slice | 1.0 |
| Breadcrumbs: | |
|   dry, grated, 1 cup (100 g.) | 5.0 |
|   †Pepperidge Farm® Herb Seasoned Stuffing, | |
|     (8-oz. pkg.) | 3.0 |
| *Corn muffins, made with enriched degermed | |
|   cornmeal and enriched flour; muffin 2⅜-in. | |
|   diameter (40 g.) | 4.0 |

Foods, Home and Garden Bulletin No. 72, U.S. Department of
Agriculture, slightly revised January 1971.
[2]Toasting bread does not alter fat content.

|  | Fat grams |
|---|---|
| *Corn muffins, made with mix, egg, and milk; muffin 2⅜-in. diameter (40 g.) | 4.0 |
| §Melba Toast, 1 average wafer (4.2 g.) | 0.2 |
| *Muffins, with enriched white flour; muffin, 3-in. diameter, (40 g.) | 4.0 |
| Rolls³: | |
|     Cloverleaf or pan, home recipe, 1 roll (35 g.) | 3.0 |
|     Commercial, 1 roll (28 g.) | 2.0 |
|     Frankfurter or hamburger, 1 roll (40 g.) | 2.0 |
|     Hard, round or rectangular, 1 roll (50 g.) | 2.0 |
| *Waffles, with enriched flour, 7-in. diameter, 1 waffle (75 g.) | 7.0 |
| *Waffles, made from mix, enriched, egg and milk added, 7-in. diameter, (75 g.) | 8.0 |

## Pasta

|  | Fat grams |
|---|---|
| §Lasagne, dry, 1 pound (454 g.) | 4.5–6.8 |
| Macaroni: | |
|     Dry, 1 pound (454 g.) | 5.4 |
|     Cooked, 1 pound (454 g.) | 3.2 |
|     1 cup (140 g.) | 1.0 |
| Noodles (containing egg): | |
|     Dry, 1 pound (454 g.) | 20.9 |
|     Cooked, 1 pound (454 g.) | 5.7 |
|     1 cup (160 g.) | 2.0 |
| Spaghetti: | |
|     Dry, 1 pound (454 g.) | 5.4 |
|     Cooked, 1 pound (454 g.) | 3.2 |
|     1 cup (140 g.) | 1.0 |

## Crackers⁴

|  | |
|---|---|
| †Cracker meal, 1 cup (85 g.) | 1.6 |
| Graham, 4 crackers, 2½-in. square, (28 g.) | 3.0 |

³See Table 4 for fat content of certain rolls.
⁴See Table 7 for fat content of crackers and cookies by brand name; information furnished by the manufacturers.

|  | *Fat grams* |
|---|---|
| †Graham cracker crumbs, 1 cup (131 g.) | 10.7 |
| ‡Norwegian flatbread® or Swedish Crispbread®, 1 slice or wafer (8 g.) | 0.1 |
| Pretzels: | |
|   Dutch, twisted, 1 pretzel (16 g.) | 1.0 |
|   Thin, twisted, 1 pretzel (6 g.) | trace |
|   Stick, small, 2¼-in., 10 sticks | trace |
|   Stick, regular, 3⅛-in., 5 sticks | trace |
| Rye wafers, whole-grain, 2 wafers (1⅞ by 3½-in., 13 g.) | trace |
| Saltines, 4 crackers (11 g.) | 1.0 |
| Soda, plain: | |
|   †2 crackers (10 g.) | 1.2 |
|   †1 cup oyster crackers (28.35 g.) | 3.1 |
|   †10 oyster crackers | 0.8 |
| Yeast (included here because it is most commonly used in the preparation of breads) | trace |

## Cereals, Flour, Grains

|  | *Fat grams* |
|---|---|
| Barley, pearled, light, uncooked, 1 cup (200 g.) | 2.0 |
| Bran flakes (40 per cent bran), 1 cup (35 g.) | 1.0 |
| Buckwheat flour, light, 1 cup sifted (98 g.) | 1.0 |
| Cornflakes, 1 cup (25 g.) | trace |
| Corn flour, 1 pound (454 g.) | 11.8 |
| Corn (hominy) grits, degermed: | |
|   Dry, 1 pound (454 g.) | 3.6 |
|   Cooked, 1 cup (245 g.) | trace |
| Corn meal, whole ground, dry: | |
|   Unbolted, 1 cup (122 g.) | 5.0 |
|   Bolted (nearly wholegrain), 1 cup (122 g.) | 4.0 |
| Corn meal: | |
|   Degermed, dry, 1 cup (138 g.) | 2.0 |
|     Cooked, 1 cup (240 g.) | 1.0 |
|   Self-rising, whole ground, dry: | |
|     With soft wheat flour added, 1 pound (454 g.) | 13.2 |

335

|  |  |
|---|---:|
| Without wheat flour added, 1 pound (454 g.) | 14.5 |
| Self-rising, degermed, dry: | |
| With or without soft wheat flour added, 1 pound (454 g.) | 5.0 |
| Corn, popped, plain, 1 cup (6 g.) | trace |
| Oatmeal or rolled oats: | |
| Dry, 1 pound (454 g.) | 33.6 |
| Cooked, 1 cup (240 g.) | 2.0 |
| Rice: | |
| Brown, raw, 1 pound (454 g.) | 8.6 |
| White: | |
| Raw, 1 cup (185 g.) | 1.0 |
| Cooked, 1 cup (205 g.) | trace |
| Instant, ready-to-serve, 1 cup (165 g.) | trace |
| Rice, wild. See Wild Rice. | |
| Rye flour: | |
| Light, 1 pound (454 g.) | 4.5 |
| Medium, 1 pound (454 g.) | 7.7 |
| Dark, 1 pound (454 g.) | 11.8 |
| Soybean flours: | |
| Defatted, 1 pound (454 g.) | 4.1 |
| Low-fat, 1 pound (454 g.) | 30.4 |
| High-fat, 1 pound (454 g.) | 54.9 |
| Full-fat, 1 pound (454 g.) | 92.1 |
| Tapioca, dry, quick-cooking, 1 cup (152 g.) | trace |
| Wheat flours: | |
| Whole (from hard wheats), 1 cup, stirred (120 g.) | 2.0 |
| All-purpose, self-rising and cake flour, 1 cup | 1.0 |
| Wheat products: | |
| Flakes, 1 cup (30 g.) | trace |
| Germ, 1 pound (454 g.) | 49.4 |
| Wild rice, raw, 1 pound (454 g.) | 3.2 |

## Chocolate, Chocolate Products

*Fat grams*

| | |
|---|---|
| Chocolate, bitter or unsweetened, 1 oz. (28.35 g.) | 15.0 |
| Semi-sweet, small pieces, 1 cup (170 g.) | 61.0 |
| Sweetened: | |
| Milk, plain, 1 oz. (28.35 g.) | 9.0 |
| Milk with almonds, 1 oz. (28.35 g.) | 10.1 |
| Chocolate-flavored beverage powder (approx. 4 heaping teaspoons per oz.), with or without nonfat dry milk, 1 oz. (28.35 g.) | 1.0 |
| Chocolate flavored syrup or topping: | |
| Thin type, 1 fluid oz. (38 g.) | 1.0 |
| Fudge type, 1 fluid oz. (38 g.) | 5.0 |
| Cocoa, breakfast, plain, dry powder: | |
| 1 pound (454 g.) | 107.5 |
| 1 oz. (28.35 g.) | 6.7 |
| 1 tablespoon (7 g.) | 1.7 |

## Condiments

| | |
|---|---|
| †Butter Flavored Salt, 1 teaspoon | 0.1–0.9 |
| Catsup, tomato: | |
| 1 cup (273 g.) | 1.0 |
| 1 tablespoon (15 g.) | trace |
| Chili sauce: | |
| 1 cup (273 g.) | 0.8 |
| 1 tablespoon (17 g.) | trace |
| †Imitation bacon bits, 1 teaspoon | 0.3–0.5 |
| ‡Mustard, 1 tablespoon (14 g.) | 0.6–0.9 |
| †Soy sauce, 1 tablespoon | trace |
| Vinegar | — |

## Crackers. See Breads

337

## Dairy Products

| | *Fat grams* |
|---|---:|
| Butter: | |
|   Regular, 4 sticks per pound: | |
|     1 stick, ½ cup (113 g.) | 92.0 |
|     1 cup (226 g.) | 184.0 |
|     1 tablespoon (approx. ⅛ stick) (14 g.) | 12.0 |
|     1 pat (1-in. sq. ⅓-in. high; 90 per lb.) (5 g.) | 4.0 |
|   Whipped, 6 sticks or | |
|     2 8-oz. containers per pound: | |
|     1 stick, ½ cup (76 g.) | 61.0 |
|     1 tablespoon (approx. ⅛ stick) (9 g.) | 8.0 |
|     1 pat (1¼-in. sq. ⅓-in. high; 120 per lb.) | |
|       (4 g.) | 3.0 |
| Cheese: | |
|   Natural: | |
|   Blue or Roquefort type: | |
|     1 oz. (28.35 g.) | 9.0 |
|     1 cubic inch (17 g.) | 5.0 |
|   Camembert, packed in 4-oz. pkg. with 3 wedges | |
|     per pkg., 1 wedge (38 g.) | 9.0 |
|   Cheddar: | |
|     1 cup grated (112 g.) | 36.1 |
|     1 oz. (28.35 g.) | 9.0 |
|     1 cubic inch (17 g.) | 6.0 |
|   Cottage, large or small curd: | |
|     Creamed: | |
|       Package of 12-oz. (340 g.) | 14.0 |
|       1 cup, curd pressed down (245 g.) | 10.0 |
|       1 oz. (28.35 g.) | 1.2 |
|     Uncreamed: | |
|       Package of 12-oz. (340 g.) | 1.0 |
|       1 cup, curd pressed down (200 g.) | 1.0 |
|       1 oz. (28.35 g.) | 0.1 |

338      Products by brand names:

|  | Fat grams |
|---|---|
| §Borden Lite-Line®: | |
|     Package of 16 oz. (454 g.) | 4.5 |
|     1 cup (227 g.) | 2.3 |
|     1 oz. (28.35 g.) | 0.3 |
| §Slim Cheez®: | |
|     Package of 12 oz. (340 g.) | 6.8 |
|     1 cup (227 g.) | 4.5 |
|     1 oz. (28.35 g.) | 0.6 |
| §Slim N' Light®: | |
|     Package of 12 oz. (340 g.) | 6.8 |
|     1 cup (227 g.) | 4.5 |
|     1 oz. (28.35 g.) | 0.6 |
| §Trim®: | |
|     Package of 12 oz. (340 g.) | 6.8 |
|     1 cup (227 g.) | 4.5 |
|     1 oz. (28.35 g.) | 0.3 |
| §Trim N' Light®: | |
|     Package of 12 oz. (340 g.) | 3.4 |
|     1 cup (227 g.) | 2.3 |
|     1 oz. (28.35 g.) | 0.3 |
| Cream cheese: | |
|   Package of 8 oz. (227 g.) | 86.0 |
|   Package of 3 oz. (85 g.) | 32.0 |
|   1 cubic inch (16 g.) | 6.0 |
|   1 oz. (28.35 g.) | 10.7 |
| ‡Gammelost, 1 oz. (28.35 g.) | 0.1–0.3 |
| ‡Harzkäse, 1 oz. (28.35 g.) | 0.3–0.6 |
| ‡Limburger, 1 oz. (28.35 g.) | 7.5–8.4 |
| ‡Mozzarella, 1 oz. (28.35 g.) | 12.8 |
| Parmesan, grated: | |
|   1 cup pressed down (140 g.) | 43.0 |
|   1 tablespoon (5 g.) | 2.0 |
|   1 oz. (28.35 g.) | 9.0 |
| ‡Sapsago, 1 oz. (28.35 g.) | 1.4–2.7 |
| §St. Otho's®, 1 oz. (28.35 g.) | 1.4 |
| Swiss: | |

**APPENDIX**

|                                                    | Fat grams |
|----------------------------------------------------|-----------|
| 1 oz. (28.35 g.)                                   | 8.0       |
| 1 cubic inch (15 g.)                               | 4.0       |
| Pasteurized processed cheese:                      |           |
| American:                                          |           |
| 1 oz. (28.35 g.)                                   | 9.0       |
| 1 cubic inch (18 g.)                               | 5.0       |
| Swiss:                                             |           |
| 1 oz. (28.35 g.)                                   | 8.0       |
| 1 cubic inch (18 g.)                               | 5.0       |
| Pasteurized process cheese food:                   |           |
| American:                                          |           |
| 1 tablespoon (14 g.)                               | 3.0       |
| 1 cubic inch (18 g.)                               | 4.0       |
| Pasteurized process cheese spread,                 |           |
| American, 1 oz. (28.35 g.)                         | 6.0       |
| Imitation pasteurized process cheese spread:       |           |
| §Chef's Delight®:                                  |           |
| 1 oz. (28.35 g.)                                   | 1.4       |
| 1 cup grated                                       | 11.2      |
| Imitation pasteurized process skim milk cheese     |           |
| spread:                                            |           |
| §Count Down®, cheddar or blue cheese flavor:       |           |
| 1 oz. (28.35 g.)                                   | 0.3       |
| 1 cup grated                                       | 2.4       |
| Cream:                                             |           |
| Half-and-half (cream and milk):                    |           |
| 1 cup (242 g.)                                     | 28.0      |
| 1 tablespoon (15 g.)                               | 2.0       |
| Light, coffee or table:                            |           |
| 1 cup (240 g.)                                     | 49.0      |
| 1 tablespoon (15 g.)                               | 3.0       |
| Sour:                                              |           |
| 1 cup (230 g.)                                     | 47.0      |
| 1 tablespoon (12 g.)                               | 2.0       |
| Whipped topping (pressurized):                     |           |
| 1 cup (60 g.)                                      | 14.0      |
| 1 tablespoon (3 g.)                                | 1.0       |

*Fat grams*

Whipping, unwhipped (volume about double
    when whipped):
  Light:
    1 cup (239 g.)            75 0
    1 tablespoon (15 g.)     5.0
  Heavy:
    1 cup (238 g.)          90.0
    1 tablespoon (15 g.)     6.0
Imitation cream products (made with vegetable fat):
  Creamers:
    Powdered:
      1 cup (94 g.)         33.0
      1 teaspoon (2 g.)     1.0
    Liquid (frozen):
      1 cup (245 g.)        27.0
      1 tablespoon (15 g.)   2.0
  Sour dressing (imitation sour cream) made with
    nonfat dry milk:
      1 tablespoon (12 g.)   2.0
  Whipped topping:
    Pressurized:
      1 cup (70 g.)        17.0
      1 tablespoon (4 g.)    1.0
    Frozen:
      1 cup (75 g.)       20.0
      1 tablespoon (4 g.)    1.0
    Powdered, made with whole milk:
      1 cup (75 g.)       12.0
      1 tablespoon (4 g.)    1.0
Ice cream, ice milk, sherbet, ices:
  Ice cream:
    regular (approx. 10% fat):
      ½ gal. (1064 g.)    113.0
      1 cup (133 g.)     14.0
    rich (approx. 16% fat):
      ½ gal. (1,188 g.)   191.0
      1 cup (148 g.)     24.0

**APPENDIX**

**341**

| | Fat grams |
|---|---|
| Ice milk: | |
| hardened: | |
| ½ gal. (1048 g.) | 53.0 |
| 1 cup (131 g.) | 7.0 |
| soft-serve, 1 cup (175 g.) | 9.0 |
| Milk sherbet, 1 pint | 5.5 |
| Water ices, 1 cup | trace |
| Popsicle | 0.0 |
| Milk: | |
| Fluid: | |
| Whole: | |
| 1 quart (976 g.) | 36.0 |
| 1 cup (244 g.) | 9.0 |
| Nonfat (skim): | |
| 1 quart (980 g.) | 1.0 |
| 1 cup (245 g.) | trace |
| Partly skimmed, 2%: | |
| 1 quart (984 g.) | 20.0 |
| 1 cup (246 g.) | 5.0 |
| Buttermilk, made from skim milk: | |
| 1 quart (980 g.) | 1.0 |
| 1 cup (245 g.) | trace |
| Canned, concentrated, undiluted: | |
| Evaporated, unsweetened: | |
| 1 cup (252 g.) | 20.0 |
| ‖Evaporated, skimmed, undiluted: | |
| 1 cup | 0.5 |
| Condensed, sweetened: | |
| 1 cup (306 g.) | 27.0 |
| Dried: | |
| Whole: | |
| 1 cup (128 g.) | 35.2 |
| 1 tablespoon (8 g.) | 2.2 |
| Nonfat instant, 1 cup (104 g.) | 1.0 |
| Malted milk, 3 heaping teaspoons | |
| dry powder, 1 oz. (28.35 g.) | 2.0 |

Yogurt:
  Made from partially skimmed milk,
    1 cup (245 g.)                           4.0
  Made from whole milk, 1 cup (245 g.)    8.0

## Eggs, Hen

Raw or cooked in shell or with nothing added:
  Whole:
    1 large (50 g.)                            6.0
    1 cup (243 g.)                          27.9
  White:
    1 egg white (large, 33 g.)           trace
    1 cup (243 g.)                    trace
  Dried:
    Whole, 1 cup (108 g.)             44.5
    White, 1 cup (56 g.)              0.1
    Yolk, 1 cup (96 g.)              54.3

## Fats, Lards, Margarine, Oils, Salad Dressing, and Mayonnaise

Fats, cooking:
  Lard:
    1 cup (205 g.)                    205.0
    1 tablespoon (13 g.)            13.0
  Vegetable fats:
    1 cup (200 g.)                  200.0
    1 tablespoon (13 g.)            13.0
Margarine:
  Regular, 4 sticks per pound:
    1 stick, ½ cup (113 g.)          92.0
    1 tablespoon (approx. ⅛ stick), (14 g.)   12.0    **343**

|  | *Fat grams* |
|---|---|
| 1 pat (1-in. sq. ⅓-in. high; 90 per lb.), (5 g.) | 4.0 |
| Whipped, 6 sticks per pound: | |
| 1 stick, ½ cup (76 g.) | 61.0 |
| Soft, 2 8-oz. tubs per pound: | |
| 1 tub (227 g.) | 184.0 |
| 1 tablespoon (14 g.) | 11.0 |
| Oils, salad or cooking: | |
| 1 cup (220 g.) | 220.0 |
| 1 tablespoon (14 g.) | 14.0 |
| Salad dressing: | |
| 1 cup (235 g.) | 99.4 |
| 1 tablespoon (15 g.) | 6.0 |
| Mayonnaise: | |
| 1 cup (205 g.) | 163.8 |
| 1 tablespoon (14 g.) | 11.0 |

## Fish, Frog Legs, Shellfish, Turtle

| | |
|---|---|
| Abalone: | |
| 1 pound (454 g.), raw, flesh only | 2.3 |
| canned | 1.4 |
| Albacore, 1 pound (454 g.), raw, flesh only | 34.5 |
| Alewife, 1 pound (454 g.), raw, flesh only | 22.2 |
| Barracuda, Pacific, 1 pound (454 g.), raw, flesh only | 11.8 |
| Bass: | |
| Black Sea: | |
| 1 pound (454 g.), raw, flesh only | 5.4 |
| raw, whole as purchased | 2.1 |
| Smallmouth and largemouth: | |
| 1 pound (454 g.), raw, flesh only | 11.8 |
| raw, whole as purchased | 3.7 |
| Striped: | |
| 1 pound (454 g.), raw, flesh only | 12.2 |
| raw, whole as purchased | 5.3 |

344

White:
| | |
|---|---|
| 1 pound (454 g.), raw, flesh only | 10.4 |
| raw, whole as purchased | 4.1 |

Blackfish. See Tautog

Bluefish:
| | |
|---|---|
| 1 pound (454 g.), raw, flesh only | 15.0 |
| raw, whole as purchased | 7.6 |

Bonito, including Atlantic, Pacific, and striped:
| | |
|---|---|
| 1 pound (454 g.), raw, flesh only | 33.1 |
| Buffalo fish, 1 pound (454 g.), raw, flesh only | 19.1 |
| Bullhead, black, 1 pound fillets (454 g.), raw | 7.3 |
| Burbot, 1 pound (454 g.), raw, flesh only | 4.1 |

Butterfish:

From Northern waters:
| | |
|---|---|
| 1 pound (454 g.), raw, flesh only | 46.3 |
| raw, whole as purchased | 23.6 |

From Gulf waters:
| | |
|---|---|
| 1 pound (454 g.), raw, flesh only | 13.2 |
| raw, whole as purchased | 6.7 |
| Carp, 1 pound (454 g.), raw, flesh only | 19.1 |
| Catfish, freshwater, 1 pound (454 g.), raw, fillets | 14.1 |
| Chub, 1 pound (454 g.), raw, flesh only | 39.9 |

Clams:

Raw:

Soft:
| | |
|---|---|
| 1 pound (454 g.), raw, meat and liquid in shell (refuse: shell) | 2.6 |
| 1 pound (454 g.), raw, meat only | 8.6 |

Hard or round:
| | |
|---|---|
| 1 pound (454 g.), raw, meat and liquid in shell (refuse: shell) | 0.6 |
| 1 pound (454 g.), raw, meat only | 4.1 |

Canned (hard, soft, razor and unspecified):
| | |
|---|---|
| 1 pound (454 g.), solids and liquid | 3.2 |
| solids only | 5.9 |
| liquor, bouillon, or nectar | 0.5 |

**A P P E N D I X**

345

Cod:
- 1 pound (454 g.), raw, flesh only — 1.4
- dehydrated, lightly salted — 12.7
- dried, salted — 3.2
- canned — 1.4

Crabs, including blue, Dungeness, rock, and king:
Cooked, steamed:
- 1 pound (454 g.), whole, refuse, shells — 4.1
- meat only — 8.6
- Canned, 1 pound (454 g.) — 11.3

Crappie, white, 1 pound (454 g.), raw, flesh only — 3.6

Crayfish, fresh water; and spiny lobster:
- 1 pound (454 g.), raw in shell (refuse: shell) — 0.3
- meat only — 2.3

Croaker:
- Atlantic, 1 pound (454 g.), raw, flesh only — 10.0
- White, 1 pound (454 g.), raw, flesh only — 3.6
- Yellowfin, 1 pound (454 g.), raw, flesh only — 3.6

Cusk, 1 pound (454 g.), raw, flesh only — 0.9

Dogfish, spiny (grayfish),
- 1 pound (454 g.), raw, flesh only — 40.8

Dolly Varden, 1 pound (454 g.), raw, flesh and
- skin — 29.5

Drum:
- Freshwater, 1 pound (454 g.), raw, flesh only — 23.6
- Red (redfish), 1 pound (454 g.), raw, flesh only — 1.8

Eel:
- American, 1 pound (454 g.), raw, flesh only — 83.0
- Smoked, 1 pound (454 g.), flesh only — 126.1

Eulachon (smelt),
- 1 pound (454 g.), raw, flesh only — 28.1

Finnan haddie (smoked haddock),
- 1 pound (454 g.), flesh only — 1.8

Flatfishes (flounders, soles, and sanddabs):
- 1 pound (454 g.), raw, flesh only — 3.6
- raw, whole as purchased — 1.2

Flounder. See Flatfishes.

Frog legs, 1 pound (454 g.), raw                            0.9

Grouper, including red, black, and speckled hind:

  1 pound (454 g.), raw, flesh only                2.3

Haddock:

  1 pound (454 g.), raw, flesh only                0.5

     raw, whole as purchased              0.2

     smoked, canned or not canned         1.8

Hake, including Pacific hake, squirrel hake,

  and silver hake or whiting:

     1 pound (454 g.), raw, flesh only    1.8

Halibut:

  Atlantic and Pacific:

     1 pound (454 g.), raw, flesh only    5.4

       raw, whole as purchased    3.2

  California, 1 pound (454 g.), raw, flesh only    6.4

  Greenland:

     1 pound (454 g.), raw, flesh only    38.1

       raw, whole as purchased    19.8

  Smoked, 1 pound (454 g.)                          68.0

Herring:

  Atlantic, 1 pound (454 g.), raw, flesh only       51.3

  Lake (cisco), 1 pound (454 g.), raw, fillets      10.4

  Pacific, 1 pound (454 g.), raw, flesh only        11.8

  Canned, solids and liquids, 1 pound (454 g.)      61.7

  Pickled, Bismarck type, 1 pound (454 g.)          68.5

  Salted or brined, 1 pound (454 g.)                68.9

  Smoked:

    Bloaters, 1 pound (454 g.)                56.2

    Hard, 1 pound (454 g.)                    71.7

    Kippered, 1 pound (454 g.)                58.5

Inconnu (sheefish), 1 pound (454 g.),

  raw, flesh only                                   30.8

Jack, mackerel, 1 pound (454 g.), raw, flesh only  25.4

Kingfish: Southern, gulf, and Northern (whiting):

  1 pound (454 g.), raw, flesh only                 13.6

**APPENDIX**

|  |  |
|---|---|
| raw, whole as purchased | 6.0 |

Lake trout. See Trout.

Lobster, Northern:

|  |  |
|---|---|
| 1 pound (454 g.), raw, whole | 2.2 |
| raw, meat only | 8.6 |
| canned or cooked | 6.8 |

Lobster, spiny. See Crayfish

Lobster paste. See Shrimp or lobster paste canned.

Mackerel:

Raw:

|  |  |
|---|---|
| Atlantic, 1 pound (454 g.), raw, flesh only | 55.3 |
| Jack. See Jack mackerel. |  |
| Pacific, 1 pound (454 g.), raw, flesh only | 33.1 |

Canned:

|  |  |
|---|---|
| Atlantic, 1 pound (454 g.) | 50.3 |
| Pacific, 1 pound (454 g.) | 45.4 |
| Salted, 1 pound (454 g.) | 113.9 |
| Smoked, 1 pound (454 g.) | 59.0 |

|  |  |
|---|---|
| Menhaden, Atlantic, canned, 1 pound (454 g.), solids and liquid | 46.3 |
| Mullet, striped, 1 pound (454 g.), raw, flesh only | 31.3 |
| Muskellunge, 1 pound (454 g.), raw, flesh only | 11.3 |

Mussels, Atlantic and Pacific:

Raw:

|  |  |
|---|---|
| 1 pound (454 g.), in shell | 2.9 |
| as meat only | 10.0 |

Ocean perch. See Perch.

|  |  |
|---|---|
| Octopus, 1 pound (454 g.), raw | 3.6 |

Oysters:

Raw:

|  |  |
|---|---|
| Eastern, 1 pound (454 g.), raw, meat only | 8.2 |
| Pacific and western (Olympia), 1 pound (454 g.), raw, meat only | 10.0 |
| Oysters, 1 cup (240 g.), meat only | 4.0 |
| Canned, 1 pound (454 g.), solids and liquid | 10.0 |

348  Perch:

Ocean:

   Atlantic (redfish):

      1 pound (454 g.), raw fillets         5.4

               raw, whole as purchased    1.7

   Pacific:

      1 pound (454 g.), raw, flesh only   6.8

               raw, whole as purchased    1.8

White:

      1 pound (454 g.), raw, flesh only  18.1

               raw, whole as purchased    6.5

Yellow:

      1 pound (454 g.), raw, flesh only   4.1

               raw, whole as purchased    1.6

Pickerel, chain, 1 pound (454 g.), raw, flesh only   2.3

Pike:

  Blue, 1 pound (454 g.), raw, flesh only   4.1

               raw, whole as purchased    1.8

  Northern, 1 pound (454 g.), raw, flesh only   5.0

                 raw, whole as purchased    1.3

  Walleye, 1 pound (454 g.), raw, flesh only   5.4

                raw, whole as purchased    3.1

Pollock, 1 pound (454 g.), raw, fillets     4.1

Pompano, 1 pound (454 g.), raw, flesh only  43.1

Porgy and scup, 1 pound (454 g.), raw, flesh only 15.4

Raja fish. See Skate.

Red and gray snapper:

  1 pound (454 g.), raw, flesh only     4.1

              raw, whole as purchased    2.1

Redfish. See Drum, red, and ocean Perch, Atlantic.

Redhorse, silver,

  1 pound (454 g.), raw, flesh only    10.4

Rockfish, including black, canary, yellowtail,

  rasphead, and bocaccio, 1 pound (454 g.), raw,

  flesh only                    8.2

Roe:

  Raw:

**APPENDIX**

| | |
|---|---|
| Including carp, cod, haddock, herring, pike, and shad, 1 pound (454 g.) | 10.4 |
| Including salmon, sturgeon, and turbot, 1 pound (454 g.) | 47.2 |
| Canned: | |
| Including cod, haddock, and herring, 1 pound (454 g.) | 12.7 |
| Sablefish, 1 pound (454 g.), raw, flesh only | 67.6 |
| Salmon: | |
| Atlantic: | |
| Raw: | |
| 1 pound (454 g.), flesh only | 60.8 |
| Canned: | |
| 1 pound (454 g.), solids and liquid | 55.3 |
| Chinook (king): | |
| Raw: | |
| 1 pound (454 g.), flesh only | 70.8 |
| steak, including bones | 62.3 |
| Canned: | |
| 1 pound (454 g.), solids and liquid | 63.5 |
| Chum: | |
| Canned: | |
| 1 pound (454 g.), solids and liquid | 23.6 |
| Coho (silver): | |
| Canned: | |
| 1 pound (454 g.), solids and liquid | 32.2 |
| Pink (humpback): | |
| Raw: | |
| 1 pound (454 g.), flesh only | 16.8 |
| steak, including bones | 14.8 |
| Canned: | |
| 1 pound (454 g.), solids and liquid | 26.8 |
| Sockeye (red): | |
| Canned: | |
| 1 pound (454 g.), solids and liquid | 42.2 |
| Salmon, smoked, 1 pound (454 g.) | 42.2 |

| | |
|---|---:|
| Sanddab. See Flatfishes. | |
| Sardines: | |
|   Atlantic: | |
|     Canned in oil: | |
|       1 pound (454 g.), solids and liquid | 110.7 |
|                      drained solids | 41.3 |
|   Pacific: | |
|     Raw: | |
|       1 pound (454 g.) | 39.0 |
|     Canned: | |
|       1 pound (454 g.) in brine or mustard, | |
|         solids and liquid | 54.4 |
|       1 pound (454 g.) in tomato sauce, | |
|         solids and liquid | 55.3 |
| Sauger, 1 pound (454 g.), raw, flesh only | 3.6 |
| Scallops, bay and sea, 1 pound (454 g.), | |
|   raw (edible muscle) | 0.9 |
| Scup. See Porgy. | |
| Seabass, white, 1 pound (454 g.), raw, flesh only | 2.3 |
| Shad or American shad: | |
|   Raw: | |
|     1 pound (454 g.), flesh only | 45.4 |
|   Canned: | |
|     1 pound (454 g.), solids and liquid | 39.9 |
| Shad, gizzard (gizzard shad), | |
|   1 pound (454 g.), raw, flesh only | 63.5 |
| Sheefish. See Inconnu. | |
| Sheephead, Atlantic, 1 pound (454 g.), | |
|   raw, flesh only | 12.7 |
| Sheephead, fresh water. See Drum. | |
| Shrimp: | |
|   Raw: | |
|     1 pound (454 g.), flesh only | 3.6 |
|     1 pound (454 g.), in shell | 2.5 |
|   Cooked, flesh only, 1 cup | 1.8 |
|   Canned: | |

*Fat grams*

| | |
|---|---|
| 1 pound (454 g.), solids and liquid, wet pack | 3.6 |
| 1 pound (454 g.), solids only, wet pack | 3.2 |
| solids only, dry pack | 5.0 |
| Shrimp or lobster paste, canned, 1 pound (454 g.) | 42.6 |
| Siscowet. See Lake trout. | |
| Skate (raja fish), 1 pound (454 g.), raw, flesh only | 3.2 |
| Smelt, Atlantic, jack, and bay: | |
| Raw: | |
| 1 pound (454 g.), raw, flesh only | 9.5 |
| raw, whole as purchased | 5.2 |
| Canned, 1 pound (454 g.), solids and liquid | 61.2 |
| Smelt, eulachon. See Eulachon. | |
| Snail, 1 pound (454 g.), raw, including Giant African | 6.4 |
| Snapper, red. See Red and gray snapper. | |
| Sole. See Flatfishes. | |
| Spanish mackerel, 1 pound (454 g.), raw, flesh only | 47.2 |
| Spiny lobster. See Crayfish. | |
| Spot, 1 pound (454 g.), raw, fillets | 72.1 |
| Squid, 1 pound (454 g.), raw, flesh only | 4.1 |
| Sturgeon, 1 pound (454 g.), raw, flesh only | 8.6 |
| smoked | 8.2 |
| Sucker, carp, 1 pound (454 g.), raw, flesh only | 14.5 |
| Suckers, including white and mullet suckers, 1 pound (454 g.), raw, fillets | 8.2 |
| Swordfish, 1 pound (454 g.), raw, flesh only | 18.1 |
| canned, solids and liquid | 13.6 |
| Tautog (blackfish), 1 pound (454 g.), raw, flesh only | 5.0 |
| Terrapin, 1 pound (454 g.), raw, muscle only | 15.9 |
| Tilefish, 1 pound (454 g.), raw, flesh only | 2.3 |
| Tomcod, Atlantic, 1 pound (454 g.), raw, flesh only | 1.8 |

Trout:

    Brook, 1 pound (454 g.), raw, flesh only     9.5

              raw, whole as purchased     4.7

    Gray. See Weakfish.

    Lake, 1 pound (454 g.), raw, fillets     45.4

    Lake (Siscowet):

        Less than 6.5 pounds, round weight:

            1 pound (454 g.), raw, flesh only     90.3

        6.5 pounds and over, round weight:

            1 pound (454 g.), raw, flesh only    246.8

    Rainbow or steelhead, 1 pound (454 g.), raw,

        flesh with skin     51.7

        canned     60.8

Tuna:

    Raw:

        Bluefin, 1 pound (454 g.), flesh only    18.6

        Yellowfin, 1 pound (454 g.), flesh only    13.6

    Canned:

        In oil:

            1 pound (454 g.), solids and liquid    93.0

                    drained solids    31.6

        In water:

            1 pound (454 g.), solids and liquid    3.6

            1 6½-oz. can dietetic-pack    3.2

                    water-pack, white    1.5

Turtle, green, 1 pound (454 g.), raw, muscle only    2.3

                        canned    3.2

Weakfish (Gray trout), 1 pound (454 g.),

    raw, flesh only    25.4

    raw, whole as purchased    12.2

Whale, 1 pound (454 g.), raw, meat only    34.0

Whitefish, lake, 1 pound (454 g.), raw, flesh only  37.2

                      smoked    33.1

Whiting. See Kingfish.

Wreckfish, 1 pound (454 g.), raw, fillet    17.7

Yellowtail (Pacific coast), 1 pound (454 g.), raw,

    fillet    24.5

**APPENDIX**

**353**

# Flour. See Cereals.

## Fruits and Fruit Juices

Fruits and fruit juices have a negligible amount of fat
per serving except for the ones listed below which
should not be used in low-fat eating:

Avocados, whole fruit, raw:

| | Fat grams |
|---|---|
| California: | |
| 1 avocado (diameter 3⅛-in.), (284 g.) | 37.0 |
| 1 pound (454 g.), as purchased | 58.6 |
| Florida: | |
| 1 avocado (diameter 3⅝-in.), | |
| 1 pound (454 g.) | 33.0 |
| Coconut: | |
| Fresh, meat only: | |
| 1 piece, approx. 2 × 2 × ½ in. (45 g.) | 16.0 |
| 1 cup (130 g.), shredded or grated, firmly packed | 46.0 |
| 1 pound (454 g.), as purchased | 160.1 |
| Dried: | |
| 1 pound (454 g.), unsweetened, as purchased | 294.4 |
| 1 pound (454 g.), sweetened, shredded | 177.4 |
| Olive, pickled: | |
| Green, 4 med. or 3 extra large or 2 giant (16 g.) | 2.0 |
| Ripe, Mission, 3 small or 2 large (10 g.) | 2.0 |

## Gelatin

Gelatin, dry:

| | |
|---|---|
| 1 envelope (7 g.), plain dry powder | trace |

|  | *Fat grams* |
|---|---|
| 1 3-oz. pkg. (85 g.), dessert powder | 0.0 |
| Gelatin dessert, prepared with water, | |
| 1 cup (250 g.) | 0.0 |

## Grains. See Cereals.

## Ice Creams, Ice Milks, Sherbets, Ices. See Dairy Products.

## Jams, Jellies, Preserves, Spreads

| | |
|---|---|
| Apple butter, 1 cup (282 g.) | 2.3 |
| 1 tablespoon (18 g.) | 0.1 |
| Honey, strained or extracted | 0.0 |
| Jams, jellies, marmalades, preserves, | |
| 1 tablespoon | trace |
| Peanut butter: | |
| 1 cup (258 g.) | 129.0 |
| 1 tablespoon (16 g.) | 8.0 |

## Lard. See Fats.

## Legumes

| | |
|---|---|
| Beans, common, mature seeds, dry | |
| 1 pound (454 g.) as purchased | |
| White: | |
| Raw | 7.3 |
| Canned, solids and liquid: | |
| With pork and tomato sauce | 11.8 |

| | Fat grams |
|---|---|
| With pork and sweet sauce | 21.3 |
| Without Pork | 2.3 |
| Red: | |
| Raw | 6.8 |
| Canned, solids and liquid | 1.8 |
| Pinto, calico, and red Mexican, raw | 5.4 |
| Soybeans, immature seeds: | |
| Raw, shelled | 23.1 |
| Canned, solids and liquid | 14.5 |
| Soybeans, mature seeds, dry, raw | 80.3 |
| Others, including black, brown, and Bayo, raw | 6.8 |
| 1 cup cooked, drained: | |
| Great Northern, lima, navy, red kidney | 1.0 |
| Lentils, mature seeds, dry, raw, whole, 1 pound (454 g.) | 5.0 |
| Peas, mature seeds, dry, raw: | |
| 1 pound (454 g.) as purchased | |
| Whole | 5.9 |
| Split, without seed coat | 4.5 |
| 1 cup cooked, drained: | |
| Cowpeas or blackeye peas, (248 g.) | 1.0 |
| Split (250 g.) | 1.0 |

## Margarine. See Fats.

## Mayonnaise. See Fats.

## Meats

### Beef

Choice grade, raw, 1 pound (454 g.) separable lean:.
  Chuck:

| | |
|---|---|
| Roast | 33.6 |

|  | Fat grams |
|---|---|
| Steak | 49.9 |
| Arm | 24.5 |
| Flank steak | 25.9 |
| Hamburger (ground beef): | |
| Lean | 45.4 |
| Regular ground | 96.2 |
| Loin or short loin: | |
| Porterhouse steak | 37.2 |
| T-bone steak | 36.7 |
| Club steak | 46.7 |
| Loin end or sirloin | 25.9 |
| Rib roast | 52.6 |
| Round, entire (round and heel of round) | 21.3 |
| Rump | 34.0 |
| Short plate | 37.2 |
| Beef, canned, roast beef: | |
| 1 pound (454 g.) | 59.0 |
| Beef, corned, boneless, 1 pound (454 g.): | |
| Uncooked | 113.0 |
| Canned | 54.0 |
| Canned corned-beef hash (with potato) | 51.3 |
| Beef, dried, chipped, 1 pound (454 g.) | 28.6 |

## Lamb

| Choice grade, raw, 1 pound (454 g.) separable lean: | |
|---|---|
| Leg | 22.7 |
| Loin | 26.8 |
| Rib | 38.1 |
| Shoulder | 34.9 |

## Pork

| Pork, fresh, raw, medium-fat class, 1 pound (454 g.) separable lean: | |
|---|---|
| Ham | 34.0 |

|                                                                      | Fat grams |
|----------------------------------------------------------------------|-----------|
| Loin                                                                 | 51.7      |
| Boston butt                                                          | 51.3      |
| Picnic                                                               | 33.6      |
| Spareribs, fresh, raw, medium-fat class:                             |           |
| 1 pound (454 g.) with bone                                           | 89.7      |
| 1 pound (454 g.) without bone                                        | 150.6     |
| Pork, cured, medium-fat class, 1 pound (454 g.)                      |           |
| Dry, long cure, country-style, without bone and skin:                |           |
| Ham                                                                  | 159.0     |
| Light-cure, commercial, separable lean:                              |           |
| Ham                                                                  | 38.6      |
| Boston butt                                                          | 55.8      |
| Picnic                                                               | 38.1      |
| Pork, cured, canned:                                                 |           |
| 1 pound (454 g.) ham, contents of can                                | 55.8      |
| Pork, salt, raw, with skin, 1 pound (454 g.)                         | 370.0     |
| Bacon, cured, as purchased:                                          |           |
| Raw:                                                                 |           |
| 1 pound (454 g.) sliced                                              | 314.3     |
| 1 pound (454 g.) slab                                                | 295.5     |
| Canned:                                                              |           |
| 1 pound (454 g.)                                                     | 324.3     |
| Cooked, (broiled or fried crisp):                                    |           |
| 2 slices (15 g.), (20 slices per lb. raw)                            | 8.0       |
| Bacon, Canadian:                                                     |           |
| Unheated:                                                            |           |
| 1 pound (454 g.)                                                     | 65.3      |
| Cooked, broiled or fried, drained:                                   |           |
| 3½ oz. (100 g.)                                                      | 17.5      |

## Variety Meats

| | |
|---|---|
| Brains, all kinds (beef, calf, hog, sheep), raw: | |
| 1 pound (454 g.) | 39.0 |
| Heart, raw, 1 pound (454 g.): | |

|  | Fat grams |
|---|---|
| Beef, lean | 16.3 |
| Calf | 26.8 |
| Chicken, all classes | 27.2 |
| Hog | 20.0 |
| Lamb | 43.5 |
| Turkey, all classes | 50.8 |
| Kidney, raw, 1 pound (454 g.): | |
| Beef | 30.4 |
| Calf | 20.9 |
| Hog | 16.3 |
| Lamb | 15.0 |
| Liver, raw, 1 pound (454 g.): | |
| Beef | 17.2 |
| Calf | 21.3 |
| Chicken, all classes | 16.8 |
| Goose | 45.4 |
| Hog | 16.8 |
| Lamb | 17.7 |
| Turkey, all classes | 18.1 |
| Sausage, cold cuts, and luncheon meats: | |
| Blood sausage or blood pudding, 1 pound (454 g.) | 167.4 |
| Bockwurst, 1 pound (454 g.) | 107.5 |
| Bologna: | |
| All meat, 1 pound (454 g.) | 103.4 |
| With cereal, 1 pound (454 g.) | 93.4 |
| Braunschweiger, 1 pound (454 g.) | 124.3 |
| Brown-and-serve sausage, before browning, 1 pound (454 g.) | 163.3 |
| Capicola or Capacola, 1 pound (454 g.) | 207.7 |
| Cervelat: | |
| Dry, 1 pound (454 g.) | 170.6 |
| Soft, 1 pound (454 g.) | 111.1 |
| Country-style sausage, 1 pound (454 g.) | 141.1 |
| Deviled ham, canned: | |
| 1 pound (454 g.) | 146.5 |

APPENDIX

|  | *Fat grams* |
|---|---|
| 1 tablespoon (13 g.) | 4.0 |
| Frankfurters: | |
| Raw: | |
| All meat, 1 pound (454 g.) | 115.7 |
| With nonfat dry milk, 1 pound (454 g.) | 116.1 |
| With cereal, 1 pound (454 g.) | 93.4 |
| With nonfat dry milk and cereal, 1 pound (454 g.) | 98.4 |
| Canned, 1 pound (454 g.) | 82.1 |
| Headcheese, 1 pound (454 g.) | 99.8 |
| Knockwurst, 1 pound (454 g.) | 105.2 |
| Liverwurst: | |
| Fresh, 1 pound (454 g.) | 116.1 |
| Smoked, 1 pound (454 g.) | 124.3 |
| Luncheon meat: | |
| Boiled ham, 1 pound | 77.1 |
| Pork, cured ham or shoulder, chopped, spiced or unspiced, canned, 1 pound (454 g.) | 112.9 |
| Meat, potted (includes potted beef, chicken and turkey), 1 pound (454 g.) | 87.1 |
| Meat loaf, 1 pound (454 g.) | 59.9 |
| Minced ham, 1 pound (454 g.) | 76.7 |
| Mortadella, 1 pound (454 g.) | 113.4 |
| Polish-style sausage, 1 pound (454 g.) | 117.0 |
| Pork and beef (chopped together), 1 pound (454 g.) | 135.6 |
| Pork sausage, links or bulk, raw, 1 pound (454 g.) | 230.4 |
| Canned, solids and liquids, 1 pound (454 g.) | 174.2 |
| Pork sausage, link, smoked. See Country-style sausage. | |
| Salami, dry, 1 pound (454 g.) | 172.8 |
| Cooked, 1 pound (454 g.) | 116.1 |
| Scrapple, 1 pound (454 g.) | 61.7 |
| Souse, 1 pound (454 g.) | 60.8 |

| | Fat grams |
|---|---|
| Thuringer, 1 pound (454 g.) | 111.1 |
| Vienna sausage, canned: | |
| 1 pound (454 g.) | 89.8 |
| 1 sausage (16 g.), 7 sausages per 5-oz. can | 3.0 |
| Tongue, raw, 3½ oz. (100 g.): | |
| Beef, medium-fat | 15.0 |
| Calf | 5.3 |
| Hog | 15.6 |
| Lamb | 15.3 |
| Sheep | 21.8 |
| Tongue, canned or cured (beef, lamb, etc.), 3½ oz. (100 g.): | |
| Whole, canned or pickled | 20.3 |
| Potted or deviled | 23.0 |
| Tongue, smoked (beef), 3½ oz. (100 g.) | 28.8 |
| Tripe, beef, 3½ oz. (100 g.): | |
| Commercial | 2.0 |
| Pickled | 1.3 |

### Veal

| | |
|---|---|
| Veal, raw, medium-fat class, without bone, 1 pound (454 g.): | |
| Chuck | 45.0 |
| Flank | 122.0 |
| Foreshank | 36.0 |
| Loin | 50.0 |
| Plate | 77.0 |
| Rib | 64.0 |
| Round with rump | 41.0 |

## Nuts

| | |
|---|---|
| Almonds, shelled, 1 cup (142 g.) | 77.0 |
| Brazil nuts, shelled, 1 cup (140 g.) | 93.7 |

|  | Fat grams |
|---|---|
| Cashew nuts, roasted, 1 cup (140 g.) | 64.0 |
| Coconut. See Fruits. | |
| Chestnuts, shelled: | |
|   Fresh, 1 pound (454 g.) | 6.8 |
|   Dried, 1 pound (454 g.) | 18.6 |
| Litchi nuts (a fruit, not a nut): | |
|   Raw, 1 pound (454 g.) | 0.8 |
|   Dried, 1 pound (454 g.) | 2.5 |
| Peanut butter. See Jams. | |
| Peanuts, roasted, 1 cup (144 g.) | 72.0 |
| Pecans, 1 cup (108 g.) | 77.0 |
| Walnuts, black or native, 1 cup (126 g.) | 75.0 |
| Water chestnuts (a vegetable, not a nut), 1 pound (454 g.) | 0.7 |

## Oils. See Fats.

## Olives. See Fruits.

## Pasta. See Breads.

## Pickles

Pickles made from vegetables and fruits have a negligible amount of fat, unless oil is added in the processing.

## Popcorn. See Cereals and Grains.

## Poultry

Chicken:
Fryers:

| | Fat grams |
|---|---|
| Raw, ready-to-cook, 1 pound (454 g.): | |
|     Whole | 15.1 |
|     Breast | 8.6 |
|     Drumstick | 10.6 |
|     Giblets | 14.1 |
|     Thigh | 19.1 |
|     Wing | 16.5 |
| Without skin, raw, 3½ oz. (100 g.): | |
|     Light meat | 1.5 |
|     Dark meat | 3.8 |
| Roasters: | |
|     Raw, ready-to-cook, 1 pound (454 g.) | 59.3 |
|     Without skin, roasted, 3½ oz. (100 g.): | |
|         Light meat | 4.9 |
|         Dark meat | 6.5 |
|     Giblets, raw, 1 pound (454 g.) | 21.8 |
| Hens: | |
|     Raw, ready-to-cook, 1 pound (454 g.) | 82.1 |
|     Without skin, stewed, 3½ oz. (100 g.): | |
|         Light meat | 4.7 |
|         Dark meat | 9.5 |
|     Giblets, raw, 1 pound (454 g.) | 52.7 |
| Capon: | |
|     Raw, ready-to-cook, 1 pound (454 g.) | 70.2 |
|     Giblets, raw, 1 pound (454 g.) | 66.3 |
|     Chicken, canned, meat only, boned, 3½ oz. (100 g.) | 11.7 |
| Duck, domesticated, raw, ready-to-cook, 1 pound (454 g.) | 106.4 |
| Duck, wild, raw, ready-to-cook, 1 pound (454 g.) | 41.6 |
| Pheasant: | |
|     Raw, ready-to-cook, 1 pound (454 g.) | 20.5 |
|     Without skin, raw, 3½ oz. (100 g.) | 6.8 |
|     Giblets, raw, 1 pound (454 g.) | 22.2 |
| Quail: | |
|     Raw, ready-to-cook, 1 pound (454 g.) | 27.8 |
|     Giblets, raw, 1 pound (454 g.) | 28.1 |

APPENDIX

|                                         | *Fat grams* |
|-----------------------------------------|------------:|
| Turkey:                                 |             |
|     Raw, ready-to-cook, 1 pound (454 g.) | 48.7 |
|     Without skin, roasted, 3½ oz. (100 g.): | |
|         Light meat      | 3.9 |
|         Dark meat       | 8.3 |
|     Giblets, raw, 1 pound (454 g.)  | 30.0 |
|     Canned, meat only, 3½ oz. (100 g.) | 12.5 |

## Preserves. See Jams.

## Salad Dressing. See Fats.

## Soups

See Table 6 for fat content of soups by brand name.
Information furnished by manufacturer.
Bouillon cubes, approximately ½ in.,
  1 cube (4 g.)                          trace

## Spreads. See Jams.

## Starches

Starches (including arrowroot, corn, etc.) contain a
negligible amount of fat.

## Sugars

Sugars contain no fat.

## Syrups

Molasses, cane, any type

Syrup, table blends (check label to be sure no
  butterfat added)                                    *Fat grams*

                                                          0.0

## Vegetables

Vegetables and vegetable juices contain a negligible
amount of fat in the natural state.

## Dry Beans and Peas. See Legumes.

### TABLE 4. FAT CONTENT OF SOME ROLLS

Table 3 in the Appendix gives an average figure for
commercial rolls as 2.0 g. fat per roll. In examining the
manufacturer's figures this is a reasonable figure for
most yeast rolls. Below are two varieties which exceed
this figure enough to be noted:

|  | *Fat grams* |
| --- | --- |
| Pepperidge Farm® | |
| Butter Crescent Roll, 1 roll, (33.1 g.) | 8.0 |
| Golden Twist Roll, 1 roll, (32.7 g.) | 7.1 |

### TABLE 5. FAT CONTENT OF SOME CANNED GOODS
### (Information supplied by manufacturers)

|  | *Fat grams* |
| --- | --- |
| Campbell® | |
| Contents of 1 cup | |
| Barbecue Beans | 3.4 |

| | Fat grams |
|---|---|
| Beans n' Beef in Tomato Sauce | 6.1 |
| Beans & Franks in Tomato & Molasses Sauce | 16.1 |
| Home Style Pork & Beans | 4.0 |
| Pork & Beans with Tomato Sauce | 3.0 |

Franco-American®

Contents of 1 cup

| | |
|---|---|
| Macaroni 'n Beef in Tomato Sauce | 8.4 |
| Macaroni & Cheese | 9.5 |
| "MacaroniOs" with Cheese Sauce | 5.7 |
| Italian Style Spaghetti in Tomato-Cheese Sauce | 2.0 |
| Spaghetti in Tomato Sauce with Cheese | 1.6 |
| Spaghetti 'n Beef in Tomato Sauce | 13.9 |
| Spaghetti with Meatballs in Tomato Sauce | 13.6 |
| "SpaghettiOs" in Tomato and Cheese Sauce | 2.3 |
| "SpaghettiOs" with Little Meatballs in Tomato Sauce | 8.9 |
| "SpaghettiOs" with Sliced Franks in Tomato Sauce | 12.7 |

Contents of ¼ cup

| | |
|---|---|
| Beef Gravy | 2.0 |
| Brown Gravy with Onions | 1.2 |
| Chicken Gravy | 3.6 |
| Chicken Giblet Gravy | 1.4 |
| Mushroom Gravy | 1.4 |

Swanson®

Contents of ½ cup

| | |
|---|---|
| Chicken à la King | 8.0 |
| Creamed Chipped Beef | 5.0 |

Contents of 1 cup

| | |
|---|---|
| Beef Stew | 5.7 |
| Chicken Stew | 5.9 |
| Chili Con Carne with Beans | 13.2 |

Contents of 1 can—5 oz.

| | |
|---|---|
| Boned Chicken with Broth | 11.0 |
| Boned Turkey with Broth | 9.0 |
| Chicken Spread | 21.0 |

366

Bounty®
- Contents of 1 cup
  - Beef stew .......................... 5.7
  - Chicken Stew ....................... 5.9
  - Chili Con Carne with Beans ......... 13.2
- Contents of ½ cup
  - Creamed Chipped Beef ............... 5.0
  - Rice (with cinnamon) Pudding ....... 6.9

Crosse & Blackwell®
- Plum Pudding, 4 oz. ................. 1.0
- Mince Meat, 1 Tablespoon ........... 0.2

Underwood®
- Contents of 1 oz.
  - Sardines in Mustard Sauce ......... 3.8
  - Sardines in Tomato Sauce .......... 2.6

R&R®
- Plum Pudding, 4 oz. ................. 1.2

B&M®
- Contents of 1 cup
  - Baked Pea Beans ................... 8.0
  - Baked Yellow Eye Beans ............ 10.4
  - Baked Red Kidney Beans ............ 8.8
  - Shelled Beans ..................... 1.6
  - Beef Stew ......................... 4.8
  - Lamb Stew ......................... 8.8
  - Chicken Stew ...................... 2.4
  - Indian Pudding .................... 0.8
- Contents of 1 oz.
  - Brown Bread—Plain ................. trace
  - Brown Bread—Raisins ............... 0.2

Morton House®
- Contents of 6¼-oz. serving (½ 12½-oz. can)
  - Heat 'n Serve Gravy and Sliced Beef ....... 11.5
  - Heat 'n Serve Gravy and Sliced Pork ....... 11.9
  - Heat 'n Serve Gravy and Sliced Turkey ..... 4.5
  - Heat 'n Serve Beef Patties and Burgundy
    Sauce ................................... 8.9
  - Heat 'n Serve Beef Patties and Italian Brand

367

|  | Fat grams |
|---|---|
| Sauce | 8.9 |
| Heat 'n Serve Beef Patties and Mexican Brand | |
| Sauce | 9.0 |
| Heat 'n Serve Meat Loaf and Brown Gravy | 12.1 |
| Heat 'n Serve Meat Loaf and Tomato Sauce | 12.2 |
| Heat 'n Serve Mushroom Gravy and | |
| Salisbury Steak | 11.0 |

## TABLE 6. FAT CONTENT OF SOME CANNED AND DEHYDRATED SOUPS
(Information supplied by manufacturers)

Campbell®

Contents of 1 cup prepared soup when diluted with water according to the directions on can: one can soup plus one can water. In recipes calling for 1 can Campbell® soup, to calculate fat content multiply figure below by 2½.

|  | Fat grams |
|---|---|
| Asparagus, Cream of | 3.2 |
| Bean with Bacon | 4.8 |
| Beef | 2.3 |
| Beef Broth (Bouillon) | 0.0 |
| Beef Noodle | 2.2 |
| Black Bean | 1.6 |
| Celery, Cream of | 4.4 |
| Cheddar Cheese | 9.4 |
| Chicken Broth | 1.8 |
| Chicken, Cream of | 5.0 |
| Chicken 'n Dumplings | 5.5 |
| Chicken Gumbo | 1.3 |
| Chicken Noodle | 1.7 |
| Chicken Noodle-O's | 1.9 |
| Chicken with Rice | 1.5 |
| Chicken & Stars | 1.5 |
| Chicken Vegetable | 2.0 |
| Chili Beef | 4.2 |

| | *Fat grams* |
|---|---|
| Clam Chowder Manhattan Style | 2.4 |
| Consommé (Beef), gelatin added | 0.0 |
| Curly Noodle with Chicken | 2.5 |
| Golden Vegetable Noodle-O's | 2.5 |
| Green Pea | 1.8 |
| Hot Dog Bean | 3.9 |
| Minestrone | 2.7 |
| Mushroom, Cream of | 9.9 |
| Mushroom, Golden | 4.0 |
| Noodles & Ground Beef | 4.2 |
| Onion | 1.6 |
| Pepper Pot | 3.6 |
| Scotch Broth | 2.7 |
| Split Pea with Ham | 3.0 |
| Stockpot | 3.9 |
| Tomato | 1.8 |
| Tomato, Bisque of | 2.4 |
| Tomato-Beef Noodle-O's | 3.3 |
| Tomato Rice, Old Fashioned | 2.8 |
| Turkey Noodle | 3.0 |
| Turkey Vegetable | 3.2 |
| Vegetable | 1.6 |
| Vegetable, Old Fashioned | 2.4 |
| Vegetable Beef | 2.6 |
| Vegetarian Vegetable | 1.7 |

Campbell® Chunky Soups
Contents of 1 cup of ready to serve soup, not diluted

| | |
|---|---|
| Chunky Beef | 6.6 |
| Chunky Chicken | 5.4 |
| Chunky Turkey | 4.0 |
| Chunky Vegetable | 3.0 |

Crosse & Blackwell®
Contents of ½ can (6½ oz.), not diluted

| | |
|---|---|
| Black Bean | 0.6 |
| Consommé Madrilene (Clear & Red) | 2.4 |
| Crab | 0.9 |

**APPENDIX**

369

|  | Fat grams |
|---|---|
| Cream of Shrimp | 5.3 |
| French Onion | 1.7 |
| Gazpacho | 2.4 |
| Lentil | 2.0 |
| Lobster Bisque | 5.2 |
| Manhattan Clam Chowder | 1.5 |
| Minestrone | 1.5 |
| Mushroom Bisque | 6.1 |
| New England Clam Chowder | 3.5 |
| Oxtail | 9.8 |
| Senegalese | 2.0 |
| Vichyssoise | 5.2 |

Swanson®
  Contents of 1 cup, not diluted

| Beef Broth | 0.8 |
|---|---|
| Chicken Broth | 1.6 |

R&R®
  Contents of 1 cup, not diluted

| Chicken Broth—clear | 0.8 |
|---|---|
| Chicken Broth—with Rice | 1.6 |

Lipton® Soup Mixes—Regular Soups
  Contents of 1 cup prepared soup when diluted
  with water according to the directions on the
  package. Some mixes yield three servings per 8-oz.
  package, some yield four. In recipes calling for 1
  package of dry soup mix, to calculate the fat
  content multiply the figure below by three or four,
  depending on the number of servings listed on
  package label.

| Beef Flavor Mushroom Mix | 0.8 |
|---|---|
| Beef Flavor Noodle Soup with Vegetables | 1.3 |
| Chicken Noodle Soup with Diced White Chicken Meat | 2.2 |
| Chicken Rice Soup | 2.1 |
| Chicken Vegetable Soup | 2.2 |
| Country Vegetable Soup with Noodles | 1.1 |

Giggle Noodle Soup with Real Chicken
    Broth    2.2
Green Pea Soup    1.7
Noodle Soup with Real Chicken Broth    1.8
Onion Soup    0.8
Potato Soup    1.2
Ring-O Noodle Soup with Real Chicken
    Broth    1.2
Tomato Vegetable Soup with Noodles    1.6
Turkey Noodle Soup    2.1
Vegetable Beef Soup    1.5

Lipton® Cup-A-Soup (instant soup)
  Contents of 1 6-oz. serving when mixed according
  to directions on package

Beef Flavored Cup-a-Broth    0.1
Beef Flavor Noodle    0.3
Chicken Flavored Cup-a-Broth    0.7
Chicken Flavor Cream Style    5.1
Chicken Noodle with Chicken Meat    0.9
Cream of Mushroom    4.5
Green Pea    1.4
Noodle Soup—Chicken Flavor    0.8
Onion    0.5
Spring Vegetable    0.8
Tomato    0.5

## TABLE 7. FAT CONTENT OF SOME CRACKERS, COOKIES, AND FRUIT–NUT LOAVES
### (Information supplied by manufacturers)

You will note that there is a wide range in the fat content of the crackers and cookies listed. Remember that there is also a wide variation in the size of the various crackers which would influence the quantity eaten. Some of the products have a low enough fat content to be suitable for snacks. Others would have

**APPENDIX**

to be used in limited quantities as accompaniments to soup or dessert. Still others have too high a fat content for use in lowered-fat eating. In any case, they should be calculated in the total fat content of the meal.

The six most suitable crackers and five most suitable cookies and loaves are starred (*).

*Fat*
*grams per cracker*

Nabisco®

| | |
|---|---|
| AMERICAN HARVEST Snack Crackers | 0.8 |
| Bacon Flavored Thins Crackers | 0.6 |
| Butter Thins Flavored Crackers | 0.5 |
| Buttery Flavored Sesame Snack Crackers | 0.8 |
| Cheese Flavored FLINGS Curls | 0.8 |
| Cheese NIPS Crackers | 0.2 |
| Cheese TID-BIT Crackers | 0.2 |
| CHICKEN IN A BISKIT Crackers | 0.5 |
| CHIPPERS Potato Crackers | 0.7 |
| CHIPSTERS Potato Snacks | 0.1 |
| CORN DIGGERS Snacks | 0.2 |
| CROWN PILOT Crackers | 1.9 |
| DANDY Soup and Oyster Crackers | 0.1 |
| DOO DADS Snacks (average) | 0.1 |
| ESCORT Crackers | 0.9 |
| French Onion Crackers | 0.5 |
| *Graham Crackers | 0.7 |
| *HOLLAND Rusk | 0.6 |
| KORKERS Corn Chips | 0.5 |
| MEAL MATES Onion Flavored Bread Wafers | 0.5 |
| MEAL MATES Rye Flavored Bread Wafers | 0.4 |
| MEAL MATES Sesame Bread Wafers | 0.7 |
| MISTER SALTY Dutch Pretzels | 0.2 |
| MISTER SALTY 3-Ring Pretzels | 0.1 |
| *{ MISTER SALTY VERI-THIN Pretzels | 0.2 |
| MISTER SALTY VERI-THIN Pretzel Sticks | trace |
| MISTER SALTY Pretzelettes | 0.1 |
| NATIONAL Arrowroot Biscuit | 0.8 |

| | Fat grams per cracker |
|---|---|
| OYSTERETTES Soup & Oyster Crackers | 0.1 |
| *{PREMIUM Crackers Unsalted Tops | 0.3 |
| {PREMIUM Saltine Crackers | 0.3 |
| RITZ Cheese Crackers | 1.0 |
| RITZ Crackers | 0.8 |
| ROYAL LUNCH Milk Crackers | 2.2 |
| SHAPIES Cheese Flavored Dip Delights | 0.6 |
| SHAPIES Cheese Flavored Shells | 0.6 |
| SIP 'N CHIPS Cheese Flavored Snacks | 0.5 |
| SOCIABLES Crackers | 0.4 |
| Sugar HONEY MAID Graham Crackers | 0.7 |
| Swiss 'n Ham Flavored FLINGS Curls | 0.7 |
| TWIGS Sesame/Cheese Flavored Snack Sticks | 0.7 |
| TRIANGLE THINS Crackers | 0.3 |
| TRISCUIT Wafers | 0.8 |
| UNEEDA Biscuit Unsalted Tops | 0.6 |
| WAVERLY Wafers | 0.8 |
| WHEAT THINS Crackers | 0.4 |
| ZWIEBACK | 0.7 |
| Pepperidge Farm® | |
| Gold Fish Crackers, 10 fish: | |
|     Cheddar Cheese (5.6 g.) | 1.3 |
|     *Pretzel (6.9 g.) | 0.6 |
|     Lightly Salted (5.8 g.) | 1.2 |
|     Parmesan Cheese (5.9 g.) | 1.2 |
|     Sesame Garlic (5.9 g.) | 1.3 |
|     Pizza (5.9 g.) | 1.4 |
|     Onion (5.9 g.) | 1.2 |
| Toasted Thins, 2 pieces (5.4 g.): | |
|     Cheese | 0.5 |
|     White | 0.4 |
|     Onion | 0.4 |
|     Rye | 0.3 |
| Ralston Purina Ry Krisp® | |
| *Original Ry Krisp®: | |

373

|  | Fat<br>grams per cracker |
|---|---|
| Per triple cracker | 0.2 |
| Per large square (family size) | 1.5 |
| Seasoned Ry Krisp®: | |
| Per triple cracker | 0.7 |
| Per large square (family size) | 5.1 |

|  | Fat<br>grams per cooky |
|---|---|
| Nabisco® | |
| Almond Flavored Crescent | 1.4 |
| BAKE SHOP Cocoanut Macaroons | 4.0 |
| BAKE SHOP Oatmeal Raisin Cookies | 3.0 |
| BARNUM'S ANIMALS Crackers | 0.3 |
| BISCOS Sugar Wafers | 0.9 |
| BISCOS Waffle Cremes | 2.1 |
| Brown Edge Wafers | 1.2 |
| Butter Flavored Cookies | 0.9 |
| CAMEO Creme Sandwich | 2.6 |
| CHIPS AHOY Chocolate Chip Cookies | 2.1 |
| Chocolate Chip Cookies | 1.6 |
| Chocolate Chip Snaps | 0.7 |
| Chocolate Chip Creme Sandwich | 3.8 |
| Chocolate Snaps | 0.7 |
| Cocoanut Bars Cookies | 2.0 |
| Cocoanut Chocolate Chip Cookies | 4.1 |
| COOKIE BREAK Assorted Fudge Creme<br>    Sandwich | 2.5 |
| COOKIE BREAK Chocolate Fudge Creme<br>    Sandwich | 2.5 |
| COOKIE BREAK Vanilla Flavored Creme<br>    Sandwich | 2.4 |
| COWBOYS and INDIANS Cookies | 0.2 |
| DANDY Shortcakes | 1.5 |
| Devil's Food Cakes | 0.8 |
| FAMILY FAVORITES Brown Sugar Cookies | 1.3 |

| | Fat grams per cracker |
|---|---|
| FAMILY FAVORITES Chocolate Chip Cookies | 1.6 |
| FAMILY FAVORITES Cocoanut Cookies | 0.7 |
| FAMILY FAVORITES Oatmeal Cookies | 0.9 |
| Famous Chocolate Wafers | 0.7 |
| FANCY CRESTS Cakes | 1.0 |
| FIG NEWTONS Cakes | 1.2 |
| Iced Fruit Cookies | 1.5 |
| *Lemon Snaps | 0.4 |
| Lemon Juble Rings | 2.3 |
| LORNA DOONE Shortbread | 1.6 |
| Macaroon Sandwich | 3.4 |
| Marshmallow Sandwich | 0.8 |
| NABISCO Oatmeal Cookies | 3.1 |
| NILLA Vanilla Wafers | 0.7 |
| NUTTER BUTTER Peanut Butter Sandwich Cookies | 3.1 |
| *Old Fashion Ginger Snaps | 0.7 |
| OREO Creme Sandwich | 2.2 |
| OREO/SWISS Assortment (average) | 2.3 |
| Peanut Creme Patties | 1.8 |
| Pecan Shortbread Cookies | 4.6 |
| PRIDE Sandwich Assortment (average) | 2.6 |
| *Raisin Fruit Biscuit | 0.6 |
| SOCIAL TEA Biscuit | 0.6 |
| SOCIAL TEA Creme Sandwich | 2.3 |
| Spiced Wafers | 1.1 |
| Sugar Rings Cookies | 2.5 |
| SWISS Creme Sandwich | 2.6 |
| Vanilla Snaps | 0.3 |
| ZUZU Ginger Snaps | 0.4 |
| Chocolate-Covered Cookies | |
| Chocolate Covered Grahams | 2.7 |
| Chocolate PINWHEELS Cakes | 5.8 |
| IDEAL Chocolate Peanut Bars | 5.4 |
| MALLOMARS Chocolate Cakes | 2.5 |

|  | Fat grams per cracker |
| --- | ---: |
| Cocoa-Covered Cookies | |
|     Creme Wafer Sticks | 2.8 |
|     CROWN Peanut Bars | 5.1 |
|     Fancy Grahams | 3.3 |
|     Fancy Peanut Creme Patties | 3.3 |
|     HEYDAYS Caramel Peanut Logs | 6.6 |
|     Marshmallow Puffs | 4.4 |
|     Marshmallow TWIRLS Cakes | 4.6 |
|     MINARETS Cakes | 2.4 |
|     MYSTIC Mint Sandwich Cookies | 4.6 |
|     PANTRY Grahams | 2.8 |
|     Striped Shortbread | 2.3 |
| Pepperidge Farm® | |
|   Bordeau | 1.6 |
|   Brown Sugar | 2.2 |
|   Brownie Chocolate Nut | 3.5 |
|   Brussels[1] | 2.4 |
|   Capri | 4.6 |
|   Cardiff[1] | 0.8 |
|   Cinnamon Sugar | 2.4 |
|   Chocolate Chip | 2.9 |
|   Chocolate Laced Pirouette | 2.1 |
|   Dresden | 4.6 |
|   Fudge Chip | 2.5 |
|   Gingerman | 1.1 |
|   Irish Oatmeal | 2.2 |
|   Lemon Nut Crunch | 3.2 |
|   Lemon Pirouette | 2.0 |
|   Lido | 5.3 |
|   Lisbon[1] | 1.5 |
|   Marquisette[1] | 2.6 |
|   Milano | 3.5 |

[1]These cookies are components of Pepperidge Farm® Assorted Cookies.

|  | Fat grams per cracker |
|---|---|
| Mint Milano | 4.4 |
| Molasses Crisp | 1.3 |
| Naples | 1.9 |
| Nassau | 4.9 |
| Oatmeal Raisin | 2.6 |
| Original Pirouette | 2.0 |
| Orleans | 1.7 |
| Rochelle | 4.5 |
| Tahiti | 5.4 |
| Shortbread | 3.9 |
| Sugar | 2.4 |
| Venice[1] | 3.3 |
| *Lady Fingers, 1 large or 2 small (14 g.) | 1.1 |
| Nabisco® Cups and Cones | |
| COMET® Cups and Cones | 0.2 |
| COMET® Rolled Sugar Cones | 0.5 |

|  | Fat grams per slice |
|---|---|
| Nabisco® Dromedary® Nut Rolls | |
| Banana Nut Roll, ½ in. slice (28.4 g.) | 2.0 |
| Chocolate Nut Roll, ½ in. slice (28.4 g.) | 2.4 |
| Date and Nut Roll, ½ in. slice (28.4 g.) | 2.1 |
| Orange Nut Roll, ½ in. slice (28.4 g.) | 2.0 |
| Nestlé Crosse & Blackwell® | |
| Chocolate Nut Loaf, ½ in. slice (28.4 g.) | 0.8 |
| Date & Nut Roll, ½ in. slice (28.4 g.) | 0.5 |
| Fruit & Nut Loaf, ½ in. slice (28.4 g.) | 0.4 |
| Orange Nut Loaf, ½ in. slice (28.4 g.) | 0.6 |
| *Spice Nut Loaf, ½ in. slice (28.4 g.) | 0.3 |

APPENDIX

377

## TABLE 8. HERB CHART

| | Basil | Bay | Marjoram | Oregano | Parsley | Peppermint |
|---|---|---|---|---|---|---|
| APPETIZERS | Tomato juice<br>Seafood cocktail | Tomato juice<br>Aspic | | Tomato | Garnish | Fruit cup<br>Melon balls<br>Cranberry juice |
| SOUPS | Tomato<br>Spinach | Stock<br>Herb bouquet | Spinach<br>Clam bouillon<br>Onion | Tomato<br>Bean | Any<br>Garnish<br>Herb bouquet | Pea |
| FISH | Shrimps<br>Broiled fish<br>Fillets of fish<br>Mackerel | Bouillon | Broiled fish<br>Baked fish<br>Creamed fish | Stuffing | Any | |
| EGGS or CHEESE | Scrambled eggs<br>Mock rarebit | | Omelette aux fines herbes<br>Scrambled eggs | Boiled eggs | Creamed eggs<br>Scrambled eggs | |
| MEATS | Liver<br>Lamb | Stews<br>Pot roast<br>Shishkebab | Pot roast<br>Beef<br>Veal | Lamb<br>Meat loaf | Lamb<br>Veal<br>Steak<br>Stews | Lamb<br>Veal |
| POULTRY and GAME | Duck | Fricassee<br>Stews | Creamed chicken | | Stuffings<br>Herb bouquet | |
| VEGETABLES | Eggplant<br>Squash<br>Tomatoes<br>Onions | Boiled potatoes<br>Carrots<br>Stewed tomatoes | Stuffings<br>Carrots<br>Zucchini<br>Peas<br>Spinach | Marinades<br>Stuffings<br>Tomatoes<br>Cabbage<br>Broccoli | Potatoes<br>Carrots<br>Peas | Carrots<br>New potatoes<br>Spinach<br>Zucchini |
| SALADS | Tomato<br>Mixed green<br>Sea food | Fish salads<br>Aspic | Chicken<br>Mixed green | Tomato aspic<br>Fish salad | Potato<br>Fish<br>Mixed green | Fruit<br>Coleslaw<br>Orange<br>Pear |
| SAUCES | Tomato<br>Spaghetti<br>Orange (for game)<br>Lemon (for fish) | All marinades | White sauce | Spaghetti<br>Tomato | | Mint |
| DESSERTS and BEVERAGES | Fruit compote | Custards | | | | Fruit compote<br>Frostings<br>Ices<br>Tea |

| | Rosemary | Saffron | Sage | Savory | Tarragon | Thyme |
|---|---|---|---|---|---|---|
| APPETIZERS | Fruit cup | | Cottage cheese<br>Cheddar spread | Vegetable juice cocktail | Fish cocktail<br>Tomato juice | Tomato juice<br>Fish cocktails |
| SOUPS | Pea<br>Spinach<br>Chicken | Fish consommé<br>Chicken | Cream soup<br>Chowders | Fish con-sommé<br>Bean | Consommé<br>Chicken<br>Tomato | Gumbo<br>Pea<br>Clam chowder<br>Vegetable |
| FISH | Salmon<br>Stuffings | Halibut | Stuffings | Broiled fish<br>Baked fish | Broiled fish<br>Mock lobster Newburg | Broiled fish<br>Baked fish |
| EGGS or CHEESE | Scrambled eggs | Scrambled eggs | Cheddar spread<br>Cottage | Scrambled eggs<br>Deviled eggs | All egg dishes<br>Omelette aux fines herbes | Shirred eggs<br>Cottage cheese |
| MEATS | Lamb<br>Veal ragout<br>Beef stew | Veal | Stews | Veal | Veal | Meat loaf<br>Veal |
| POULTRY and GAME | Turkey<br>Chicken<br>Duck | Chicken | Turkey<br>Stuffings | Chicken<br>Stuffings | Chicken<br>Duck | Stuffings<br>Fricassee |
| VEGETABLES | Peas<br>Spinach<br>French-fried potatoes | Spanish rice<br>Rice | Lima beans<br>Eggplant<br>Onions<br>Tomatoes | Beans<br>Rice<br>Lentils<br>Sauerkraut | Salsify<br>Celery root<br>Mushrooms<br>Baked potatoes | Onions<br>Carrots<br>Beets |
| SALADS | Fruit | Fish | | Mixed green<br>String bean<br>Russian | Mixed green<br>Chicken<br>Fish | Pickled beets<br>Tomato<br>Aspics |
| SAUCES | White sauce<br>Jelly | Fish sauce | | Horse-radish<br>Fish sauces | Béarnaise | Creole |
| DESSERTS and BEVERAGES | Fruit compote | Cake<br>Frostings | Sage tea | Stewed pears | | Herb bouquets |

Source: Adapted from the Spice Islands Herb Chart, and printed by permission of the Spice Islands Company, South San Francisco, Calif.

# Supplementary Information for Special Diets Prescribed by Physicians

SUPPLEMENTARY INFORMATION

SUPPLEMENTARY INFORMATION

# Sodium-Restricted
# Low-Fat Cookery

Diets with both sodium restriction and fat restriction are often prescribed by physicians. The degree to which sodium is limited may vary from a mild restriction to a very strict one. We will not attempt to outline diet plans at the different levels. In this section we give general information about seasoning without salt, and we show how one can adjust recipes in *Low-Fat Cookery* for sodium restriction.

Salt substitutes and low-sodium meat tenderizers should not be used unless prescribed by your physician. Salt substitutes or salt substitute products such as low-sodium seasoning are best if added to food after it is cooked. If added during cooking, they may impart a bitter taste.

Bouillon cubes are used in many recipes in the book. Regular bouillon cubes, both beef and chicken, are

383

very high in sodium content. There are low-sodium chicken and beef bouillon cubes, Cellu-Featherweight® brand. The chicken contains 1.7 mg. sodium per cube, and the beef 10 mg. sodium per cube. Beef or chicken broth, made from fresh meat and cooked without added salt, may be substituted for bouillon cubes. This broth should be chilled, and the solidified fat removed.

The restriction of sodium in the diet gives one an opportunity to experiment with herbs and seasonings for new flavors. You will find that one-quarter to one-half teaspoon dried herbs is sufficient to enhance the flavor of dishes made to serve four; two to three times as much will be needed if fresh herbs are used. In meat, fish, and poultry dishes lively flavors can be created by using herbs and wine, or a dash of lemon juice to spark the natural flavor of the food. A wine-herb blend can be used as a marinade for meat, fish, or poultry. Allow at least two hours for these savors to soak into the food. Save the marinade and use as a basting sauce or as a gravy. Experiment with a dash of allspice or cloves in your ground meat loaves or stews. A teaspoon of vinegar in the water for poaching eggs adds flavor. Eggs may be scrambled with a pinch of mixed herbs, or with fresh tomato cut up with them.

If you are placed on a low-sodium diet, we suggest you first try new dishes rather than remove the salt from your regular favorites. After you become accustomed to the taste of low-sodium foods, reintroduce the foods previously eaten but with their sodium content reduced.

## Herbs and Seasonings Which May be Used

Allspice
Almond extract

Anise seed
Basil
Bay leaf
Bouillon cube, low-sodium dietetic
Caraway seed
Cardamon
Catsup, dietetic
Chili powder
Chives
Cinnamon
Cloves
Cocoa, Hershey®, plain
Cumin
Curry
Dill
Fennel
Garlic
Ginger
Horseradish root or horseradish prepared without
    salt
Juniper
Lemon juice or extract
Mace
Maple extract
Marjoram
Meat extract, low-sodium dietetic
Meat tenderizers, low-sodium dietetic
Mint
Mustard, dry
Nutmeg
Onion, fresh, juice, or sliced
Orange extract
Oregano
Paprika
Parsley
Pepper, fresh, green or red
Pepper, black, red, or white

Peppermint extract
Pimento
Poppy seed
Poultry seasoning
Purslane
Rosemary
Saccharin
Saffron
Sage
Salt substitutes
Savory
Sesame seeds
Sorrel
Sugar
Sugar substitute, calcium
Tarragon
Thyme
Turmeric
Vanilla extract
Vinegar
Wine
Walnut extract

## Suggestions in the Use of Herbs and Flavors

Beef:       Bay, basil, caraway, curry, dill, garlic, onion, parsley, rosemary, sage, savory, sweet marjoram, thyme, turmeric

Chicken:   Cranberries, mushrooms, paprika, parsley, poultry seasoning, thyme, sage

Fish:       Bay leaf, curry, dry mustard, green pepper, lemon juice, marjoram, mushrooms, paprika

| Lamb: | Cloves, curry, dill, garlic, onion, parsley, rosemary, sage, sweet marjoram, mint |
|---|---|
| Liver: | Chives, onions, parsley |
| Veal: | Basil, garlic, onion, parsley, summer savory, sage, thyme |
| Asparagus: | Chives, caraway, lemon |
| Green beans: | Marjoram, rosemary |
| Corn: | Green pepper, parsley, tomato |
| Potatoes: | Chives, leeks, lentils and tops, mace, rosemary |
| Squash: | Lemon juice, ginger, mace, onion |
| Tomatoes: | Basil, onion, parsley, thyme, sugar |

## Some Foods Which Are High in Sodium Content

Salt Preserved Foods
  Anchovies
  Dried Beef
  Smoked and seasoned meats and poultry
  Koshered meats
  Olives
  Salted fish
  Sauerkraut
  Bacon
  Ham
  Canned fish, meat, poultry, soups, and vegetables (unless specially prepared without salt in the processing)
Highly Salted Foods
  Bouillon cubes
  Crackers
  Pretzels
  Potato and corn chips
  Frozen fish fillets

Catsup
Celery, garlic and onion salt
Pickles
Prepared mustard
Relishes, as chow-chow
Worcestershire or meat sauces
Foods preserved with benzoate of soda
Soda
Baking powder
Self-rising flour

## Some Sodium-Restricted Items[1] Available on the Market Which May Be Used on a Low-Fat, Sodium-Restricted Eating Plan—Read the Label Carefully

Cellu-Featherweight® Products[1]
  Low Sodium Non Fat Dry Milk
  Low Sodium/Salt Free Meats & Stews
    Salmon
    Tuna Fish
    Shrimp
    Boned Chicken
    Cooked Ham
    Beef Stew
    Chicken Stew
    Lamb Stew
    Spanish Rice

[1]All of these items are specially prepared for sodium-restricted diets. Other brands may be available on special food shelves. Check labels for fat and sodium content. If you are unable to find the products locally, check with the manufacturers: Cellu-Featherweight® Products, Chicago Dietetic Supply, Inc., 405 East Shawmut Ave., LaGrange, Illinois 60525; Tillie Lewis® Tasti-Diet Products, Tillie Lewis Foods, Inc., Drawer J, Stockton, California 95201.

Low-Sodium Salt-Free Vegetables and Juices
  Tomato Juice
  Cut Asparagus
  Green Beans, Cut
  Cut Wax Beans
  Green Lima Beans
  Sliced Beets
  Whole Beets
  Golden Cream Style Corn
  Whole Kernel Corn
  Mixed Vegetables
  Mushrooms
  Peas
  Spinach
  Tomatoes
  Yams
  Asparagus Spears Whole
  Tomato Paste
Low-Sodium Salt-Free Soups
  Chicken Noodle
  Green Pea Soup
  Tomato Soup
  Mushroom Soup
  Vegetable Beef Soup
  Tomato Rice Soup
  Chicken Broth
  Beef Bouillon
  Chicken Bouillon
Specialties, Low Sodium Salt Free
  Chili Sauce
  Mustard
  Tomato Catsup
  Pickles, Sliced, dill and whole
  Cucumber Relish
  Fancy Fruit Dressing
  Seasoned Salt Substitute
  Salt Substitute

**SUPPLEMENTARY INFORMATION**

Low-Sodium Baking Powder
Desserts—Low Sodium Salt Free
Gelatins, variety of flavors
Low-Sodium Salt-Free Breads and Crackers
Melba Toast
Rice Wafers
All Rye Wafers
Tillie Lewis® Tasti-Diet Products[1]
Fruits, variety
Jellies and Preserves
Vegetables, variety
Soups
Chicken Noodle
Tomato
Split Pea
Vegetable
Chicken of the Sea® Dietetic Tuna[1]
Holland Honey® Cake
Premium Honey Cake
Honey Fruit Cake
Raisin Date Loaf
Prepared Dry Cereals
Puffed Rice
Puffed Wheat
Shredded Wheat

## Recipe Adjusted to Lower Sodium Content

**Baked Stuffed Flounder**        *6 servings (page 106)*

2 whole fresh flounder, heads removed,
cleaned (2 pounds)
½ package Pepperidge Farm® bread
dressing (4 ounces)

½ cup cut-up boiled shrimp*
1 chicken bouillon cube
½ cup water

Adjust by omitting the following ingredients:

½ package Pepperidge Farm® bread dressing
1 chicken bouillon cube
½ cup water

Substitute for omitted items the following ingredients:

2 cups dried salt-free bread crumbs, seasoned with diced onion, thyme, savory, sage, and ground black pepper
½ cup unsalted fresh chicken broth or 1 low-sodium bouillon cube dissolved in ½ cup water

*At some very low levels of sodium restriction it may be necessary to omit the shrimp from the dressing.

# The Use of Unsaturated Vegetable Oils with Low-Fat Cookery

## A Program Which May Be Recommended for Atherosclerosis but Which Is Not Effective for Weight Control

Physicians may recommend the addition of unsaturated vegetable oils to one's diet. There is no difference in caloric content between unsaturated and saturated fats. Indeed, there is *no such thing as a low-caloric fat*. In order to keep the calories at an adequately low level, unsaturated vegetable oils must be added to an otherwise low-fat diet. The fats which appear to be effective in lowering the blood cholesterol are liquid oils such as corn, cottonseed, safflower, soy, and sunflower. Corn oil, readily available in groceries as Mazola®, has been shown to be one of the most effective.

Vegetable oils yield approximately 125 calories per tablespoon and contain 14 grams of fat per tablespoon. The quantity of oil prescribed may vary with the

393

individual. Studies have indicated that to be effective in lowering cholesterol the oil must be consumed in about a 2-to-1 ratio to the so-called "saturated" fats such as butter, hydrogenated shortening, margarine, or animal fat. The fat in seafood is "unsaturated." One must eat a diet lower in "saturated" fat than the so-called "normal" to achieve this ratio.

Some of the ways in which vegetable oil can be used in conjunction with *Low-Fat Cookery* are:

1. Frying. Follow the correct rules for frying:
    a. Moist foods such as potatoes should be dried before frying.
    b. Batter dipped foods should be drained of excess batter.
    c. For even cooking and browning, food should be of uniform size.
    d. Preheat oil over medium heat, before any food is added. Correct frying temperature is 375°. In general an 8-inch skillet takes about 6 minutes; a 10-inch, 8 minutes; and a 12-inch, 10 minutes to preheat. Fry to a golden brown before turning. Use more oil for foods which require longer cooking.
    e. Drain foods on paper towels.
2. Mayonnaise. Try the one below as it is both tasty and easy to make.


**Mayonnaise**                    *Yield: 2¼ cups*

   **1 teaspoon sugar**
   **1 teaspoon dry mustard**
   **¾ teaspoon salt**
     **Pinch cayenne**
   **1 egg**
   **2 cups corn oil**
   **3 tablespoons vinegar**

Combine sugar, mustard, salt, and cayenne in a bowl. Mix well. Add egg; beat well with rotary beater. Continue beating and add oil, a little at a time, beating continually until 1 cup is used. Then add one table-spoon vinegar and continue adding remaining oil, a little at a time. Beat in last two tablespoons vinegar.

3. Salad Dressing. This is an excellent oil-and-vinegar dressing for salad greens. Variations in the recipe can be made by using wine vinegars or dehydrated salad dressing mixes (pages 167 and 170.)

**Salad Dressing**                    *Yield: ¾ cup*

   ¼ **cup vinegar**
   ½ **cup corn oil**
   **Garlic clove**

Shake ingredients and let stand for several hours before using.

4. White Sauce. Use corn oil for the butter in most recipes to blend with the flour. The milk used should be liquefied skim milk to keep the animal fat low.
5. Pastry

**Pastry: 2-Crust 8- or 9-inch Pie**

   2 **cups sifted flour**
   1 **teaspoon salt**
   ½ **cup corn oil**
   5 **tablespoons ice water.**

Sift together flour and salt. Combine oil and ice water in measuring cup. Beat with fork until thickened and creamy. To avoid separation, immediately pour all at once over flour mixture. Toss and mix with fork. The dough will be moist. Form into ball; divide in half. Roll out between wax paper. Bake in hot oven (475°) 10 to 12 minutes. For filled pie bake at temperature require for filling used. Note: Always prepare pastry just before ready to use. Do not store.

6. Eggs. Now available in the grocery store is an egg substitute, Fleischmann's® Egg Beaters. This is a product which is essentially cholesterol free, but which has a slightly higher calorie and fat content than fresh eggs. The fat is unsaturated and therefore suitable for use when unsaturated fats are to be added to the diet.

As pointed out earlier in this section, there is *no such thing as a low-caloric fat*, and that fact must be taken into account when planning menus in which unsaturated fat is incorporated.

# INDEX

*Consult Table 3, pp. 332–365, for Fat Content of Foods.*

INDEX

*Consult Table 3, pp. 332–365, for Fat Content of Foods.*  **399**

**I N D E X**

*Consult Table 3, pp. 332–365, for Fat Content of Foods.*

401

*Consult Table 3, pp. 332–365, for Fat Content of Foods.*

Consult Table 3, pp. 332–365, for Fat Content of Foods.

*Consult Table 3, pp. 332–365, for Fat Content of Foods.*

I
N
D
E
X

405

*Consult Table 3, pp. 332–365, for Fat Content of Foods*

*Consult Table 3, pp. 332–365, for Fat Content of Foods.*

*Consult Table 3, pp. 332–365, for Fat Content of Foods.*

Consult Table 3, pp. 332–365, for Fat Content of Foods.

## Catalog

If you are interested in a list of fine Paperback
books, covering a wide range of subjects
and interests, send your name and address,
requesting your free catalog, to:

McGraw-Hill Paperbacks
1221 Avenue of Americas
New York, N.Y. 10020